Cities by Contract

D1528267

Cities by Contract
The Politics of Municipal Incorporation

Gary J Miller

The MIT Press
Cambridge, Massachusetts
and London, England

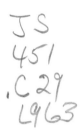

This book was set in Fototronic Baskerville
by Colonial Cooperative Press
and printed and bound in the United States of America.

Library of Congress Cataloging in Publication Data
Miller, Gary J
    Cities by contract.
    Includes bibliographical references and index.
    1. Municipal incorporation—California—Los Angeles Co.—History. I. Title.
JS451.C29L963   320.8′09794′94   80–25611
ISBN 0–262–13164–1

Contents

Contents

Preface

Beginning in 1954, a rash of municipal incorporations took place in Los Angeles County, the first in the city of Lakewood. Most of these new cities contracted for their major services from the county government rather than create their own municipal bureaucracies, a mode of service delivery that came to be called the Lakewood Plan. Over the years there has been a great deal of interest in the Lakewood Plan. It has been used as a prime example of efficient administration within the context of fragmented metropolitan government.

Much less interest has been shown in the political history of the Lakewood Plan cities themselves. The drama behind the incorporation movement has been completely overlooked. Each incorporation effort was marked by various forms of political conflict and protest—sometimes internal, sometimes external—involving a wide variety of political actors. Interestingly enough, the efficiency or inefficiency of county contracting was rarely the most salient issue in the debate that surrounded incorporation. The first purpose of this book is to tell the story of these incorporation efforts and to explain the political struggle surrounding them with reference to the conflicting interests of homeowners, bureaucrats, industrialists, businessmen, and elected and appointed officials at various levels of government.

Chapters 1 through 5 constitute a political analysis of the Lakewood Plan incorporations that goes beyond the question of efficient contracting. The book suggests that the primary purpose of the incorporations was the same as that of the Jarvis-Gann tax revolt of 1978: to limit the property tax burden on homeowners and businesses and to limit the expansion of governmental bureaucracies and social welfare programs.

Chapters 6 through 9 deal with the effects of the Lakewood Plan incorporations. By making suburbanization of residences and businesses more attractive, the new cities served to weaken the tax bases of several older cities such as Compton, which were increasingly unable to provide services to the low-income groups that constituted an increasing proportion of their populations. Thus, in effect, as well as in motivation, the incorporation movement was analogous to Proposition 13.

I am greatly indebted to the 46 citizens of Los Angeles County who talked to me so freely about their memories of the incorporation proceedings. The creation of these new cities was an exciting, often life-changing event to those involved, and they were wonderfully effective in sharing that excitement with me.

I had no interest whatsoever in the problem of metropolitan area government until Elinor Ostrom and the other members of Indiana University's Workshop in Political Theory and Policy Analysis introduced me to the subject. The year of my fieldwork for them was made enjoyable by their graciousness, good humor, and contagious enthusiasm.

I am deeply grateful to my former colleagues at California Institute of Technology, especially Bruce Cain and Bob Bates, who read my entire manuscript and whose lunchtime conferences provided me with food for thought and boosts for my morale. In addition, Bruce Cain suggested the title for this book. Dee Scriven typed innumerable chapter drafts while I was there, and was editor, proofreader, and the world's greatest creator of table 5 as well.

My wife, Anne, must be thanked for consenting to live in Los Angeles smog for three years, and for making those three years very happy ones for me.

As always, I am grateful to Joe Oppenheimer, whose enthusiastic teaching kept me interested in political science and who provided excellent criticism on this project throughout multiple drafts.

Cities by Contract

Municipal Incorporations in Northeastern Los Angeles County

Cities incorporated prior to 1954
Cities incorporated since 1954

Los Angeles County
San Bernardino County

N

0   2   4 Km.
0   2   4 Mi.

Claremont
La Verne
Pomona
San Dimas
Glendora
Walnut
Azusa
Covina
West Covina
Industry
Duarte
Irwindale
Baldwin Park
La Puente
Bradbury
Monrovia
Sierra Madre
Arcadia
El Monte
Temple City
South El Monte
Whittier
Rosemead
San Gabriel
Montebello
Pico Rivera
Pasadena
San Marino
Monterey Park
Alhambra
South Pasadena
East Los Angeles (unincorporated)
Commerce
Bell Gardens
La Canada-Flintridge
Glendale
Los Angeles
Maywood
Bell
Vernon
Huntington Park

Municipal Incorporations in Southern Los Angeles County

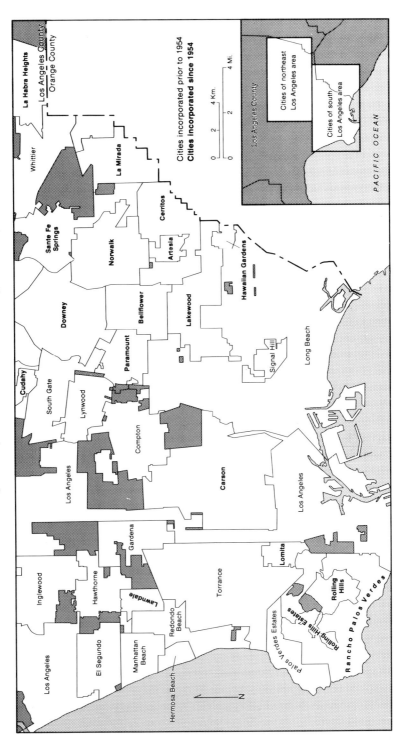

La Habra Heights

Los Angeles County
Orange County

Whittier

La Mirada

Cities incorporated prior to 1954
Cities incorporated since 1954

4 Km.

4 Mi.

2

2

0

0

Los Angeles County

Cities of northeast
Los Angeles area

Cities of south
Los Angeles area

PACIFIC OCEAN

Sante Fe
Springs

Cerritos

Norwalk

Artesia

Downey

Bellflower

Lakewood

Hawaiian Gardens

Signal Hill

Long Beach

Cudahy

South Gate

Lynwood

Paramount

Compton

Carson

Los Angeles

Los Angeles

Gardena

Lomita

Inglewood

Hawthorne

Lawndale

Torrance

Rolling
Hills

Rancho Palos Verdes

Rolling Hills Estates

Palos Verdes Estates

Redondo
Beach

El Segundo

Manhattan
Beach

Los Angeles

Hermosa Beach

N

Introduction

Voice and Exit
in the California
Tax Revolt

On Thursday, September 16, 1977, the California Senate failed to pass Governor Brown's property tax relief bill. As a "circuit-breaker" relief measure, the bill would have linked the homeowner's property tax bill to family income as well as to the value of the home. The bill also would have granted relief to renters with incomes less than $12,000, while denying tax relief to all families with incomes greater than $40,000. All of the Senate's Republicans voted against the bill, preferring uniform, across-the-board property tax relief for all homeowners. The Republicans also claimed that the real need, unmet by Brown's bill, was to place a lid on government spending and bureaucracy.

The failure of this tax relief measure in the final moments of the 1977 session accelerated a grass-roots revolt against property taxation. Within months, at a cost of only $28,000, over one and one-quarter million people signed a petition to place the Jarvis-Gann property tax limitation initiative on the ballot of the June 6 election.

The initiative, labeled Proposition 13, was to cut property taxes to 1 percent of market value, for all forms of property, both commercial and residential. Tax assessments would return to levels from the year 1975–76, and could climb no faster than 2 percent a year as long as the property did not change owners. Only when property did change hands could assessments again be set by market value.

Tax Revolt As "Voice"

The property tax revolt of 1978 was an example of what Alfred Hirschman calls "voice," the articulation of citizen dissatisfaction with the politics of an economic or political institution.[1] Voice, in order to be effective, requires the organization of like-minded individuals in an effort to change the institution. Because a change in institutional policies typically displaces a previous policy that was to someone else's benefit, voice is dramatic and conflictual; the dynamics of organization for institutional change often resemble a sudden upheaval. Voice also tends to be redistributional; that is, the institutional change it involves may affect the publicly conferred rights that help determine individual income. Thus, the organization for institutional change incorporates a bias; in fact "organization is itself a mobilization of bias in preparation for action." [2]

The "mobilization of bias" in the organization of the property tax revolt was evident. The fundamental issue, according to Jarvis, was the defense of "the most essential human right . . . the right to own property." [3] Government legislators and bureaucrats threatened this right by taxing property to provide inessential services that redistributed income, regardless of the preferences of the property-owning majority. Proposition 13 would fight this built-in bureaucratic bias in favor of government expansion by cutting off the flow of property tax revenue; that is, it would alter the built-in redistributional bias of governmental activity. Jarvis was opposed by those groups who benefited from the increasing scale of government and its redistributional programs: city officials, government employee unions, low-income renters, the recipients of welfare services. The alternatives were not neutral; the question facing the voters on June 4, 1978, was which way the redistributional bias in local and state politics would tilt.

As could be expected for such an issue, voting was very much on class lines. Property owners voted for the initiative by a margin of 72 percent; a majority of renters opposed it. Margins of support were greatest among those with annual incomes between $8,000 and $25,000. Members of public employees' households were against the Jarvis initiative, as were a majority of blacks. Whites, especially whites in households with no public employees, favored it. While Democrats were split, Republicans voted for Proposition 13 by a three-to-one margin. When asked on election day which services they would be most willing to have reduced, the bias against redistributional, social welfare programs was once again apparent. The most frequently selected program was welfare (54 percent), followed by parks (26 percent), libraries (25 percent), and public transportation (21 percent). Schools, fire departments, and police were rarely mentioned.[4] The redistributional nature of the conflict was summarized by John Kenneth Galbraith's observation that Proposition 13 was a "revolt of the rich against the poor." [5]

The Exit Option

Not all conflicts are as dramatic as those characterized by vocal, organized electoral campaigns; nor is voice the only way for citizens to express their dissatisfaction. Hirschman suggests that an alternative mode of expression is "exit." Rather than collectively articulating dissatisfaction with institutional behavior, the alternative is for individuals, as individuals, quietly to leave the domain of the institution. Exit relies on the presence of alternative institutions; given alternatives, the individual can choose to leave an institution with which he or she is dissatisfied, in favor of another, preferable institution. Voice is the only means of expressing dissatisfaction in the absence of choice. Exit is less dramatic, less visible, and much less newsworthy, as a means of protest.

As Hirschman noted, exit belongs to the realm of economics, which typically studies exit in the form of customers abandoning one firm's product for another.[6] Voice, on the other hand, is a typically political response; if dissatisfied customers form an interest group to lobby a manufacturing firm to improve its product, that is political, voice-like protest.

"The economist tends naturally to think that his mechanism is far more efficient and is in fact the only one to be taken seriously." [7] The roots of this attitude toward exit can be traced to Adam Smith and his attack on the mercantile system, with its authoritarian, centralized direction of the economy. The mercantile system had, he wrote, made the mistake of giving the state "the duty of superintending the industry of private people, and of directing it towards the employments most suitable to the interest of the society"; however, in the proper performance of this duty "no human wisdom or knowledge could ever be sufficient." Instead, Smith proposed "the obvious and simple system of natural liberty," in which "Every man, as long as he does not violate the laws of justice is left perfectly free to pursue his own interest his own way, and to bring both his industry and his capital into competition with those of any other man." [8] By using his capital and industry "in such a manner as its produce may be of the greatest value, he intends only his own gain, and he is in this, as in many other cases, led by an invisible hand to promote" the society's interest.[9] Smith's system had the moral advantage of individual freedom and promoted societal efficiency as well.

This was a remarkably revolutionary idea, even for the Enlightenment. But modern welfare economics has justified Smith's leap of faith by its discovery that rational individual choice, in a free competitive market for private goods, results in an efficient, Pareto optimal distribution of goods and services. Goods and services are distributed so well that it would be impossible to conceive of a transaction involving two or more parties that would leave everybody any better off. Any transaction that would benefit one person would necessarily leave another person worse off.[10]

The success of the "invisible hand" has naturally left economists convinced of the superiority of the exit option. Because competition and self-interest work so well in normal market settings, the argument is that competition should be encouraged in other settings (in order to provide the alternatives necessary for the exit option to work) and individuals be allowed to leave one organization for a preferable one. Some economists have even suggested that greater competition and a greater range of individual choice would increase the effectiveness of the political process. For instance, some people are not really interested in the outcome of political elections, while others are. There is no guarantee that the people who are not really interested will outvote a minority of individuals who would greatly benefit by a particular outcome of the election. The performance of elections could be improved, then, by allowing individuals the option of selling their votes. No one would be deprived of the franchise except by free will. Those who are not particularly interested in the outcome of an election could be made better off by selling their votes to the highest bidder. The interested minority could be made better off by paying the price necessary to win the election. The creation of a market allows the invisible hand to make some people better off, without really hurting anyone.

However, the invisible hand has not been demonstrated to be efficacious in all possible settings. In fact, with regard to one kind of goods, public goods, there is a very clear argument that the concept of the invisible hand does not apply. Before dealing with exit and voice as they apply to the property tax revolt, it is necessary to understand something about public goods.

Public Goods and the Necessity of Coercive Organization

Public goods are viewed as problematic by economists precisely because they spoil the efficacy of the invisible hand. Public goods may be defined as those goods which can be consumed jointly; that is, one person's consumption of the good does not "use it up" so that another person does not have it available for his own consumption. For example, a stereo is a public good for a group of students living in the same apartment. One individual in the apartment may enjoy the music without depriving other students of its benefits. This is altogether unlike a purely private good such as a candy bar, which may be fully consumed by only one individual.

For normal private goods the requirement of Pareto optimality includes the requirement that each individual consume enough so that the marginal cost to him is equal to the marginal benefit. For instance, if an individual regards the first candy bar as being worth 50 cents, the second 30, and the third 20 cents, and if the price of candy bars is a quarter, he will buy only two candy bars, because at this quantity, the net benefit (30 cents) is greatest.

For public goods, however, the requirement for Pareto efficiency is that the sum of the marginal benefits of all those individuals who jointly consume the good should equal the marginal cost. This conflicts with net benefit maximization on the part of the individuals in that group, because these individuals will still equate individual marginal benefit and marginal cost. Thus, if a stereo costs $250 and each individual values it as being worth $100, then no individual alone would buy the stero. However, three individuals living together can achieve the benefits of the public good if they organize themselves as a group rather than act as individual net-benefit maximizers. The paradox is that individuals must be forced by organizations to abandon individual net-benefit maximizing behavior in order to realize the benefits of public goods. Without this organization, individuals will act as "free riders" to get the benefits of whatever level of public good consumption is made available by the purchases of other individuals. The necessity of coercive organization to share marginal costs (and the consequent inefficacy of the invisible hand) is the hallmark of public goods.[11]

The Invisible Hand in Metropolitan Fragmentation

The most common coercive organization which requires cost sharing in order to procure public goods is the state. However, the coercion which is implicit in the state's taxation of its citizens poses an ethical problem to those economists who believe that the state could more efficiently perform its function (and, at the same time, increase the range of individual freedom) with a dose of the invisible hand. For instance, Milton Friedman's famous proposal of a voucher system for education is in this vein. Under this proposal, parents of school-age children could buy an education at any private or public school with vouchers provided by government. This would not only increase the competitiveness of the education industry; it would greatly increase the range of choices of schools. It also amounts to creation of an effective exit-like option in this area. "Parents could express their views about schools directly, by withdrawing their children from one school and sending them to another." [12]

Another way of building choice and greater efficiency into the coercive governmental production of public goods was suggested by an economist named Charles Tiebout in 1956.[13] It involved allowing individuals to choose which government they will live under within a given metropolis. Tiebout was suggesting that if it is necessary to have coercive organizations (governments) to supply public goods efficiently, individuals should at least be able to choose which coercive organization they wish to join. In a metropolitan area, with modern transportation systems, this is a practical possibility. An individual can keep his or her job while residing in virtually any municipality, even in a metropolis as large as Los Angeles. The remarkable claim made by Tiebout is that giving individuals a choice in this way serves not only to reassert individual autonomy but also to restore efficient individual autonomy, that is, the invisible hand. When faced with a choice of jurisdictions, each providing a different mix of public services, the people of a metropolitan area will sort themselves out on the basis of similar tastes for public goods. Given a wide enough range of choice, no individual need live in a jurisdiction where he obtains a set of services markedly different from what he prefers, and each jurisdiction can efficiently meet the tastes of its homogeneous population.

This view was in direct opposition to the traditional reform position with regard to metropolitan government. The traditional reform position was that too many governments operating in a single metropolitan area inhibited efficiency, accountability, and equity. The numerous small governments were thought to be too small to achieve economies of scale and too numerous to deal effectively with area-wide problems. Furthermore, fragmentation inhibited accountability because there were too many officials for even an alert, intelligent citizenry to keep track of. And finally, a tendency was observed for some governmental jurisdictions to have the lion's share of resources in a metropolitan area, while others were unable to meet basic service needs.[14]

The followers of Tiebout, who came to be called the public choice school, dismantled much of the traditional consolidationist argument. Small local governments, they maintained, are more accountable than large, comprehensive governments with their immobile, unresponsive bureaucracies. While it is necessary to have some large, comprehensive layers of local government to deal with metropolitan problems such as air pollution, other problems can be dealt with by progressively smaller layers of local government right down to the neighborhood level. And while it may be desirable to realize economies of scale in production, these economies are available to even the smallest jurisdiction by means of contracting. For instance, in Los Angeles under the Lakewood Plan, small local governments can contract with the large county sheriff's office for the provision of law enforcement services.[15] Taken all together, "a public economy composed of multiple jurisdictions is likely to be more efficient and responsive than a public economy organized as a single area-wide monopoly." [16]

Exit and the Property Tax Revolt

In the presence of a range of alternatives, exit is a viable means of registering discontent with a local governmental policy. Since the property tax revolt of 1978 was primarily directed against local governments, it is worthwhile asking if, in fact, exit was not used as an alternative, quiet means of registering middle-class discontent with local property taxes.

It is the theme of this book that the same property owner discontent with bureaucracy, social services, and taxes was anticipated, at least in Los Angeles County, by a full quarter century of "quiet" tax revolt, in which property owners expressed dissatisfaction individually by means of "exit" rather than collectively through the use of the statewide initiative. During this quarter century, middle-class homeowners, motivated by the same frustrations that were behind Proposition 13, responded to these frustrations through their choice of residential communities. They "voted with their feet" for low taxes, low levels of bureaucratic activity, low levels of government spending on welfare and other social services; they did this by choosing to live in those municipalities that offered this mix of policies. By doing so, they were also able to create suburban communities that escaped the ravages of crime and urban blight. The municipalities that allowed them to express this demand in this way were, for the most part, not in existence before 1954. This book tells the story of the creation of these cities, beginning with the city of Lakewood in that year.

The book also discusses the effects of exit-like protest on the distribution of individuals and resources within the Los Angeles metropolitan area. While few would deny that Proposition 13, as an instance of voice, was primarily a redistributional conflict, it is less generally maintained that the creation of the Lakewood Plan cities and the subsequent exit of middle-class homeowners to these cities was equally redistributional in nature. On the contrary, the Lakewood movement is generally regarded as an experiment in the efficiency of contracting, which was the means by which these cities procured their essential services.[17] The question, then, is whether exit-type protest can be as redistributional as voice-type protest. Can exit be a quiet means of mobilizing bias?

Clearly, the incorporation of the Lakewood Plan cities and the migration of homeowners to small-scale, low taxation cities was not dramatic or conflictual in the same way as the Jarvis-Gann tax revolt. Municipal incorporations, despite often intense local opposition, proceeded rather automatically by established rules. Individuals chose to move to these new cities, or they did not. Discontent with the old-line cities was not organized, mobilized, or dramatically articulated. Yet it is the theme of this book that the twenty-five years of exit-type protest was just as redistributional, just as political, and just as far-reaching in its consequences as the openly conflictual Jarvis-Gann initiative. The municipal incorporation of the Lakewood Plan cities was a "revolt of the rich against the poor," carried out by exit rather than voice.

This interpretation, if accurate, throws into doubt both the traditional urban consolidation position and the position of the followers of Tiebout, for both positions use "efficiency" as the norm to attack or to defend metropolitan fragmentation. This book, on the other hand, suggests that consolidated metropolitan government and fragmented urban government, are both biased, but toward different societal groups.[18] It treats the political considerations of metropolitan organization as paramount. It does not assume that an ideal structure of metropolitan government exists which, if realized, can produce an efficiency gain sufficient to make everyone better off. The basic question in this book—left largely unaddressed by either the traditional urban reformers or the public choice theorists—is not how to bring into being the perfectly efficient metropolitan organization, but how politics tends to interact with any form of metropolitan organization to produce alternative biases in outcomes. Who will be helped, and who will be hurt, by the organization of government in metropolitan areas?

1   The Political Origins
of the Lakewood Plan

Until the Civil War, Southern California was a land of huge ranchos, whose owners maintained the life-style of the Spanish dons. With the bankruptcy of the cattle industry and the abrupt elimination of the native Californian as an economic factor, came an entirely new order based on land development, economic growth, and boosterism. The dominant interests were those pushing for economic development: the construction industry, banks, commercial interests, property owners, and real estate salesmen. Babbitt replaced the California don.

Boosterism is an essentially parochial force. Economic growth in San Francisco was viewed as a threat, not a complement, to economic growth in Los Angeles. The major metropolitan areas viewed themselves as competing for resources. San Diego, in particular, became Los Angeles's antagonist in a great and bitter 1880s feud for railway connections and preeminence in Southern California.

Boosterism led to conflict not only between metropolitan areas but also within them. The political history of Los Angeles County in the twentieth century can be viewed as a struggle for the leadership of that metropolitan region, a struggle that pitted the City of Los Angeles against those other units that resisted its bid to annex the rest of the communities of the basin.

Los Angeles: A City Surrounded

The foremost booster of Los Angeles was Harrison Gray Otis. Otis bought complete control of the Los Angeles *Times* in 1886, just in time to promote the area's greatest land boom. Advertisements in the East and Midwest called Los Angeles "a land of perpetual spring" and a "veritable sanatorium," with plenty of work and cheap land.[1] A railroad rate war led to one dollar tickets from Kansas City to Los Angeles. The resulting flood of people caused skyrocketing land prices (and an explosion of lucrative real estate advertising for the *Times*). Although many were ruined in the resulting crash, Otis came out ahead and ready to continue promoting development in Los Angeles.

From the first, economic development was linked to territorial expansion of the city limits. Since Los Angeles was a landlocked 43 square miles at the beginning of the century, Otis and others felt that development of a port was a prime requisite. This necessitated the so-called "shoestring" annexation in 1906 that connected the city with the proposed site of the port in San Pedro-Wilmington and consolidation with those port cities in 1909. It also resulted in a break between Otis and the Southern Pacific Railroad political machine, which dominated state and local politics and opposed a free harbor for Los Angeles.

The break with the Southern Pacific and Otis's hatred of a growing labor movement led to a marriage of convenience between Progressive reformers and Otis, whom Roosevelt had called "a consistent enemy of every movement for social and economic betterment." [2] George Alexander, the reform candidate, beat the labor candidate in 1909, and was reelected in 1911 after the Times building was dynamited and three local laborites confessed to the crime.

Having fought for a port in Los Angeles and an antilabor local government, Otis regarded water as another requisite of economic growth. With his son-in-law and partner, Harry Chandler, he formed a secret combination with other businessmen to buy land in the San Fernando Valley in an attempt to convince the city of Los Angeles to bring water to the valley from the Owens Valley, 225 miles to the north. Using his newspaper to publicize the idea of a water famine, he got voter approval for a $23 million bond issue for the Owen River Aqueduct in 1906. Then a series of

court decisions ruled that the city of Los Angeles also controlled the water
of the Los Angeles River, granting the city a virtual monopoly on water.
When Owen River water began to flow in 1913, the city adopted the recommendation of the Municipal Annexation Commission that Los Angeles
provide water only to those adjoining communities that agreed to be annexed (if unincorporated) or consolidated (if incorporated). For almost
two decades, Los Angeles used water as the key weapon in its program of
expansion.

In addition to Wilmington and San Pedro, Los Angeles engulfed the
cities of Hollywood, Venice, Lordsburg, Sawtelle, Watts, Eagle Rock,
Hyde Park, Tujunga, and Barnes City. It also annexed huge tracts of unincorporated territory, most notably the San Fernando Valley in 1915,
which further increased the value of the Otis land investments. By 1930,
the city covered 442 square miles, more than ten times its area at the turn
of the century. The land, water, and antilabor policies had apparently
paid off in economic growth, as the Los Angeles economy was one of the
strongest in the country.

But by the mid-1920s, after a drought in the Sierras, the city's Department of Power and Light began to doubt its ability to supply water to the
entire Los Angeles basin, and the process of expansion began to slow. In
1927, Los Angeles and the adjacent cities joined in pressuring the state
legislature to form the Metropolitan Water District (MWD). By the time
the MWD brought Colorado River water to the county in 1941, the city of
Los Angeles was no longer able to force the annexation of its thirsty
neighbors.

Furthermore, Los Angeles's neighbor cities had gained in population
and in economic and political clout. In 1900 there had been only 28,000
people in ten cities outside of Los Angeles. By 1910 there were 107,000
people in 24 other cities; and by 1930 there were 646,000 people in 43
other cities. Eleven of these were beach cities hemming in Los Angeles on
the west. A nearly solid line of 14 cities, from Burbank in the north to Long
Beach in the south, blocked expansion to the east. Where there were no
cities on Los Angeles's borders, there were hills or mountains.

By 1930, Los Angeles was a city surrounded. While it had achieved at
least 60 percent growth each of the previous six decades, after 1930 it was
never again to grow faster than 31 percent in a single decade. By the 1970s,

like other cities with fixed boundaries, it was experiencing a continuous population decline with an accompanying loss of retail trade and industry. While its government still served a larger population than that of any other city in the county, it had fallen far short of a majority of the county's population. Los Angeles was never to achieve its early hopes of hegemony; its metropolitan area, called "forty suburbs in search of a city," was to become the prime example of the fragmented metropolis.

Long Beach

Long Beach, originally developed by a Los Angeles syndicate in the 1880s, was incorporated in 1888, disincorporated in 1896, and reincorporated in 1897. A pattern of intense competition with Los Angeles was established almost immediately, as Long Beach fought with the "northern menace" for the right to develop the neighboring San Pedro-Wilmington harbor area. Its defeat in the initial skirmish seemed merely to strengthen its resolve. During the decade after 1900, it grew faster than any city in the nation, reaching 17,000 by 1910. By 1920, it had permanently replaced Pasadena as the second largest city in the county. During Los Angeles's period of greatest territorial growth in the 1920s, Long Beach responded in kind, annexing major residential developments and industrial sites, tripling its population to reach 140,000.

Long Beach suffered a temporary setback in 1921, when the great Signal Hill oil field was discovered right in its backyard. The oil companies successfully stopped Long Beach's attempts to annex the oil fields by incorporating Signal Hill as a separate city, even though it was surrounded by Long Beach.[3] But even more petroleum was to be found beneath Long Beach's tidelands. In the 15 years after the Wilmington oil field was discovered in 1938, 750 pumps raised $110 million in oil. The city spent $40 million of its share of the oil money by developing the Long Beach harbor to compete with that of Los Angeles.

During the Second World War, Long Beach became the site of major Navy and Air Force installations, and the Douglas Aircraft Company located just north of Long Beach in the Lakewood area. With the postwar housing boom, Long Beach began to contemplate a second period of territorial growth. While Los Angeles had been closed in by neighboring municipalities, Long Beach enjoyed the prospect of almost limitless expansion in the growth region of southeastern Los Angeles County. This particular region—handy to all the major railways and highways, close to the ports, bordering the established manufacturing area east of Los Angeles, and the only possible route of expansion for the housing boom—seemed to be Long Beach's for the taking. It began a new annexation campaign. Between 1947 and 1953, it was, after Glendale, the fastest annexing city in the county, growing from 34 to 40.5 square miles. It is no wonder that Long Beach boosters contemplated the possibility of a new county to be created out of the southeast portion of Los Angeles County, with Long Beach as the county seat.

Los Angeles County

If Long Beach hoped to be the big winner in the postwar game of metropolitan politics, Los Angeles County promised to be the big loser. Every annexation by Long Beach and other cities further deprived the county of part of its reason for being.

Like Long Beach, the county government had long been competing with the city as a source of political leadership for the metropolitan area. Its method of competition was to seek new services to provide to larger proportions of its population. Soon after Los Angeles Progressives obtained one of the first county home rule charters in the country, the county established a library system and a public health system. During the Depression, it received the responsibility for administering welfare. County cultural services, such as the art museum, were developed with state authorization, and the county's responsibility for justice further guaranteed its political influence.

As one veteran county supervisor put it, all of these service responsibilities help to explain "the prominence of county government in the area, its vigor and power." But a further source of power (and arena for competition) was guaranteed when the county procured state statutes permitting it "through various channels to perform all municipal functions of unincorporated territory, much of which became urban in character." [4] During the 1920s, for instance, despite the vigorous annexation campaign of the

City of Los Angeles, the population of the unincorporated territory jumped from 118,000 to 323,000. It was during this time, too, that the county sheriff's office became much larger and more efficient, and streets and roads were improved in many unincorporated communities, in an effort to demonstrate to the inhabitants of these areas that they need not pay municipal taxes to receive adequate urban services. As municipal taxes rose, the financial inducement to stay unincorporated became significant, as the county's services were paid for out of a uniform county-wide tax that citizens continued to pay even after annexing to an incorporated city. The board of supervisors became noticeably more reluctant to allow municipal incorporations. In fact, there was only one successful incorporation in the 24-year period between 1930 and 1954.

For instance, in 1931, an attempt was made to incorporate a community in east Los Angeles. The board of supervisors in this case arbitrarily refused to call an incorporation election on the grounds that the petition was not filed in good faith, although it had no legal grounds for such a denial. In 1932, another attempt was made to incorporate a sizeable territory in east Los Angeles consisting of 75,000 individuals. The attempt died by strangulation, as the board of supervisors took no official action on it for three years.[5] (East Los Angeles is still unincorporated, but has not prospered under county administration. It has become one of the largest slums in the Southwest.)

In 1935, soon after county reluctance to encourage incorporation became obvious, the city of Los Angeles pointed out that the urban services provided by the county to the growing unincorporated communities of Los Angeles County were paid for by the county property tax at a uniform rate for everyone, including the citizens of incorporated cities who were also providing their own services by means of municipal property taxes. The city's Bureau of Budget and Efficiency proposed that the state force unincorporated communities to incorporate or be annexed to neighboring cities, in order to stop the subsidization of unincorporated areas by municipalities. It is a measure of the county's political strength that this proposal was not approved by the state legislature either on this occasion, or at any one of the numerous other times it was made during the next forty years. (The equity problem caused by this method of financing services to unincorporated areas has yet to be resolved in 1980, when the population of these areas has risen to over one million.)

After World War II, the population in the unincorporated areas again jumped, and still the county was reluctant to approve new incorporations. When the citizens of Willowbrook tried to incorporate in 1945 (apparently to restrict the immigration of blacks from Los Angeles), the board of supervisors was at pains to point out the financial weakness of the city and used its political influence to help kill the incorporation movement.[6] In 1949–1950, Bell Gardens, a community of 27,000 dust bowl immigrants and wartime job seekers, sought incorporation as a means of regulating the rates of the local water company. Although the county board of supervisors approved the election, the county employees (especially county firefighters) successfully killed the incorporation attempt. The county's success in discouraging incorporations was to lead two political scientists to remark in 1952, "it is becoming extremely difficult to create a new city." [7] (This was only two years before the biggest flood of new cities in the county's history, a flood that the county itself helped to create.)

By 1950, the county property tax rate rose, for the first time, above $2.00 per $100. The cities believed that much of this tax burden represented the cost of providing improved county services to ever larger numbers of unincorporated free riders. In 1957, the League of California Cities introduced a bill that would have required unincorporated communities to establish tax districts to finance municipal services. The bill was opposed by the County Supervisors Association, which knew that it was just this free ride that made nonincorporation attractive. Those incorporation attempts that did go to election were easily defeated by the argument that incorporation would mean adding a municipal property tax to provide services that the county provided by charging everyone in the county. The reason given by the County Supervisors Association for opposing the bill was that it would be impossible to work out the costs of providing services to these municipal service districts. The only bill that came out of the session was the Community Services Act, which made the creation of such municipal services districts possible, but voluntary. It is not surprising that none of these self-taxation districts were formed on a voluntary basis.

Seeing that they had no power to force unincorporated communities to either incorporate or tax themselves for the provision of municipal services, the incorporated cities had only one option left: annexation. While Los Angeles was effectively blocked from significant annexation on most fronts, Long Beach and other municipalities were rapidly annexing much of the urbanized population which the county depended on to maintain its political importance. Thirty-one square miles were added to the territory of the incorporated cities between 1947 and 1953. This accounted for much of the million or so added to the population of the incorporated cities during this period. This trend was a real threat to the county's influential fire, police, and other departments. An example of this threat to the county's power was Long Beach's designs with respect to the Lakewood Park development.

The Lakewood Park Development

North of Long Beach City College and the Douglas Aircraft plant was a small group of houses, among the bean fields and hog farms, called Lakewood Village. In 1949, one of the inhabitants of Lakewood Village was a young lawyer named John Todd. He was a member of the Lakewood Taxpayers' Association, a group which, in Todd's words, "had a strong feeling that Lakewood Village should remain unincorporated. They professed some fear of the city of Long Beach, but expressed a much greater fear of incorporation of the area as the city of Lakewood. To even mention or suggest the same was worse than slurring motherhood." [8]

In 1950, however, a developer named Ben Weingart and two partners purchased (with the aid of FHA-secured loans) 3375 acres of farm land in the Lakewood area and the local water company. In the same year, in the middle of those empty acres, they built the country's largest shopping center. They then initiated the largest single-owner housing development in the country to create a market for the shopping center. They planned a community of 17,000 homes for a population of 70,000, twice as big as the famous planned community of Levittown, and roughly one-third as large as Long Beach's population. Ten thousand homes were built by 1952. Despite the skepticism of some contemporaries, young house-hungry veterans were soon buying as many as one hundred homes in an hour.

In July of 1951, in the midst of this rapid development, the City of Long

Beach released "An Analysis of the Advisability of Annexing All or Part of the Lakewood Area to the City of Long Beach," otherwise known as the Wentz Plan after its author, the administrative assistant to the city manager. This plan was based on the argument that Lakewood was economically, socially, and geographically part of Long Beach and should be annexed in small increments. A sympathetic majority for annexation should be obtained in each of the increments. Since organization to oppose annexation would be difficult in small units, it would become obvious that there was no viable political alternative to annexation.

Furthermore, it was argued that annexation would be beneficial for the citizens of Lakewood, who would be unable to provide themselves with police, fire, and garbage collection services at a low cost without the advantages of Long Beach's strong revenue base. Long Beach's tax rate, at $1.00 per hundred in 1950–1951, was not considered especially high; in Los Angeles the tax rate was $1.85. Indeed, in 1953 a report by the Los Angeles Bureau of Municipal Research pointed out that "Long Beach has unusual resources and tideland oil," and that "if Lakewood has the opportunity of annexing to Long Beach on satisfactory terms, it is a choice given to few communities in a similar situation." [9] The *Saturday Evening Post* projected the same image of Long Beach in a 1952 article called "The Town with Too Much Money." [10]

Despite this image of wealth, there was opposition to annexation among the citizens of Lakewood. Ben Weingart, the developer, was convinced that his investment was being threatened by the commercial interests of Long Beach, who, he believed, were using annexation to get control of the Lakewood Shopping Center. With the strong financial support of Weingart, and under the leadership of the young attorney, John Todd, the Lakewood Civic Council was incorporated to fight the annexation battle.

It was decided that the way to fight the piecemeal annexation strategy was to obtain the signatures of property owners representing 50 percent of the land in each annexation increment. These signatures would automatically stop an annexation attempt, even if the property owners represented a small proportion of the population. This property owner protest, as it was called, would make it unnecessary to run election campaigns for each of the multiple increments, a task which Wentz had correctly foreseen was beyond the organizational abilities of Long Beach's opponents. However, getting these signatures required time. Todd, after researching the law, found that these protest petitions could be circulated immediately after the annexation proponents had published a notice of intention to circulate annexation petitions, although the annexation petitions themselves could not be circulated until 21 days after publication of the notice. In other words, the law seemed to allow the opponents of annexation a three-week organizational headstart over the proponents.

Basing their entire organizational strategy on this interpretation of an obscure point of law, the opponents committed thousands of dollars and hundreds of hours to the task of early and prompt circulation of protest petitions. The city of Long Beach immediately challenged this interpretation, which let protest petitions be circulated prior to the annexation petitions themselves. Long Beach's protest was found to be invalid, and Lakewood was permitted its organizational advantage. (In numerous other incorporation and annexation battles, the technical details governing the process of annexation and incorporation proved to have similarly significant effects on the ability of one side or the other to organize and mobilize an effective campaign.) The organizational advantage proved decisive, as Lakewood's method of fighting annexation was used "in countless annexation proceedings with the same story being enacted time after time." Prior to each annexation election, the Lakewood organizers would obtain a court order invalidating the Long Beach election based on the property owner protest. "As a matter of fact, it got to the point where we were invalidating elections that probably really had been validly held by the city of Long Beach. We just couldn't seem to lose." [11]

But in 1952, Long Beach was able to make a deal with Douglas Aircraft Corporation, exchanging expanded runways for Douglas's agreement to annexation of their plant. This annexation connected two of Long Beach's "shoestrings" of incorporated territory, completely enclosing South Lakewood. This proved to be an insurmountable obstacle, and South Lakewood was eventually annexed to Long Beach. This was the gravest single blow to the antiannexationists.

Ben Weingart suddenly proposed incorporation as the only way to stop the annexation of the shopping center and North Lakewood. But local taxpayers continued to oppose incorporation, for how could a primarily residential city afford to incorporate?

The Lakewood Plan Saves the County

While fighting annexation, Lakewood had also been fighting for the location of a municipal court building to be built by the county in Lakewood to serve the growing southeastern region. A developer named Herb Legg ran for county supervisor, with a platform that included getting the court building in Lakewood, and won. In discussing this issue with one of Legg's assistants, Todd was told that the Lakewood site was not really a good one, because Lakewood would eventually have to be annexed to Long Beach. In response, Todd suggested that Lakewood could afford to incorporate if it could contract with the county for the performance of municipal services, in order to avoid costly investments in buildings and equipment. Legg's assistant, somewhat surprised, thought this might be feasible. "This, then, was the beginning of the Lakewood Plan." [12]

By mid-1953, with South Lakewood lost to Long Beach, sentiment for incorporation on the basis of county contracting was growing. An incorporation committee was formed, and the businessmen who backed Todd hired a contracting firm called Boyle Engineering to study the possibility. In December, 1953, the Boyle Report was issued, and became the "Bible for the incorporation movement." [13]

The Boyle Report recommended that the city contract with Los Angeles County for road maintenance, health services, law enforcement, a building department, and planning services. The city could remain in the Lakewood sewer maintenance district, the county library district, and the local recreation and park district, and it could contract with a private firm for garbage collection.

Having carefully developed public sentiment for incorporation, the incorporation committee set out to obtain signatures for an incorporation petition. They obtained the signatures of 37 percent of the property owners in 14 days.

On January 7, 1954, the board of supervisors held a boundary hearing for the proposed incorporation, to discuss exclusions requested by several residential areas which feared a municipal property tax. In a dramatic departure from its antiincorporation stance of the past two decades, the county supervisors voted down all exclusions, and three days later approved an incorporation election for Lakewood. An election was held in March, and the people of Lakewood voted for incorporation by a 60 percent majority. Said Todd, "no one in the city of Long Beach had given the Lakewood incorporation movement a ghost of a chance." [14]

The Lakewood Plan As a New Option

With the successful conclusion of their contract negotiations, both Lakewood and the county set out to publicize the arrangement. While the county had claimed in 1951 that the municipal service districts were unworkable because it was impossible to calculate the cost of services given to specific areas within the county, it now found no problems with contract pricing. Indeed, it established the office of county-city coordinator to encourage new incorporations and to promote county contracting. [15]

Thus, a new option was presented to the residents of unincorporated urban areas in Los Angeles County. Previously, the options had been basically three in number: (1) remaining under county jurisdiction, without local control over local services and without the power to zone and determine land-use patterns; (2) being annexed and effectively swallowed up by an older neighboring city with large municipal tax rates and perhaps a large population of individuals with different life-styles; or (3) incorporating, and trying to support a police force, fire department, and other urban services with a small tax base. Under pressure from an intense annexation campaign, the first alternative seemed to disappear. The new option, which came to be called the Lakewood Plan, provided the advantages of local autonomy that went with incorporation, but without the expense of creating new bureaucracies to provide necessary services. Tax rates could be kept low by relying on services provided cheaply by the county.

This plan became even more attractive in 1956 with the passage of the Bradley-Burns sales tax, which allowed both cities and counties to participate in a uniform sales tax program at the fixed rate of 1 percent. By thus encouraging a uniform local sales tax, it provided a source of revenue for cities that had previously feared that a local sales tax would force shoppers to other cities. The revenue from the sales tax suggested the possibility of paying for county contracts with sales tax revenue, thus avoiding a municipal property tax altogether.

The popularity of this new option was immediate. In 1956 four new cities incorporated; in 1957, ten; in 1958, two; in 1959, four; in 1960, five. Twenty-six new cities had been created in seven years. Over 580,000 people lived in these cities. By 1970, six more cities had been created, and the population of the combined 32 new cities was over 870,000. All but one of the new cities (Downey) relied primarily on contracting rather than the creation of new bureaucracies for the delivery of urban services.

Law Enforcement: The Politics of Pricing

Opposition to the Lakewood Plan from the established cities continued, despite its popularity in urbanizing areas. The old-line cities were still determined to annex the most profitable of the newly developing areas, and to a great extent, they succeeded. In fact, after 1954, more land was annexed to established cities than incorporated into new cities in every year but five. Over 175 square miles were annexed during the two decades after Lakewood, while less than 140 square miles were incorporated. But still, the Lakewood Plan made annexation much more difficult and much less likely to succeed.

There were initial attempts by the older cities to stop the Lakewood Plan in both the legislature and in the courts. One of these attempts successfully forbade the California Highway Patrol to contract services to municipalities. But the most dramatic conflict between the independent cities and the contract cities was (and is) the continuing attempt to demonstrate that the taxpayers of incorporated cities were in effect subsidizing the inhabitants of the Lakewood Plan cities, just as they were the inhabitants of the unincorporated communities, through artificially cheap county services.

The county's incentives to subsidize Lakewood Plan cities would, of course, be strong. While Lakewood Plan cities would get the benefits of inexpensive services, the county would be in a strong competitive position as supplier to the contract cities. By keeping charges below the true costs of providing services, the county could guarantee a continued demand for its bureaucratic services in developing urban areas and simply pass on the difference to county taxpayers as a whole. The county sheriff's office, which was early regarded as one of the strongest supporters of the Lakewood Plan, became the focus of the contract pricing controversy.

The sheriff of Los Angeles County is one of the few local officials in the United States to be elected by seven million people. He is one of the most important and powerful elected officials in the county. The sheriff's support for the Lakewood Plan was marked, and, at times, overwhelming.

In 1958, the newly formed city of Norwalk revised its police service policy. The city administrator, E. Frederick Bien, felt that the sheriff's services were expensive and unresponsive. A resolution to form a municipal police department was proposed and eventually defeated by a three-two vote of the Norwalk council. Interestingly, the decisive vote was cast by the measure's author. According to one councilman, the sheriff applied strong pressure to the group to reject the resolution, a view supported by other knowledgeable observers. In this case, the sheriff used his powerful position in county politics to prevent a city from exercising its formal right of withdrawal from the plan. One point emerges clearly—a city cannot always withdraw from the contract system if it wants to. Its actions are not internally controlled; rather they are subject to outside political influence, particularly from actors in the county government.[16]

The county sheriff's office, which does over 70 percent of the county's contracting by revenue, has also been the county department most eager to minimize the costs charged to contract cities. When Lakewood incorporated in 1954, the county sheriff's contract required that he provide the same level of service that he provided in unincorporated areas, and that he be paid an amount equal to the fines collected by the city, previously collected by the county. In other words, the arrangement was to maintain status quo ante. As in an unincorporated community, Lakewood's inhabitants made no contribution to the cost of law enforcement but the fines they paid for traffic violations. The preincorporation level of subsidy was maintained.[17]

By the end of 1957, 14 more cities had incorporated. At this time, the county decided to consolidate the previously separate law enforcement and traffic patrol contracts, and a new arrangement was made. Contracting cities paid the salaries of all patrolmen and their supervisors, the cost of the patrol cars and supplies and equipment, and 50 percent of county overhead. The equal split of county overhead was based on the presumption that the contracts were mutually beneficial to both the city and the county. This resulted in a charge per patrol car, operated on a 24-hour basis, of $79,400.

By this time, the issue of contract pricing became a very salient one to both the independent cities (which felt they were now subsidizing the overhead law enforcement costs of contract cities as well as the total law enforcement cost of unincorporated communities) and to the contract cities, which felt that their contracts were necessary for their financial viability. Both sides organized to press their claims.

In 1957, Johnny Johnson, the public relations consultant who had organized a half-dozen of the early incorporations, and who was to be involved in many more incorporations in succeeding years, brought together the mayors of three of "his" cities (Paramount, Norwalk, and Bellflower) in the back room of the Paramount mayor's store, and organized the California Contract Cities Association "to take appropriate action on problems involving cities contracting for the performance of services," as the by-laws were to read. In response, the Independent Cities Association was formed, "to try to break the contract cities," as Johnson was to remember; more specifically, they fought the issue of contract pricing for law enforcement from the other side.

By 1962, the Los Angeles County grand jury was brought into the conflict. At this time, a compromise solution was reached, in which the grand jury rejected the argument formerly used by the county, which held that the contract cities should be charged only for the services received in addition to basic policing. "On the other hand it accepted the argument that since the sheriff had areawide responsibilities, which should be supported by all the areas in the county, these costs should not be in the contract price." [18] This compromise position resulted in an increase in the price charged, to $94,000 per patrol car.

While the grand jury reexamined the issue every succeeding year of the 1960s, no major changes occurred until 1969. In this year, a private study indicated that, even under the grand jury's compromise formula, contract cities were still being subsidized at the rate of $5 million a year. The county grand jury then suggested that the county make a major review of its pricing methods. Another private consultant was hired to do this, reviewing various methods from marginal costing (which charged the contract cities only for the additional costs they incurred) through formulas which added different aspects of overhead costs, up to full cost pricing. The supervisors' response, over the objections of the sheriff's office and the contract cities, was to increase the patrol car rates by 65 percent, to $230,000.

This represented such a significant jump in law enforcement costs for contract cities that several cities began to consider abandoning the contract plan or looking for other contracting agencies. The Contract Cities Association, hoping to bolster its position with supervisors, hired its own consultant with the aid of a federal grant under the Safe Streets Act. In one of the few recorded instances of consultants bringing in a report unfavorable to the clients who hired them, the consultants rejected the concept of marginal cost pricing because the contract program was not, in fact, marginal to the Los Angeles Sheriff's Department. It accounted at that time for 31 percent of the population served by the department, 36 percent of the patrol cars, and 48 percent of the case load. The consultants' report, known as the Booz-Allen and Hamilton Report, became a landmark in the continuing controversy surrounding contract pricing. Its recommendations were attacked by the sheriff's department, which suggested several other costing models that would have been less expensive for the contract cities.[19] However, the report's suggestions were adopted by the county board of supervisors, which was increasingly concerned with balancing the county budget, rather than subsidizing the Lakewood Plan cities.

At this time, the city of Lakewood hired a new city administrator, Milton Farrell, who had previously been a county firefighter and county lobbyist. His first and foremost responsibility, placed on him by the city council, was to do something about the Booz-Allen Report and the high cost of law enforcement contracts. His immediate response was to seek relief in the state legislature, with a bill to make a clear legislative policy statement that contract cities were not to be charged with overhead expenses that would continue whether or not contract services were provided, thus undercutting the result of the Booz-Allen Report. He approached the assemblyman from Lakewood, who also represented Long Beach and chose not to sponsor the bill. He then approached Joe Gonsalvez, the assemblyman whose district included six contract cities including a small part of Lakewood. Although Gonsalvez was at first not eager to take on the task, he soon found out that this was a major bill in the minds of his constituent cities, and became a very effective lobbyist for what was to be the Gonsalvez Bill.[20]

Because the Gonsalvez Bill would bring about a substantial reduction in the contract price by excluding certain countywide costs from overhead, it would also mean a substantial reduction in county revenue, estimated at $1.2 million a year. The county supervisors, focusing on this revenue loss, opposed the Gonsalvez Bill. The county sheriff, focusing on the loss of contracts, favored it. With heavy lobbying by contract cities as well, the bill passed the state legislature twice, once vetoed by Governor Reagan, who preferred that the state stay out of the local conflict, and then signed into law by the same governor in 1973.

To this success for the contract cities in the state legislature, the city of Los Angeles and other independent cities responded in the courts. They claimed that the Gonsalvez Bill was unconstitutional and that it denied the citizens of the independent cities equal protection of the law. The suit was successfully defended by a committee of contract city attorneys, led by John Todd. At the present time the independent cities are seeking a change in the law from the state legislature.

Fire Protection: Firefighters Local No. 1014

While the sheriff may have helped the contract cities by keeping law enforcement rates to a minimum, the contract cities have had other friends among the county staff. Perhaps more than any other single agency, the County Firefighters Union played a key role in the incorporation of many of the Lakewood Plan cities.

While the county firefighters had been successful in stopping the incorporation of Bell Gardens in 1949, they were unsuccessful in stopping the annexation of large chunks of developing land around Long Beach and elsewhere. Where this occurred, county fire stations were closed, and county firemen lost their jobs. By 1950, it was common practice for county firemen to take the city firefighter's exam, in expectation of losing their jobs with the county. In fact, it was widely believed that the county fire department would fold within a very short while.

The problem was more severe for the county firemen than for the county sheriff's deputies, because fire protection was not supported by the county general funds, but by a special consolidated fire district. When a city annexed a piece of prime revenue-producing land, that land was automatically taken from the rolls of the fire district, leaving the district with that much less revenue with which to pay for its services.

Partly because of this, and partly because county firemen are much more likely to be career men in their department than are sheriff's deputies in theirs, the firefighters' local took a much more strident, political stand against city annexation. In fact, the activities to protect the boundaries of the fire district, organized within the union's Boundary Committee, became the most significant job protection program of the union. Despite the fact that (until 1969) direct political action on the part of governmental employee unions was illegal, firemen would walk the streets during annexation campaigns explaining the advantages of remaining unincorporated.

In 1954, the firefighters found it much more promising to support an incorporation than fight one when Lakewood incorporated with the avowed intention of staying within the consolidated fire district. When they were unable to stop Downey and Santa Fe Springs from incorporating and creating their own fire departments, this failure, contrasted with the success of Lakewood, caused them to reassess their activities. The result was that the firefighters decided to support the Lakewood Plan. In fact, their commitment was so strong that one union leader felt that "we generated the whole thing," meaning the Lakewood Plan.

The firefighters became the chief catalysts for most of the Lakewood Plan incorporations, bearing much of the organizational cost that had to be overcome to mount a successful incorporation effort. When news of a possible annexation became known, the firefighters would be at the first small meeting of concerned citizens, providing the information that residents needed in order to organize. They would provide guidelines for creating a permanent organization; emphasize the importance of bringing in the local newspapers and generating a time schedule; and relay information about other county organizations that would provide assistance, such as the city-county coordinator. They also would emphasize the importance of having professional public relations consultants brought in to run the campaign—consultants with whom the firefighters had established good working relationships. They even would provide some of the $50,000 it took to run a year-long incorporation campaign, although that was not always necessary. More frequently, they would provide information about sources of financing for the campaign from people who would profit from an incorporation, including people who could be expected to seek garbage and street-sweeping franchises from the city, and water companies and other utilities whose very existence depended on the right governmental policies. When it was awkward for these firms to make outright contributions to an incorporation campaign, the firefighters would even supply their services as middlemen.

One of the most important requirements of an incorporation campaign is dedicated volunteers to walk the streets to pass out pamphlets and convince voters. The firefighters provided invaluable help at this. One public relations consultant, who ran the incorporation campaign in South El Monte, reported having teams of firefighters (from other parts of the county so that they would not be recognized as firefighters) canvass the neighborhoods for him. Both consultants I talked to were emphatic in their belief that few, if any, Lakewood Plan incorporations would have been successful without the help of the firefighters.

Besides helping in individual incorporations, the union supported a lobbying campaign in Sacramento to make sure that there was adequate legislative support for the plan. One member of the union, a captain, was kept at Sacramento full time during the legislative sessions after Lakewood's incorporation. Other captains in the union substituted for him during this entire period.

Furthermore, after they had helped the Lakewood cities incorporate, "our feelings about annexation changed," as one union member remembers. They began to actively support annexations by Lakewood, Norwalk, and other contract cities that were a part of the county fire district.

Finally, the county firefighters and the county fire department actually encouraged established cities to consolidate with the county fire district. The main feature of this policy was that it guaranteed employees in city fire departments jobs with comparable pay and greater chance of promotion, if the city would switch to consolidated fire protection. This policy guaranteed some support, instead of undying opposition, for consolidation with the county from the politically influential municipal firefighters. As a result, a number of cities began joining the county fire protection district in the 1960s and 1970s, especially smaller cities such as Signal Hill, Bell, and Huntington Park, where the salaries were low and consolidation would mean a raise in pay.

This politically astute action on the part of the county fire department, and especially the union, resulted in the success of their primary goal of saving jobs. By the mid-1950s, the number of fire stations had stopped decreasing and had actually begun to increase. In fact, they increased from 80 in the mid-1950s to approximately 130 at the present time. This robust growth on the part of a county agency that was expected to die was matched by expansion in other county agencies. While there were still a million people in unincorporated county territory in 1970, there were over 827,000 in cities contracting for fire protection, and over 700,000 in cities contracting for law enforcement, building inspection, industrial waste services, street maintenance, lighting maintenance, and even personnel services. It is no wonder that County Supervisor Ford applauded the Lakewood Plan as "one municipal innovation that gave great promise of preserving local independence, and at the same time providing benefits of administration by seasoned career men in county service." [21]

Was the Lakewood Plan Imposed from Above?

The evidence presented so far, which places the Lakewood Plan incorporations within the context of an ongoing struggle for leadership of the metropolitan area, allows a clearly elitist interpretation of the incorporations. According to this interpretation, developers and/or owners of utilities (in Lakewood, Ben Weingart was both) realize that incorporation will lead to increased land values and make an investment secure. While they may not be able to lead an incorporation battle themselves, they can finance an incorporation campaign to be run by public relations consultants or lawyers. These professionals can organize the legal and public relations aspects of the campaigns, and county employees worried about their jobs can provide manpower. And in fact, in Los Angeles County, all of these actors did cooperate in numerous incorporations, and all benefited from them. All that was required in the way of local participation were a few local figureheads in each community to head the incorporation campaign and to run for local office; a few status-conscious community leaders of this sort could be found in any community. (For those willing to take bribes, the incorporation of a new community offers the promise of financial gain; several of the ardent incorporationists in various Lakewood Plan cities were arrested for corruption, including city council members.) With the legitimacy provided by a few local leaders, the well-oiled incorporation machinery could move into gear. According to this view, the Lakewood Plan cities were essentially a "plot" organized for the financial gain of a group of outsiders, not different from the plot to irrigate and annex the San Fernando Valley, earlier in the century.

The role of the public relations consultant is central to this elitist interpretation of the incorporations. These consultants admitted to running authoritative campaigns. The reason for this approach, they claim, is that the locals are likely to ruin an incorporation campaign, if not kept under a firm hand. Johnny Johnson, who "ran" more incorporation campaigns than any other, claimed that all the problems of such a campaign are internal organizational problems, because external opponents of incorporation are conveniently irrelevant to the legal incorporation procedure. Without a professional, he claims, local incorporationists will split into rival factions within thirty days of the inception of a campaign, and guarantee failure. For this reason, the consultants I talked to emphasized the importance of being handed the controls of an incorporation campaign even before the incorporation committee is created, before the incorporation movement is underway, "before the proponents have a chance to quarrel with themselves." Johnson ran the campaigns in a rather dictatorial way to keep any issue besides incorporation from being brought out. Various people have different ideas about what to do with the city once it is formed; these differences must be kept hidden until after the incorporation is successful. Potential and actual enemies must be kept separated; Johnson told the incorporation committees he formed, "you sleep with snakes until after the incorporation election." [22]

Since they were brought in at the very beginning of the discussion of incorporation, the consultants were in on (or made single-handedly) all the important decisions. They put the incorporation committee together, making sure all important community groups were represented and no factions left out. They helped select a slate of candidates for the council.

They decided how the money would be used in advertising and how to present the benefits of incorporation to the public.

With enough "cooperation" from the locals and with enough volunteer help and money (which could be supplied by firefighters, utilities, industry, or franchise seekers), the consultants felt confident of their ability to win virtually any election. The consultants viewed the voters as an obstacle to success, but an obstacle that was infinitely malleable, given enough time and money. If three mail-outs were not sufficient to convince a majority of the voters, then perhaps four would do it. (Johnson estimated that the three to five mail-outs which were the central expense in his campaigns were normally sufficient to convince the electorate.) And, of course, consultants could be hired by cities to convince the electorate of the benefits of annexation to established cities, with similar hopes for success. The electorate could be talked into going either way, the consultants thought.

Given the dominant role of developers, industry, firefighters, and other external forces, and given the consultants' confidence in the flexibility of the voters, it is no wonder that many people close to the action in these incorporation campaigns view them as being imposed from above. John Todd, the apparent organizer of the Lakewood incorporation, admitted to me that without the developer Weingart "we never could have incorporated." An early city manager of Lakewood felt that the incorporation was imposed.[23]

I fully agree that the organizational costs of an incorporation campaign are extremely large, and that without the external forces of developers, firefighters, PR consultants, and the ability of these external actors to work together as a team, virtually none of the Lakewood Plan cities would have been successfully incorporated, and there would now be approximately forty-five large, fiscally similar cities in the county, instead of eighty-one diverse cities of various sizes.

However, the fact that the local citizenry did not voluntarily take on the organizational costs of an incorporation campaign does not necessarily mean that they were exploited, or irrational, or unaware of their best interests, or even that they were controlled like puppets by outside forces. On the contrary, since the creation of a city government is a nonexcludable, public good, it is in fact rational for most citizens to act as "free riders,"

allowing others to bear the organizational costs associated with incorporation, even if they themselves would benefit by it. Each individual is likely
to feel that his or her own contribution to an incorporation campaign is
tiny compared to the total organizational costs involved. The small probability of making a difference in the outcome and the fact that each individual will enjoy the benefits of incorporation if it succeeds whether or not he
or she contributed to its success combine to make it unprofitable for most
individuals in a community to undertake the start-up costs associated with
incorporation.[24]

If this is the case, then the initial passivity of local communities when
compared with the activity of the external actors does not necessarily imply manipulation of the local communities by those external actors. Instead, if local citizens did in fact benefit from incorporation, then their
passivity could be viewed as exploitation of the outside elites, who have
provided an invaluable service free of charge.

A more serious case for the elitist view of incorporation can be based on
the confidence of the PR firms that they could manipulate voters toward
either position by means of biased or incomplete information. It is true
that without adequate information, voters can never be certain that they
are voting in their own best interests. Furthermore, since one vote counts
so little, it is not clear that the rational voter will spend much time or effort
to supplement the free information that is being supplied by public relations firms. But this does not mean that voters are unable to vote in their
best interests when the information from both sides in an incorporation
campaign is made available to them.

The case studies of the Lakewood Plan incorporations in this book reveal that, once the issue of incorporation was sparked, the voters in these
communities were in fact informed by arguments on both sides. Despite
what Johnson said, the antiincorporation position was generally presented
in each case, either by neighboring cities hoping to annex the community
if incorporation failed, or by local property owners' associations which
feared a property tax, or by apartment developers who feared zoning restrictions in a new city. Turnout at the polls was generally higher than for
regular local elections, and highly organized incorporation campaigns
were defeated again and again in certain communities.

In the next few chapters, all of the "elitist" actors discussed so far will appear in the narratives of incorporation campaigns. Developers, utility companies, firefighters, and public relations consultants play a constant and predictable role. They appear because they are the actors who find it to their own advantage to overcome the organizational costs associated with incorporation. However, it is not assumed that rationality is the characteristic of these elites only; on the contrary, the primary focus of the next few chapters will be on the average voter in the community to be incorporated: the individual who will be paying the taxes and receiving the services provided by the new city in the years to come. What kinds of issues are presented to the average voter to convince him or her to vote for incorporation? What kinds of citizens have an economic incentive to vote for or against incorporation?

The incorporations in the next few chapters suggest that the individuals involved in incorporation campaigns behaved very much like cool, calculating economic actors. Indeed, given the emotional intensity that was evident in incorporation campaigns, the prevalence of rational calculation was striking. While the rhetoric of incorporations was very much in terms of generalities like "community control," it was very clear that the desire for community control was meaningful only in the context of economic incentives. There were many incorporations that were voted down when the voters were convinced that "community control" was not in their best economic interest; in these campaigns, elitist actors were not able to stampede the rational voter.

2

Commercial Incorporations

Long Beach was not the only city that actively sought to expand its population and resource base by annexation. After the Bradley-Burns sales tax act was passed, developing land offered not only the promise of expanding property tax assessments, but also increasing sales tax revenue, for development brought commercial centers like the Lakewood Mall to the suburbs. A fierce, competitive struggle for attractive land developed. In the eastern part of the county, Whittier annexed over five square miles in the eight years after the Lakewood incorporation, and as a result, it was able to reduce its tax rate from $1.00 to $.50. In the San Gabriel Valley, eight cities fought actively for more land, and succeeded in annexing over 26 square miles between them. In the central and southwestern portions of the county, there was less unincorporated land left to acquire; but Hawthorne, Inglewood, Gardena, and Torrance sought to acquire what land there was.

In the face of this frantic competition for land, why were so many urban communities determined to resist annexation to established cities? Why was incorporation under the Lakewood Plan the preferred option? Most proponents of incorporation explain this preference as springing from a desire to "preserve a local identity" or to "gain local control"; but neither

of these responses is entirely satisfactory. For instance, many incorporations did not preserve an identifiable local community. On the contrary,
incorporations like those of Bradbury and Irwindale were secessions
from long-established unincorporated communities. Others represented
agglomerations of several communities, like Pico Rivera and La Canada-
Flintridge. Still others, like Commerce and Cerritos, were completely
artificial constructs, unrelated to any traditional community. Some clearly
identifiable communities like Lancaster voted down incorporation repeatedly, while Centinela, East Whittier, and other established localities
quietly let themselves be annexed. Those cities that did incorporate
around traditional community boundaries, Downey and Lakewood, for
example, often immediately sought annexation of territory far beyond the
boundaries of the original community. So "preservation of local identity"
is related in no systematic or satisfactory way to municipal incorporation.

The motive of "gaining local control" is also too vague to be satisfactory. Certainly, the creation of an autonomous, authoritative local government is undertaken in order to ensure that local rather than nonlocal
interests control decisions—but which decisions? What aspects of municipal government are so crucial that some people will devote hundreds of
hours a year, for as many as ten years, to ensure that the local community
be incorporated rather than annexed?

Providing Local Services

There are three steps in providing local services: demand articulation,
funding, and actual delivery of the service. In the United States, local governments have historically been responsible for all three.

Are any of these functions especially relevant to the proponent of incorporation? When the incorporationist says he favors incorporation to gain
"local control," over which function does he wish to gain control? It is
possible that the incorporationist wants to gain control over the agencies
which actually deliver the services. That is, Lakewood, for instance, might
have incorporated because its citizens felt that the Long Beach police and
fire departments, as large bureaucracies, would provide their services in an
unresponsive or inefficient manner. However, Lakewood and almost all
other cities incorporated as contract cities, which means that the same

county agencies provided essentially the same services before and after incorporation. Furthermore, these bureaucracies were at least as large as the Long Beach bureaucracies, and (at least with the county sheriff's office) subject to at least as many charges of bureaucratic unresponsiveness. While one incorporation (Downey's) did result in the creation of locally controlled service delivery agencies, the motivation for the creation of these agencies can be attributed to the funding aspect of local government. (See a later section in this chapter.) Local control of service delivery was clearly not the primary motivator of contract city incorporation.

Demand articulation is a function completely separate from that of service delivery. Local governments, in the form of elected representatives of the population, make authoritative decisions about the combination of services to be delivered to the population, and arrange for their delivery (either by creating a service delivery bureaucracy or contracting with an existing agency).

The Tiebout argument (see the Introduction) is based on the centrality of the demand articulation function. That is to say, different groups and communities of people have different levels of demand for local services, but a single government can normally decide on a single mix of services. Therefore, if two different communities exist within a single government structure, one or another, or both, communities will be unhappy with the level of services provided. A community that is annexed is faced with the prospect of having its preferences absorbed (and ignored) by the larger community. Incorporation, on the other hand, lets a community articulate its distinct preferences with regard to local services. As Robert Bish applies this argument, the incorporation of the Lakewood Plan cities was advantageous "because their preferences for municipal goods and services were quite different from those of neighboring areas, and they wanted to meet these demands as efficiently as possible." [1] The explanation for these new cities, according to the Tiebout interpretation, is that "families with similar tastes locate together, and often, incorporate as a municipality." [2]

However, the main argument of this and the next chapter is that this "demand articulation" interpretation of the Lakewood Plan cities is of secondary importance, and that the primary motivation for the Lakewood Plan cities has followed from the way in which local services are funded. American municipalities have traditionally been responsible for funding the services they provide through "local" resources. That is to say, the state grants local governments a "property right" to locally owned property. These governments can tax locally owned property to provide the services to that property. The Bradley-Burns sales tax act of 1956 used the same "point of origin" mode of distributing sales tax revenue to localities. The localities were viewed as having an autonomous right to a share of the sales tax revenue generated within their borders, rather than (for instance) receiving funds through statewide distribution to localities on a per capita basis.

Both the sales tax and property tax generated an intense competition for resources among local governments. Indeed, the renewal of intense annexation wars among the cities of Los Angeles County after World War II was due not so much to the "booster" mentality of earlier decades, but to a very simple calculation. Obtaining new sources of funding local services was at the root not only of the annexationist intentions of Long Beach, but also of the incorporationist motivations of Lakewood.

The explanation for municipal incorporations lies not in differences in tastes among individuals for public services, requiring local autonomy over demand articulation units; rather, it lies in the basic similarity of individuals summarized by the economic notions of price and income elasticity of demand. Incorporating around a considerable revenue resource allows inhabitants to procure services at a low tax price. Even incorporations around a small tax base can be explained in terms of the centrality of the revenue function and the relative redistributional advantage of incorporating as opposed to being annexed to another community. However, an explanation of low-resource incorporations must wait for a later chapter.

Downey and an Economic Model of High-Resource Incorporations

One of the first high-resource incorporations was that in Downey, in the rapidly developing east-central portion of the county between Long Beach and Whittier. In the 1950s Downey experienced both the rapid residential growth and industrial development that were the fate of this region. Located between the San Gabriel and Los Angeles rivers, it was one of the few regions in the county with an excellent ground water supply. This, along with its location, was one of the reasons industries (including aero-space, chemical, and fertilizers) were attracted to Downey. It had achieved a population of almost 50,000, mostly newcomers since World War II.

This area was naturally plagued with problems, including a high crime rate. The city was reportedly one of the centers for narcotics trafficking in California. In addition, fire protection was poor because of fragmented water delivery. Although there were over fifty water districts in the area, many served only a half-dozen houses. Many bits of land had no water, and many others were served by wooden water mains. In addition, the county served the area with only two patrol cars and a single fire station, for its 12.5 square miles.

A rapidly rising demand for more services was one of the clear motivations for incorporation. At first, this would seem to be indicative of a clear "demand articulation" effect. The citizens of Downey were unique among the citizens of unincorporated areas because they demanded more in the way of municipal services. Their preference structure was different, and municipal incorporation election allowed them to reveal this difference.

However, is this accurate? When an individual votes (with a ballot or with his feet) for a new jurisdiction, does this always say something about that individual's distinct tastes for public goods?

To find out, let us imagine that each jurisdiction supplies some per capita level of service Q_J to the jurisdiction's population N_J. The total quantity of the service is $Q_J N_J$; if the per unit price is r, then total cost of the service is $rQ_J N_J$. If each individual pays a proportion t_i of the total cost of the jurisdiction's service, and spends the rest on some private good z available at a price p_z, then each individual's budget constraint is given by

$$y_i = p_z z_i + t_i(rQ_J N_J),$$

where y_i is the individual's income. Now if Ms. Smith's tax share t_i is equal to the ratio of the value of her property h_i to the total assessments in the jurisdiction H_J (that is, $t_i = h_i/H_J$), her budget constraint can be graphed on a commodity space as in figure 2.1. As the graph shows, both the slope of the budget constraint and the Q_J intercept are a function of the per capita assessments (H_J/N_J) in a given jurisdiction. That is, the individual's budget constraint depends on jurisdictional wealth, and is different in different jurisdictions. So when considering annexation to city K with lower

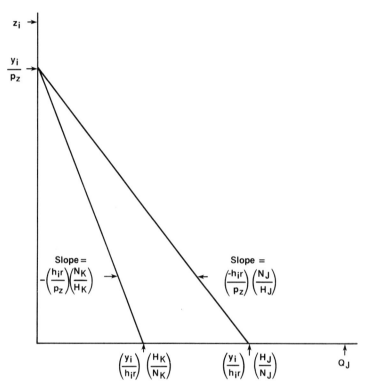

Figure 2.1
The Effect of Jurisdictional Resources on Individual Budget Constraints

per capita assessments (as opposed to incorporation as a separate jurisdiction j with higher per capita assessments), Ms. Smith may well be
influenced by the fact that a given level of municipally supplied services
can be made available to her at a lower effective tax price in the richer
municipality. That is, she can get the same services at a lower tax price or
more services at the same tax price.

Thus, a group of people may seek incorporation because they are
uniquely endowed with a resource base, rather than because of differences
in tastes for municipal services. This is exactly what happened in the creation of the city of Downey. Downey's per capita assessed valuation was
high enough so that Downey could afford more services at a lower tax

price by erecting institutional barriers around its property tax base. Before incorporation, the community paid a tax rate of $.85 for the county fire district, and for that they had the benefit of one station with one pumper. The strong tax base in Downey was diluted by being pooled in a jurisdiction that included many areas with much weaker tax bases. After incorporation, the citizens of Downey withdrew from the county fire district and created their own fire department. They paid a municipal tax of $.29 per hundred and acquired four fire stations, and a 100-man police department as well. "Our assessed valuation was trmendous. We never wanted for money." [3]

The incorporation of Downey says nothing about the preference structure (i.e., the structure of indifference curves) of the citizens who voted for it, or who subsequently moved to the town. It does say something about the relatively inexpensive per unit tax price facing these people, given their location in a resource-rich community. It is not clear that the individuals of Downey have a greater interest in police and fire protection than the citizens of resource-poor Willowbrook and East Los Angeles, who have tried and failed to incorporate on numerous occasions. Presumably, the citizens of these latter areas dislike being robbed or burned out of their homes just as much as the more affluent citizens of Downey. But, the citizens of Downey were located in such a way as to make it possible for them to procure protection from these threats at less cost. The incorporation reveals something about a difference in means, not a difference in tastes.

In addition, only months before the incorporation election, the League of California Cities had pushed the Bradley-Burns sales tax through the legislature. This made it possible for every city to tax 1 percent of the sales revenue within the city limits, without fearing that local business would relocate in a neighboring city where the sales tax burden would be smaller. By 1960, this tax resulted in more than $1 million in revenue a year within the city limits. That money made it possible to provide even better services; without incorporation, the money would have gone to the county, where the rich sales tax potential of Downey would have been diluted over such a broad population that it would have had no significant effect on the quality of services within Downey itself.

Because of this, the city council candidates and the incorporation committee ran a 1956 campaign based on the promise of providing more services at a smaller tax cost through municipal departments. Downey was to be the only city to incorporate after 1954 with its own complete set of service departments, rather than with a set of contracts with the county.

One of Downey's early projects was to expand its tax base even further. The first council considered annexation of Bell Gardens to the west. However, on a per capita basis, Bell Gardens was a poor investment; besides, Downey's police chief informed the council that out of every 100 ex-convicts in the state, 90 were in Bell Gardens.[4] This dramatic, but exaggerated, claim swung the council into opposition to the annexation requests by various Bell Gardens groups, who were subsequently rebuffed by South Gate as well. The prospect of having to provide expensive police services to a city that couldn't pay its own way ran counter to the principle on which Downey was organized.

By 1959, however, Downey's city council had picked a more profitable target: the industrial and commercial area north of Bell Gardens and northwest of Downey known as the Central Manufacturing District on county zoning maps. This was, in 1959, the only large piece of unincorporated territory in the industrial corridor stretching along the main transportation routes east of Los Angeles, and it was also one of the richest areas in the county. Downey "really went after it. If we really had been successful, we would have been one of the wealthiest cities in the country—a terrific thing." [5] However, when the Central Manufacturing District incorporated as the City of Commerce, the officials in Downey realized that the kind of economic calculation they had used could cut both ways.

Commerce: "It's Your Money"

The idea of the city of Commerce originated with Warren Bedell, to whom it was suggested by a publication of Berkeley's Bureau of Public Administration called *Annexation? Incorporation? A Guide for Community Action.*[6] Unlike the incorporationists in most of the Lakewood Plan cities, Bedell had a history of political involvement. He had been LaGuardia's Fusion Party chairman for Queens in 1930 and 1932. Bedell became convinced that the commercial property surrounding the two residential neighborhoods of Bandini and Rosewood Park was a resource which would support an excellent set of municipal services without undue strain on business. He regarded the interests of business and of citizens as not necessarily incompatible.

However, Bedell immediately ran into a differing interpretation from local businesses. They preferred to remain unincorporated. Where Bedell's arguments failed, however, the threat of annexation was to succeed in inspiring business interest in incorporation. In the mid-1950s, the city of Montebello to the east made an attempt to annex a great deal of empty territory up to, and including, the site of the Lever Brothers plant, which was, along with the railroads, one of the largest firms in the area, and which had repeatedly turned down Bedell's suggestions of incorporation. It cost industry about $15,000 to fight that incorporation, and that cost became one of Bedell's "strong points with industry." It would become easier to incorporate as a city with a small population to support rather than to continue to resist annexation from large cities. When Charles Atwood, manager of the Lever Brothers plant, heard that Downey was going to seek to annex the area, he was immediately converted. He called up Bedell and the two of them "whipped up a notice of intention" to incorporate.[7] Bedell got 30 signatures of support and filed the notice of intention just four minutes before the Downey city clerk and city manager reached the county offices to file their notice of intention to annex. Since only one proposal could be pursued at a time, the annexation bid had to be postponed until the incorporation proceedings were concluded one way or another.

The basis for the coalition between the homeowners, such as Bedell, and the representatives of industry, such as Atwood, was clearly understood on both sides. Bedell felt that the resource base in Commerce could provide services to the residents. As in the model presented earlier, more services could be provided at a cheaper tax price if the resource base was not diluted with the larger population and smaller tax base of Downey. Industry would rather provide no services; however, sales tax revenue, diverted from the state coffers, would be sufficient to provide services for a small population without *any* property tax. Eighty thousand people in Downey, however, paid property taxes. Although Downey's tax rate was low, compared to those of the older cities, it was higher than would be necessary if industry kept control of the smaller, local incorporation. This point was made clearly when one of Downey's councilmen asked Atwood of Lever

Brothers why he wanted to sponsor a local incorporation; the reply was "to control the tax rate." [8]

Bedell's notice of intention to circulate a petition was filed in the spring of 1959. Downey tried to influence industrialists to be annexed, rather than to incorporate, with a statement of industrial policy, assuring industry of "representation in government and tax and municipal service benefits." [9] While this inducement was sweet enough to get some Bell Gardens industrial firms to ask Downey to annex them, it was not enough to get Lever Brothers and the railroads to change their minds. Downey then enlisted its own industrialists to try to sell Downey.

Even after a date for the election was set by the board of supervisors, Downey continued to oppose the incorporation. However, as Giddings remembers, "we were up against the railroads and Lever Brothers, and they whipped us. They promised them [the residents] a park and a recreational area in the mountains." [10]

Within the business-homeowner coalition was a division of labor that reappeared in many high-resource incorporations. Local industry supplied the money to organize the incorporation; it hired the public relations firm that ran the incorporation election; and it financed the filing of incorporation papers and the mapping of incorporation boundaries. Bedell organized a committee of homeowners to circulate the petitions required of residents, and to supply some of the support needed by the public relations firm for his election drive.

In Downey, the residents had had enough autonomous political leadership to stay in control of the incorporation proceedings and of the city government. In Commerce, on the other hand, with a small population to draw on, with fewer interested residents, and a better organized industrial group, the initiative quickly passed from Bedell to what became known as the Industrial Council, which was to keep political power during the incorporation and for a dozen years afterward.

Much of the credit for the Industrial Council's dominance must be given to the professional public relations consultant. The professional hired by the Industrial Council was named John Gold, called by Bedell "one of these opportunity boys from Harvard Business College." One of Gold's first jobs was to select a slate of council candidates to be backed by the Industrial Council.

The council candidates selected by Gold were all Republicans; none were Mexican-American, and none had ever belonged to a labor union. This group contrasted sharply with the overall population of Commerce, which was about 60 percent Mexican-American, over 90 percent Democratic, and mostly working class. Nevertheless, all five of the members of the business-backed slate won, and were sworn into office in January of 1960.

As virtually every incorporation proponent told me, the first few months of a new incorporation are overwhelming. The new five-member council, composed normally of five individuals who have never had anything to do with politics before, are suddenly charged with creating the law and providing the services for a government of up to 80,000 people. Nearly all the incorporation leaders I talked to referred to someone to whom they turned for advice during these months: an experienced city attorney, or the political consultant who helped them incorporate. Since Gold had helped select the candidates in the first place, they were perfectly willing to listen to his advice as executive director for the Industrial Council. Bedell admits that his own increasingly outspoken opposition to the Industrial Council's slate eliminated him as a source of leadership. "They had to turn to Gold because they were afraid he was going to drop them and then they wouldn't know what the hell to do." [11] Within a year, however, Maurice Quigley, one of the original council candidates, became involved in a power struggle, in both Commerce and a bank in which he and Gold were officers, and replaced him as the source of leadership on the council and, in the opinion of observers, as the city's liaison with industry.

Conflicts between industry and a group of the residents became evident very soon after incorporation. One local editor discussed this conflict in a column called "Commerce, a Horrible Example of What a City Should Not Be":

The basic problem, of course, is the obvious one. There is a definite, widespread and virtually unbridgeable conflict of interest in the "city." The industry group—largely nonresident—originated and pushed the idea of a city strictly on the basis of obtaining a reduction in taxes, while providing a minimum of community services. The residents, on the other hand, had a city government, with all the wealth of industry behind it, pictured as a one-way free ride to Utopia. Both groups would have been infinitely better off had they accepted the offer they received at the outset to join Downey, a well-established, well-run city with enough prudence to provide both a tax savings and improved standards of municipal services.[12]

As evidence of the "mess" Commerce was in, the editor pointed to the gag rule. Initiated months after incorporation, it prohibited any citizen from addressing the city council unless he had submitted a written statement 72 hours in advance.

While Bedell still insisted that there was no necessary conflict of interest between industry and residents, less than two years after incorporation he was filing recall petitions for four out of the five members of the city council, on the grounds that they were "subservient to special powerful industrial interests, using city revenue for the benefit of big interests and refusing to give attention and cooperation to the needs of the residents." When Bedell filed 790 recall signatures with the city clerk, city administrator Lawrence O'Rourke withdrew all but 41 of the names because of "irregularities." Bedell pointed out that the city administrator was not authorized to eliminate signatures because of irregularities, but should point them out to the city council, which should then report them to the proper authorities. Bedell also charged that many individuals had been intimidated and harassed into withdrawing their names. While the district attorney looked into Bedell's charges, nothing came of it, and the recall attempt died from "lack" of signatures.

One of the reasons for the passivity of the citizens, according to Bedell and a few other dissidents, was that the city was able to deliver a large number of free or inexpensive services out of the revenue that flowed automatically into the city's coffers from the sales tax and other state sources. This revenue allowed them to build a large swimming pool, run a large recreation program that included a summer camp program in the mountains and free bus service.

These services were all supplied without a municipal property tax. In fact, the city was able to provide a tax reduction by taking over the functions of special districts that were not authorized to use the automatic sources of revenue that came to Commerce. In the first two years after the city of Commerce incorporated, 14 special districts were eliminated in the area, including a park and parkway district, a road district, and several lighting districts. While almost every other Lakewood Plan city stayed in the consolidated fire district, Commerce withdrew from the county fire district (which had a tax rate of about $.85 at that time). It then contracted with the fire district to provide fire protection. Again, this maneuver allowed the city to pay for a major service out of the automatic revenue sources. Commerce also undertook another maneuver that was more common among Lakewood Plan cities. It withdrew from the county library district, on the grounds that it could get better service by relying on its own revenue sources rather than pooling its property tax resources with a large chunk of the county. Overall, this resulted in an average actual reduction of about $1.00 per $100 in the property tax rate for different parts of the new city.

Despite the lack of support from other Commerce citizens, Bedell continued to fight to displace Quigley and O'Rourke, uncovering what he thought was adequate evidence of irresponsible and even corrupt behavior. He even complained to the leaders of industry whom he regarded as the principal source of support for the city council and administration:

I spent twelve years, talking with people and meeting people and finally, I told industry, "You're all supposed to be pillars of the community, I'm sure you're the leading lights of your communities, but in Commerce you don't give a damn, because it's just a place where your company makes money. And you figure you're riding the gravy train." [13]

In 1973, however, Bedell's campaign against Quigley and O'Rourke came to a stop. In that year, O'Rourke approached a refrigeration contractor for a $300 a month allowance, for himself and Quigley, which was to guarantee a city refrigeration contract. The contractor tape-recorded the conversation on his phone as well as subsequent conversations in which he confirmed the offer with Quigley himself. The resulting district attorney investigation led to revelations of other misconduct, including misuse of city employees and city money. A grand jury tabulated $22,203 in personal expenses charged by Quigley to the city, but did not indict him for these undocumented expense accounts because they had been approved routinely by the other members of the city council. They did indict him for bribery, however, and both officials spent some time in jail.

While this quite naturally changed the makeup of the city council considerably, Bedell is still not satisfied. In his opinion, the resources that have multiplied themselves many times over since incorporation are still not being used appropriately. Bedell believes the citizens have been "bought off" by bread and circuses, much as the Tammany Hall machine which he fought in 1932 secured the support of voters by means of particularistic services without sharing power. When Bedell complains of council policies to other citizens of Commerce, they are likely to respond to the recreation area in the mountains and the free bus service, and say "look what they have given us." Bedell replies, however, that they have given the citizens of Commerce nothing: "it's your money." As for the much vaunted recreation program in Commerce, he says it should be able to do more, since it spends one million dollars a year on 3,000 children. For the most part, however, he regards the recreation program as being "only on paper." The present city council, like past city councils, makes sure that the 300 city workers are very happy and satisfied, as they constitute the single most powerful voting and electoral bloc in the city. With their support, and the support of the still untaxed industrial interests, they don't have to worry about dissidents like Bedell.

The unrepresentative and often corrupt local government of Commerce, dominated to a great extent by city workers and local industry, makes it impossible to maintain that incorporation took place to create a responsive government capable of smoothly interpreting the unique demands of the area's citizenry. This does not mean that the citizens of Commerce were necessarily irrational, manipulated, or naive in (passively) supporting the creation of that city; it simply means that the dominant factor justifying the incorporation was a uniquely endowed tax base, rather than a unique set of preferences for public goods and services. Commerce, like Downey, incorporated to realize the benefits of a large local tax base that automatically supplied large amounts of sales tax revenue for the city government while protecting local industry and homeowners from municipal property tax burdens.

La Puente: Gaining Control of Land and Land Values

The struggle between incorporationists and annexationists after the Lakewood incorporation struck one contemporary observer, a county official, as essentially a struggle for resources. In 1960, this county official estimated that the land being fought over in this manner was worth at least $25 billion: "Owners and developers, actual and potential, of this vast deposit of natural wealth are locked in a tug-of-war to rezone or unzone, or annex or incorporate with the basic aim of gaining control of land and hence land values." [14] One of the areas of the county where this struggle was most bitter was the San Gabriel Valley, the historic eastern access route to Los Angeles, close to the industrial and commercial center of the county and containing the tracks of the Union Pacific and Southern Pacific railroads.

La Puente was a growing suburban community just north of the Whittier Hills in the central San Gabriel Valley. The year after Lakewood's historic incorporation in 1954, the Chamber of Commerce and other groups in La Puente met to discuss the possibility of incorporation.

With the Lakewood success story held before their eyes, the citizens of La Puente saw little to discourage their own plans for incorporation. They should be able to finance the same services with much the same revenue sources that Lakewood had used. This was especially true since their proposed incorporation included many miles of prime industrial development along the railroad tracks. The property tax base of a community lucky enough to incorporate around this prime resource would be one of the best in the county, and the sales tax revenue would be expected to grow munificently as well.

But the landowners along the tracks were not pleased by the prospect of supporting a growing suburban population. Besides being taxed to support services for the residential population, municipal incorporation raised the specter of proresidential zoning and residential encroachment on land that could most profitably be used for industrial growth. One of the large landowners was James M. Stafford, a member of the Los Angeles County Regional Planning Commission and a friend of Supervisor Herbert Legg, from the county supervisorial district that included La Puente.

The first two incorporation proposals to the board of supervisors were rejected for technicalities in the petitions involving boundary description errors and inadequately assessed property valuation. Legg cut the area covered by the third incorporation proposal from 13.5 square miles to 3.2 square miles. Eliminated were the properties along the railroad track that were intended to be the prime resource base of the new city. The proponents of the incorporation were shocked, but proceeded with the incorporation anyway, hoping to recover their lost tax base later, by subsequent annexations. This hope proved to be futile, because that potentially lucrative tax base incorporated independently as the unusual City of Industry.

The Incorporation of Industry: A Gimmick

Stafford is quoted as saying, "We started [the incorporation of Industry] in order to block La Puente's incorporation, but as we looked into it, it began to look like a good thing." [15] The incorporation petition was drawn to include virtually no residents, but as much of the prime industrial land along the railroads as possible. The boundaries were so neatly drawn, in fact, that with all its six square miles of land, the area had less than the requisite 500 inhabitants. Consequently, the proposal was drawn to include the 169 patients and 31 employees of a mental sanitarium, making the total population 629. The signatures on the incorporation petition included signatures representing realty firms and the two railroads. Over 50 percent of the land was owned by absentee landlords.

Incorporation provoked a great deal of opposition from outside the city, which saw walls being erected around the prime municipal revenue resource in the San Gabriel Valley. However, this opposition, while vocal, had no effective means of protest. The only means by which to block incorporation was through the county board of supervisors, which had to approve the petition. At the supervisors' meeting, Supervisor Kenneth Hahn argued that the incorporation would create a town which would employ thousands of citizens of the San Gabriel Valley, but would provide a voice to virtually none of them. As Supervisor Legg was quick to point out, it was the board's custom to defer to the representative of the district which included the proposed incorporation, which happened to be Legg himself.

Opposition to the board's approval of the incorporation petition was immediately voiced by neighboring communities. However, the only hope of that opposition was in a suit that claimed that Industry had fewer than the required 500 inhabitants. It was argued that the patients at the mental hospital, because they were not permanent residents, were not inhabitants. The court ruled, however, that the law did not require 500 *permanent* residents, and that the patients qualified as inhabitants. (The law has since been changed to require permanent residents.)

The incorporation of Industry immediately deprived the citizens of La

Puente of any hope of a sizeable tax base. In 1961, the city of Monrovia had the median per capita assessment for the county's cities, with $1624. La Puente's figure was barely over half that, at $849. Industry's per capita assessed valuation was $41,865. If La Puente had successfully annexed Industry, its per capita assessed valuation would have been satisfactorily above the median at $1918.

Since that time, the discrepancy between the two cities has grown as Industry's tax base multiplied time and again, to the per capita figure of $309,970 in 1977. La Puente's per capita assessed valuation has remained among the lowest in the county at $1512. If La Puente had annexed Industry, its tax base would instead be one of the highest, with over $8000 per capita. Industry, with approximately one ten-thousandth of the county's population, controls nearly one-tenth of the county's industrial land. Yet, in some sense, it is absurd to speak of the per capita assessments in Industry, since the incorporation of Industry was obviously not designed to serve a residential population. No residential building has been allowed there since incorporation.

The official reason for the existence of Industry is to preserve some of the county's prime industrial land from residential encroachment. It was argued that if this industrial land were kept in the same boundaries with a residential population, there would be inevitable political pressure to allow residential zoning and other incompatible land uses that would limit the industrial use of the land. The declared purpose was, in effect, land-use planning by incorporation.

However, as one urban planner has reported,

There is a contradiction between the city's announced purpose of establishing a community designed exclusively for the needs of industry and the policies it is pursuing. On one hand, it claims to protect industry from incompatible uses; on the other it makes provisions in its zoning ordinance for uses which will interfere with the effective functioning of industry.[16]

A prime example of this incompatibility of land use is the city's wide range of commercial and retail activities, including food markets, florists, and home furnishing stores. Retail stores were virtually nonexistent at the time of Industry's incorporation, but by 1974 the city had attracted 15 percent of the retail sales for a market area of over one and a half million.[17]

Since that time, the city has created the Puente Hills regional shopping mall. In addition, the city has fostered cattle-feed yards and other agricultural activities, and city councilmen have themselves been in the livestock business. Industrial zoning provisions do not assure that the operations of an industrial plant will be protected from land uses on adjacent plots of land that interfere with plant operation.

In a 1973 survey, it was found that inappropriate land use and inadequate zoning protection had caused industrial unhappiness with local government in Industry. Representatives of local industry complained of "provincial, autocratic city government" and its "dictatorial powers." Respondents claimed that "industrial firms have very little, if any, voice" in Industry, but that "the City Council is thus able to effect any ordinance they choose which would enrich their group." [18]

This last complaint provides a hint of the true reasons for the incorporation of Industry and the policies that its government has pursued since that time. The City of Industry is dedicated to the interests of the property owners who organize it. When these interests call for industrial development, that is what happens; but when the interests require incompatible land-use development, the purported purposes of Industry are neglected.

Typical of this close relationship between city government and the property owners who organize it are the city's business affairs with the Utility Trailer Company. The first meeting of the Industry City Council was held in the Utility Trailer plant in 1956. Over 20 years later, in 1978, when Utility Trailer tried unsuccessfully to buy vacant land next door to its plant, the city's Urban Development Agency bought the much soughtafter land and resold it to Utility Trailer for the same price. The sale agreement also committed the City of Industry to condemn four additional acres of land to resell to Utility Trailer if the agency had to use any of the firm's land to widen a street. Utility Trailer was one of the clients of the law firm Simmon, Ritchie, and Segal. Graham Ritchie of that firm was acting city manager and city attorney for Industry, and attorney and executive director for the Urban Development Agency in Industry.

Graham Ritchie graduated from UCLA Law School in 1955, the year after Lakewood's incorporation. In 1959 he represented the organizers of the city of Lawndale in their incorporation effort. He became interested in municipal law, and by 1970 was city attorney for Hawaiian Gardens, San

Gabriel, and the City of Industry. He was also acting city manager in Baldwin Park and urban development attorney in four cities.

His style, as acting city manager of Industry, was unusual. He has been quoted as saying "I really don't see any need for a budget." And so the City of Industry has no published budget. Nor does the city council have published agendas. He has told reporters that the assistant city manager is not an authorized spokesman for the city, and indeed, few people in Industry seem to regard themselves as authorized spokesmen. The author of a master's thesis on Industry found few people willing to be quoted. "The whole affair gave the author the feeling of operating in a 1984 type of environment where everybody was in mortal fear of showing any opposition to, or criticism of, the city fathers or administration." [19]

Ritchie, however, felt that the city's policies had paid off. As evidence, he cited the 1,000 percent increase in land values in the first 20 years of the city's history.

Perhaps Ritchie's boldest innovation in municipal policy was his unique use of the city's Urban Development Agency. Redevelopment was intended to support the eradication of urban blight; it is difficult to see how Industry, which is either undeveloped or newly developed in its entirety, could benefit from blight-eradication programs. But Ritchie had the entire city placed in one of three redevelopment districts to deal with such manifestations of urban blight as drainage problems on vacant land. He was quoted as saying that redevelopment is "a gimmick every city ought to look at."

The redevelopment agency, established in 1971, has worked on such projects as the creation of elaborate recreation centers, the construction of a regional shopping mall, and the renovation of the El Encanto Convalescent Center, where a large proportion of Industry's citizens live.

By March of 1977, Industry's bonded indebtedness to support these "redevelopment" projects amounted to over $100 million, almost as much as the total bonded indebtedness of the county of Los Angeles. None of these bond issues were voted on, thanks to a system called tax increment financing. Under this system, the property assessments in a redevelopment district are fixed, and the taxes on the increase in property value are allocated to the redevelopment district. This is true for the school district and county taxes as well as municipal taxes. Thus, when property values in the redevelopment district have doubled, half of the county tax revenue raised from that district goes to the redevelopment district rather than the county or school district coffers. However, all of Industry is in one of three development districts. By this means, the entire county has subsidized Industry's fight against "blight" to the amount of $20 million, in the first five years after the inception of Industry's redevelopment project. This amounts to a county subsidy of almost $30,000 for every inhabitant of Industry.

The tax-increment bonds were not used simply to finance the "blight eradication" projects in Industry. Over half of the bond proceeds were invested in Treasury bond securities of ten years or more. It is clear that the bonds were floated not for redevelopment, but for the production of income.

Abuses of the redevelopment program led to state legislation aimed at regulating redevelopment. One bill introduced in 1977 by an El Monte legislator would have required numerous reports on Industry's redevelopment finances, including information that was not forthcoming from Ritchie. The author of the bill was quoted as saying, "There is just one reason for the bill: the abuses of one Graham Ritchie. The City of Industry is Graham Ritchie personified." [20] Ritchie responded by calling the requirement for a redevelopment budget "a childlike thing. Cities don't have to have budgets." [21]

Although the bill had been aimed at Industry, Senator Bill Campbell (from the neighboring community of Hacienda Heights) successfully shielded Industry from this threat with an amendment exempting all cities with populations under 1,000 from the provisions of the bill. (The relationship between Campbell and the citizens of Industry goes back several years. Influential citizens of Industry supported Campbell as a potential replacement for the late County Supervisor Bonelli in 1972, but were beaten by the forces favoring developer Pete Schabarum.)

In June of 1978, passage of the Jarvis Amendment promised greatly to reduce the rate of increase of property assessments and the total tax rate on property. Both these innovations promised in turn to eliminate the usefulness of tax-increment financing. Accordingly, the Industry City Council, thinking of the future, proposed to float $250 million in general obligation bonds. This more than doubled the bonded indebtedness of the city, and in fact made Industry's bonded indebtedness greater than the total bonded indebtedness of all the cities in the county except for Los Angeles itself.

Because general obligation bonds require voter approval, the City of Industry required a speedy election between the passage of Proposition 13 on June 4 and the day the proposition went into effect on July 1. The need for haste led the council to mail out ballots to the city's 138 registered voters, despite the opinion of the one dissenting councilman that unauthorized persons might obtain the ballots and vote. The bond election was successful. The ability of the City of Industry to engage in programs that enhanced the land value for local landowners without requiring property taxation was guaranteed for the foreseeable future.

Baldwin Park and Irwindale: Twenty Holes in the Ground

Baldwin Park was an older unincorporated community with a history of failed attempts to incorporate and an excellent location with regard to potential tax base. It lies between the prime industrial land that was to become the City of Industry to the south, and another industrial district to the north, owned largely by several large gravel companies. In its first postwar incorporation attempt in 1950, dissension over the issue of the gravel companies resulted in failure. Because one proincorporation group threatened to stop the gravel companies from using a main access road that went through a Baldwin Park neighborhood, Consolidated Rock Company (ConRock) and other gravel companies funded a strong opposition campaign which succeeded in killing the incorporation attempt.

By 1956, relationships with Consolidated Rock Company had improved. The head of the local water company, Donald Holmes, had worked with Consolidated Rock and with the county to secure the construction of an alternate route for the trucks that bypassed the residential neighborhood. On the basis of this demonstration of their willingness to work with the gravel companies, the incorporationists under Holmes secured a promise from ConRock that the gravel companies would not oppose a new incorporation attempt. Furthermore, while the gravel pits were not included in the original incorporation limits, the incorporationists hoped that the gravel companies would be willing to consider annexation to the city of Baldwin Park after incorporation. Since the incorporationists had every intention of keeping property tax rates low, they hoped that they would be able to demonstrate to the gravel companies a compatibility of interest sufficient to warrant annexation.

The original incorporation did not include the prime industrial land along the railroad tracks either, but it was once again supposed that annexation of this tax base would be the first order of business upon incorporation. This supposition was much of the basis for Supervisor Legg's opposition, which emerged during the course of the incorporation proceedings. The incorporation attempt succeeded, however, without organized opposition from the gravel companies· or elsewhere, and in January of 1956, Baldwin Park became the second Lakewood Plan city.

To the dismay of local leaders such as Holmes, however, the newly elected city council did not make annexation of the vacant tax base to the south its first order of business. Instead, the city council insisted on first attending to the issue of developing a municipal zoning ordinance. While the reasons for this were not clear at first, they became evident within two months of incorporation. Within that length of time, three city councilmen were indicted for taking bribes to corrupt the zoning ordinance to which they had insisted on giving priority. As it turned out, two of the councilmen had asked for bribes of $200 each from the promoter of a local massage parlor. The promoter, evidently guessing from the small size of the bribes requested that he was dealing with green, untrustworthy officials, decided to report the bribes before one of them did. Before the dust settled from this case, the tax base to the south had incorporated as Industry, and Consolidated Rock Company had definitely eliminated the possibility of annexation to Baldwin Park.

After foregoing the opportunity to annex to Baldwin Park, the gravel pits became the object of the annexationist attentions of Monrovia, Azusa, and West Covina. In addition, the unincorporated community of Duarte was itself beginning incorporation proceedings in response to annexation bids by Azusa, and it felt that the gravel pits were historically a part of their community. ConRock saw the handwriting on the wall, and perceived that annexation could be permanently precluded only by means of separate incorporation. They organized a proindustry incorporation that eliminated most of the residential areas surrounding the gravel pit, leaving a population of only 1500 people, almost half of whom were in a migrant labor camp located among the gravel pits. They also ran a slate of five proindustry council candidates.

The citizens of Irwindale were quite satisfied to be incorporated within a resource-rich industrial city. However, they were not satisfied to let the management of those resources be undertaken by the employees of the gravel companies and the proindustry council candidates. An alternative slate of candidates disputed the contest, and in the election only one of the industry candidates won a city council seat. This was the first warning signal that the inhabitants of Irwindale intended to run that city in their own best interests, which were not necessarily coincident with the interests of the gravel companies.

The first occasion for conflict between the citizens and the gravel companies came over actual regulation of the mining operations. Before incorporation, the mining companies had been subject to very lax enforcement of mining regulations by the county. However, the city undertook more stringent enforcement of regulations regarding setbacks from homes and other matters. Furthermore, it instituted a mining tax on tonnage that began at a half-cent a ton and gradually rose to 5 cents a ton, amounting to 30 percent of the city's revenues. While the mining companies objected that they were already providing revenue through sales tax and property taxation to the county government and school district, the citizens of Irwindale felt that the extraction of their only resource required a special tax, to prepare for the day (estimated to arrive before the year 2000) when that resource would be exhausted and Irwindale would be left with 20 holes in the ground.

In addition, in the middle of the 1970s the city instituted a municipal property tax for the first time. This was violently opposed not only by industry, which owned 92 percent of the property, but also by homeowners. However, the city council argued that the property tax was necessary as seed money for the Community Redevelopment Agency to get plans for projects started that could be paid for by tax-increment financing. The city council was eventually successful in getting this passed and soon began the diversification of industry within the city by condemning some property for a $150 million brewery. The property in question was condemned over the vigorous opposition of its owner, Consolidated Rock Company.

In Irwindale, as in Industry, the basic premise of incorporation was a shared interest in limiting the benefits of a rich tax base to as small a population as possible. In Irwindale, however, it was demonstrated that this shared interest in incorporation is not always sufficient to ensure the peaceful management of that tax base after incorporation. South El Monte is another case of a commercial incorporation which became increasingly divided on the issue of how to use the resource base that motivated incorporation.

South El Monte: Business Backed It

Located between the old industrial zone of east Los Angeles and the new industrial zone that was to become Industry, South El Monte began its commercial and industrial development in a situation of benign neglect on the part of the county. County zoning practices tended to leave undeveloped areas like this swampy area in the San Gabriel Valley zoned M-3 until zoning changes were requested by business or residential developers. This zoning status allowed any kind of economic activity whatsoever. Consequently, after World War II the area south of El Monte attracted a large number of entrepreneurs who initiated, often on very small investments, a diverse set of businesses: sand-blasting, cabinet-making, small livestock operations, feed-making companies, dozens of kennels, and others. By the mid-1950s, the economic potential of the area was attracting the attention of the El Monte weekly newspaper, which began to suggest annexation. El Monte, a city of about 10,000 people, had been making numerous small annexations for several years, between one and eighteen pieces of territory every year since 1945. In the process it grew from slightly less than one and one-half square miles at the end of the war to two and one-quarter square miles when Lakewood was incorporated. It grew as much again in the three years after Lakewood's incorporation, but always in numerous, tiny plots of land, fearing that large annexation attempts would generate an incorporation movement on its boundaries.

The entrepreneurs in the South El Monte area were immediately concerned that annexation would result in higher taxes; El Monte had a tax rate of 1.13 in 1956–1957. Other property owners in the area could agree with this concern, even if their only property was their homes. One of the leading activists against annexation, Frank Stiles, was an owner of an animal feed business who was concerned that annexation would result in imposition of El Monte's antilivestock ordinances. Having a flair for the dramatic, he began writing articles against annexation in his advertising newsletter, which he sent regularly to the owners of chickens, rabbits, goats, and other small livestock in the area, warning them that annexation would deprive them of their livestock and cost them more in taxes as well. After Lakewood's incorporation, it became obvious to Stiles that "if we don't want to annex, we'll have to incorporate." [22]

Stiles discovered that Max Shapiro, who owned the sand-blasting operation and had organized the local business association, had similar concerns. El Monte's business tax, as well as its property tax, concerned Shapiro and his friends. In addition, El Monte's poor water supply had given it a very low fire rating, while county fire service gave South El Monte a very high fire rating. In voicing these concerns to a county building inspector, the inspector suggested incorporation. With the help of the inspector, Shapiro organized the early meetings to look into the possibility of incorporation.

The group sent Stiles to Lakewood, where he discovered that it would be possible to run a city on the sales tax to be raised after incorporation, with other state subsidies. Despite the intense opposition of El Monte at every step of the incorporation proceedings, the group managed to raise a petition, and get county approval for an election. Because they lacked professional help and money, there was a consensus that the incorporation would fail. However, Shapiro managed to raise $3000, and Stiles managed a small public relations campaign. The campaign was aided by heavy-handed lobbying by El Monte which alienated local voters. The 1958 election was a surprise victory for the incorporationists. Because of his well-known advertising, Stiles was the vote leader in the council election, and became mayor. Shapiro was on the council.

For the first 15 years, the council reflected this businessman makeup. However, over the opposition of Stiles, South El Monte embarked on a campaign of annexation which resulted in several residential areas being brought into the city, with a resulting population growth from 5,000 to 13,000 in the 1960s. By the end of that decade, the residential citizens were beginning to make themselves felt politically, fighting for business taxes, among other things. This tendency increased when inflation hit in the 1972–1973 fiscal year, forcing the city to impose a municipal property tax for the first time. In addition, the new residents imposed zoning require-ments that eliminated much of the livestock from the city. By the end of the seventies, Shapiro felt that Stiles had been right to oppose the annex-ation of residential areas: "All of a sudden the businessman is an orphan in his own home." [23] Unlike the situation in Industry and Commerce, in South El Monte the business interests that had provided the impetus for incorporation were losing control of "their" city.

El Monte, deprived of the South El Monte industrial area, continued to expand, growing from 3.26 square miles in 1958 to almost ten square miles by the end of the 1960s. However, this expansion resulted less in a growth of the tax base than in population growth, as the city reached a population of almost 70,000. Most of this population increase represented low- and middle-income renters; a large proportion were illegal aliens. By 1970, a majority of El Monte's population were renters; a majority of South El Monte's were homeowners.

The difference in the two cities' resource bases continued to grow, as well. By 1976, South El Monte's property assessments per capita were $3590, compared to El Monte's $2296. The sales tax revenue per capita was $716 in South El Monte and $41 in El Monte. It is no wonder that some El Monte officials still entertained the idea of combining the two cities. When candidates for the city councils of both cities appeared on the same forum in February 1978, one El Monte councilman said, "I have a beauti-ful thought. I would like to see El Monte and South El Monte become one great, big, beautiful city." [24] Although the idea was proposed seriously, it was met with laughter, at least by the South El Monte part of the audi-ence. While delicately overlooking El Monte's indebtedness, a South El Monte council candidate replied, "South El Monte has $2 million in re-serve. El Monte would have to offer us quite a lot to merge with them, and even then we'd have to call it South El Monte." [25]

The Common Denominator of High-Resource Incorporation

The incorporations discussed in this chapter are not the only high-resource incorporations that could have been mentioned. The dairy farmers incorporated Dairy Valley to forestall annexation to the business community of Artesia. This incorporation allowed the landowners to keep the land for agricultural purposes until a sufficiently high profit could be made from development. As the farmers cashed in on this strategy, the population in Dairy Valley almost tripled between 1960 and 1970, reaching 15,000, and then tripled again in the next seven years, reaching 45,000. The city also decided to change its name to Cerritos. With the business generated by a large shopping mall, sales tax revenue has grown even faster than population (see table 2.1).

Located next to Whittier, the city of Santa Fe Springs incorporated as a proindustry town in 1958 when the citizens of South Whittier protested industrial development too near Sunnyside School. The Industrial League in that community, as in the City of Industry, drew the boundaries to include the industry south of Whittier and to exclude those residents who were likely to complain. Santa Fe Springs was zoned 82 percent industrial, and became "the city that is bought, sold, and paid for by industry," according to one observer. "What mama wants, mama gets." [26] Said one city councilperson, "The residents—most of them, anyway—understood that the industry is good for us . . . I think it's a good place to live because the taxes are low and we furnish a lot of free services. We're the envy of a lot of cities." [27] They are especially the envy of the citizens of Whittier, who now suffer the externalities brought to them by any south wind, but none of the benefits of the tax revenue.

The nature of the coalition agreement worked out between homeowners and industry has varied in the different high-resource communities. In some, as in Industry, the commercial interests are definitely in the driver's seat. In others, like Irwindale, that place is taken by the homeowners. In still others, there is some sort of compromise, either amicable, as in Downey, or otherwise, as in South El Monte. But the original premise of cooperation was the same in all cases: to define a set of tax resources as "belonging" to a more local, rather than a wider, community in order to keep them from being diluted.

Table 2.1
Relative Tax Bases of Annexing Cities and Selected Incorporations

City	Assessed valuation per capita		Sales tax revenue per capita	
	1959–1960	1970–1971	1959–1960	1970–1971
La Puente[1]	$ 849	$ 1,248	$ 6	$ 14
Industry	$41,866	$163,000	$511	$2,077
(Ratio)[2]	(49.3)	(130.6)	(85.2)	(148.4)
Monrovia	$ 1,625	$ 2,437	$ 17	$ 23
Irwindale	$ 8,682	$ 36,000	$276	$ 698
(Ratio)	(5.3)	(14.8)	(16.2)	(30.3)
Whittier	$ 1,001	$ 2,451	$ 25	$ 27
Santa Fe Springs	$ 3,533	$ 9,277	$ 25	$ 127
(Ratio)	(3.5)	(3.8)	(1.0)	(4.7)
El Monte	$ 1,171	$ 1,891	$ 51	$ 29
South El Monte	$ 2,017	$ 3,060	$ 42	$ 44
(Ratio)	(1.7)	(1.6)	(.8)	(1.5)
Artesia	$ 904	$ 1,412	$ 8	$ 10
Cerritos	$ 5,029	$ 4,346	$ 18	$ 27
(Ratio)	(5.6)	(3.1)	(2.3)	(2.7)
Downey	$ 1,482	$ 2,520	$ 14	$ 30
Commerce	$18,056	$ 27,171	N.A.	$ 405
(Ratio)	(17.9)	(16.6)	(—)	(22.5)

Sources: 1960 data from Winston Crouch and Beatrice Dinerman, *Southern California Metropolis,* Tables 2 and 3. 1970 data from *Financial Transactions Concerning Cities of California, 1970* (California State Controller, 1971).
[1] City in bold type is city that attempted annexation of newly incorporated city.
[2] Ratio is the resource level of the newly incorporated city as a proportion of that of the older city.

Contrary to the interpretation of the Tiebout camp, the articulation of a unique set of local interests was not the common denominator of these incorporations. No one I talked to was able to point to differences in preferences for public services between the citizens of Industry and the citizens of La Puente sufficient to justify a separate jurisdiction for the former city. If indeed any of these new cities have populations with different sets of preferences for public services, it is doubtful whether the institutions of local politics are representative or subtle enough to make these differences manifest. Instead, all of these incorporations turned on redistributive advantages guaranteed by the collective ownership of a set of local resources. Consequently, one of the most important norms to be used in analyzing these incorporations must be redistributional equity, rather than the norm of allocational efficiency which is paramount for the followers of Tiebout. Shall the citizens of La Puente share in the benefits of the resources along the Southern Pacific railroad tracks or not? Allocational efficiency can have little to say one way or another; redistributional equity may have a great deal to say.

The paramount importance of such redistributional questions is easy to justify for the high-resource incorporations discussed in this chapter. A good many of the incorporations in Los Angeles County, however, have been incorporations of relatively resource-poor communities. To explain these will require a more complicated model which must include variations in income among individuals, the preferences of different income groups for the scale of activity of local governments, and the redistributional effects of local governmental activity.

3

Homeowners, Renters, and Bureaucrats

The motivation for incorporation in the communities discussed in the previous chapter had little to do with the gratification of distinct collective tastes for public goods. Incorporation of high-resource cities can easily be explained in economic terms as the gratification of the shared desire to have adequate or better urban services at little or no tax price by maximizing resources per capita. When they are presented with the alternative of annexation to a relatively poor city with a high tax rate, incorporation (and protection of the tax base) seems preferable to landowners, industry, and residents alike.

But there were as many low-resource incorporations after 1954 as high-resource. Some of these might be explained as strategic miscalculation, as when La Puente felt it would be possible to annex an ample tax base subsequent to incorporation. But for the most part, low-resource incorporations were undertaken with ample understanding of the inadequacies of the local tax base.

Not only did these cities incorporate with small tax bases; most of them actually turned down an opportunity to be annexed to a wealthier city to do so. Lakewood, for instance, resisted annexation to Long Beach, which was in the public image a recreational Shangri-la with money to burn. In

1960, the citizens of Long Beach were getting the benefit of $110 per capita of municipal services, with a tax bill of only $49 for the median home-owner. The citizens of Lakewood, on the other hand, got a return of only $26 worth of services per capita for their median tax bill of $18. Had the citizens of Lakewood made an economic miscalculation when they incor-porated? Weren't they getting a worse fiscal deal than the citizens of Long Beach?

If they had made a mistake, they had plenty of company. The citizens of at least a dozen other cities refused annexation to cities with much better tax bases where their tax dollars would have been converted into higher levels of services. This seems economically perverse on both sides. Why should a wealthier, established city seek to annex a poor, new community? And why should the poor, new community fight so hard to maintan its identity?

It would be possible, of course, to explain these low-resource incorpora-tions in terms of the intrinsic value of local government to local citizens, just as it is possible to explain the voting act by saying that citizens get intrinsic pleasure out of the act of voting. These explanations, however, are somewhat tautological. It is more challenging to attempt explanations of political phenomena in terms of their instrumental or investment value. For instance, John Ferejohn and Morris Fiorina were able to advance an economic theory of voting, based solely on the instrumental value of vot-ing, that approximates observed voting rates.[1] Similarly, it is the purpose of this chapter to explain low-resource municipal incorporations in terms of the instrumental, rather than intrinsic, value of such local governments. Because most of these incorporations took place as alternatives to annex-ation to relatively high-resource old-line cities, my explanation will require a comparison of tax and expenditure policy in both types of cities. The argument will be that, because of the redistributional effect of government expenditures, different kinds of people prefer different scales of local gov-ernmental activity. The foundation of this argument will be based on an analysis of demand for municipal expenditures.

Demand for Municipal Expenditures

Demand for municipal expenditures can be estimated by replicating the Bergstrom-Goodman regression analysis of 1970 municipal expenditures in the 70 Los Angeles cities with populations greater than 2500.[2] The Bergstrom and Goodman analysis assumes that local expenditures are supplied at the level demanded by the median voter and that individual demand is a function of median tax shares (T), median family income (I), and municipal population (N).[3] (Median tax share is operationalized as the median home value divided by total property in the municipality.) Results of the model's estimation by means of a double log regression are presented in table 3.1.[4]

As formulated by Bergstrom and Goodman, municipal population enters into the demand function both because of its "crowding" effect γ and because greater population decreases the tax share cost to the individual, depending on both the crowding effect and the tax share elasticity. Together, the observed population elasticity α is equal to $\tau(\delta + 1)$, and the crowding parameter is estimated as $\alpha/1 - \delta$. With this estimation, police, parks, and streets are crowdable goods, as are overall municipal expenditures.

But further, demand for these municipally supplied goods is highly elastic with respect to tax share and income, as suggested by the models already described. As income goes up, demand increases, but as tax share increases, demand decreases. The conditions for redistributional provision of municipal goods are met. Middle-class families with a large investment in their homes will prefer to have less municipal provision of goods.

But renters do not pay the property tax directly, and may be subject to "fiscal illusion," in that they do not perceive that the property taxes paid by their landlords are passed on to them, or they may not be as aware of the size of the property tax on the property, as is the landlord who actually pays it.[5] In either case, they would demand more municipal services than they would if they owned similar property. Therefore, demand for expenditures may increase with the likelihood that the median voter is suffering from fiscal illusion. The proportion of homeowners in the municipality is taken as a proxy for this variable.

As can be seen from table 3.1, this variable adds significantly to the analysis of local government expenditures, and in the right direction. As the probability that the median voter is a homeowner increases, demand for municipal expenditures decreases sharply.

Table 3.1
Estimates of Demand for Municipal Expenditures, 1970

	Police	Streets	Total
	$\text{Exp} = kI^\epsilon T^\delta P^{\gamma(1+\delta)}$		
Income[a]	.29	.36	.54*
Elasticity (ϵ)	(.18)[b]	(.27)	(.20)
Tax Share[c]	$-.59$*	$-.52$*	$-.85$*
Elasticity (δ)	(.08)	(.12)	(.09)
Population	.52*	.55*	.34*
Elasticity ($\gamma(1+\delta)$)	(.08)	(.12)	(.09)
Crowding Term (γ)	1.3	1.14	2.27
k	1.70	.76	.67
R^2	.91	.81	.91
F	225.9	91.3	209.7
	$\text{Exp} = kI^\epsilon T^\delta P^{\gamma(1+\delta)}H^\alpha$		
Income	.78*	.55	.98*
Elasticity (ϵ)	(.18)	(.31)	(.21)
Tax Share	$-.58$*	$-.51$*	$-.84$*
Elasticity (δ)	(.07)	(.12)	(.08)
Population	.52*	.56*	.34*
Elasticity ($\gamma(1+\delta)$)	(.07)	(.12)	(.08)
Home Ownership	$-.62$*	$-.24$	$-.57$*
Elasticity (α)	(.12)	(.21)	(.15)
Crowding Term (γ)	1.3	1.14	2.13
k	.21	.33	.10
R^2	.94	.81	.92
F	241.0	69.15	195.0

[a] Income and population data from *Census of Population, 1970,* vol. 1, pt. 6, Tables 89, 107, 118 (U.S. Bureau of the Census, 1971).
[b] Figures in parentheses are standard errors; estimates followed by asterisks are statistically significant at the .05 level.
[c] Tax rates from *Financial Transactions Concerning Cities of California, 1970,* Table 19 (California State Controller, 1971).
[d] Home ownership data from *Census of Housing, 1970,* vol. 1, pt. 6, Tables 10, 20, 24 (U.S. Bureau of the Census, 1971).

One of the most important implications of the Bergstrom-Goodman analysis is that public services are crowdable goods; there is no benefit to be derived from providing the good to a group rather than to individuals. It costs at least as much to provide it to a group of ten people as it would to provide it to ten individuals. As James Buchanan[6] and Robert Spann[7] have noted, this raises the question: "why are municipal services provided by jurisdictions at all, instead of being provided by normal market mechanisms?" Are there any circumstances under which a majority of individuals in a jurisdiction would collectively agree to provide private goods publicly?

The answer is yes, and the circumstances are redistributional in nature. The cost sharing implicit in collective provision of a good at a uniform level makes it possible for lower classes to get more of the good, at the expense of subsidies from the upper-income classes, than they could get through market mechanisms.

To show how collective provision of a municipality implies a pooling of resources, we need only look at the budget constraint discussed in the last chapter.

$$y_i = p_z\, z_i + t_i(rQ_J N_J).$$

The budget constraint in a private market is simply

$$y_i = p_z\, z_i + rQ_J.$$

The two budget constraints are equal if $t_i N_J = 1$; that is, if his tax share is exactly equal to $1/N_J$. If his tax share is greater than $1/N_J$, then his budget constraint is less favorable, and if it is less than that figure, then it is more favorable. (See figure 3.1.)

Let us suppose that the tax share is given by h_i/H_J, where h_i is individual property valuation and H_J is total property valuation. If a poor individual, e.g., Ms. Doe, owns less than an "average" amount of property she may well prefer collective provision of the public good because of the decrease in apparent "price" to her. On the other hand, if a rich individual owns a great deal of property, then the individual's jurisdictional "price" will be greater than the per-unit market price. (To link the results of this model with those of the last chapter, suppose the jurisdiction includes a great deal of valuable property owned by absentee landlords. Then H_J will

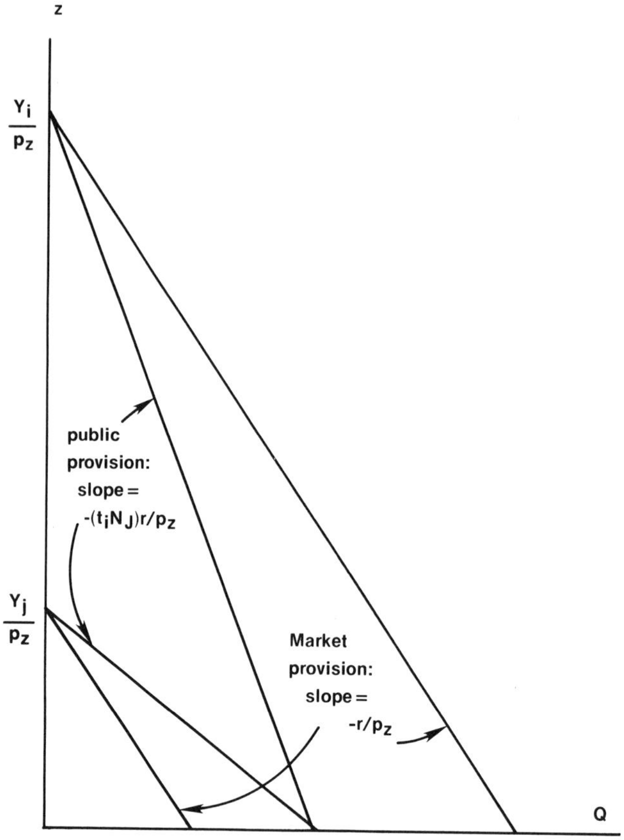

Figure 3.1
Individual Budget Constraints with Market and Public Provision of Q

be so large that it will be in everyone's interest to prefer collective provision of the good. But if H_J consists only of locally owned property, then the average property owner marks the breaking point between preferring market provision over jurisdictional provision of the public good.)

It is important to notice that the implications of this model are fully supported by the Bergstrom-Goodman analysis, which reveals that demand for public expenditures increases with income, but decreases very fast with property ownership and with the value of the property owned. Thus, the demand of a high-income individual may actually be lower than that of a middle-income individual, depending on the regressivity or progressivity of tax shares.

Chapter 2 and this chapter are, therefore, oriented toward the two different effects that the "pooling of resources" has on an individual's preferences for community type. In the last chapter, it was argued that the pooling of a high-resource base with a low-resource base is generally to be avoided. In this chapter, the individual's contribution to that resource pool becomes central. An individual owning an expensive house in a less affluent community may well be hurt by the automatic redistribution that takes place when that community incorporates and begins paying for resources out of a common pool of which his house is a disproportionately large portion.

Who Gains from the Public Provision of Private Goods?

What this analysis suggests is that cities with a large number of renters and low-income individuals will tend to have a very high demand for governmental services. But these groups are not noted for their activity in local government. Robert Dahl, for instance, finds that political participation among these groups is low.[8] The Census Bureau finds that homeowners vote at twice the rate of renters, and that people earning more than $25,000 outvote those earning less than $5,000 by the same rate.[9]

It is true, of course, that these groups do become involved in salient issues, such as rent control. Santa Monica, the city with the highest level of rentership in the county—80 percent—became the first city in the county to pass a rent control ordinance in the wake of post–Proposition 13 rent increases. But if these groups are neither active nor organized in the normal course of events, how does their demand for increasing the scale of activity of local government become translated into budget increases? Surely the assumption that the median voter's preferences are perfectly met in an urban democracy is too heroic to be taken literally. Is demand articulation that perfect? Or do supply factors also help to determine patterns of governmental expansion? Can suppliers be viewed as representing the redistributional demands of lower-income groups in urban governments?

In the independent cities of Los Angeles County, city officials (both elected and appointed) tend to gain from the expansion of governmental activity in the same way that low-income groups do. Low-income groups benefit by relying on pooled resources rather than their own meager resources to buy services—any services. City officials find their career goals advanced by expanding the scale of governmental activity.

Bureaucrats, most obviously, wish to guarantee employment and promotion opportunities by pushing their governmental programs. But do bureaucrats have the political influence to promote the bureaucratic provision of public services? The power of bureaucrats in the independent cities of the Los Angeles area can best be illustrated by the fact that, of the 45 independent cities in 1954, only one (the tiny city of Avalon on Santa Catalina Island) took advantage of the county sheriff's inexpensive policing rates by switching to a contracting mode of providing police services. The political influence of local fire departments is also evident. When Signal Hill's city council sought to take advantage of the economies of subsidized contracting by switching to county contracts for police and fire service, the Signal Hill police and fire departments initiated a recall campaign that resulted in the recall of two Signal Hill councilmen. The new majority canceled the contract and rehired the police and fire personnel.[10]

That lesson was no doubt in the mind of the Bell City Council, when it became in 1970 the next old-line city to consider county contracting as a means of economizing. The arrangement worked out was that Bell would switch to the county fire department, on condition that that department would immediately hire all of the Bell city firemen at an increase in salary and with improved chances for advancement. While the city's population took on an additional county fire district tax rate of $.65, the city's property tax rate went from $1.29 to $.26 with this change, for a beneficial net change of $.38. (This beneficial change was possible because the shift in responsibility was also a redistributional change. The citizens of the low-resource city of Bell were not paying all the costs of their fire protection at a tax rate of $.65; the costs were simply shared among the entire fire district, which has a higher average per capita poverty value than does Bell.)

For the most part, a dramatic confrontation between bureaucrats and city council is not necessary because the city councils recognize that it is not in their interest to initiate such a fight. They can best secure their reelection by making sure that their constituents get what they want out of local government, not by making city employees their enemies in the next election. This is especially important for representatives from low-income areas, where, despite the absence of an integrating party machine, politicians tend to get reelected by providing the same kinds of particularistic services that characterized old-time party machines.

Art Snyder, for instance, represents the Hispanic working-class district of northeast Los Angeles. He has been opposed by Hispanic candidates, and grass-roots Hispanic organizations such as the United Neighborhood Organization (UNO), which charged him with "filling the area with visible projects that build his fame but [leave] major problems unsolved." For instance, Snyder failed to act on the issue of housing until UNO protested in 1977. He did, however, emphasize swimming pools and libraries. He would arrange paint jobs for local schools, community centers, parks, and soccer fields. "Snyder sends over a big box of apples for every Wilson High School football game and pays for high school jackets for those who can't afford them. He has a staff of 30, eight of them CETA workers, all of them from the communities in which they work. Tirelessly, he attends parades and meetings. He has in effect, bought the people and he has bought the people with their own money," stated one member of UNO.[11]

At any rate, this strategy of providing particularistic services is highly successful politically. Snyder is one of the best fund raisers in the city. While critics typically fail to raise enough campaign money to field an opposition candidate, his campaign treasury is large enough to create the possibility of a much more expensive, citywide mayoral campaign.

The result is that Los Angeles's city politics and administration are still much as they were when described by Edward Banfield.

Council candidates depend mainly upon personal followings. Incumbents are able to build followings by "giving service" (that is, "doing favors") for constituents, and normally an incumbent who looks after his district is sure of reelection. . . . The councilmen are, of course, interested in the problems of their districts, not those of the city as a whole. . . . A constituent who thinks the palm trees along the street need trimming, who is bothered by a barking dog, or who wants bigger storm drains, calls the councilman, who takes the matter up with the appropriate city department. "By custom," a councilman said, "the councilman is considered the administrator of the city services in his district." As much as 25 percent of the work of a public works office, a recent check showed, is done at the request of a councilman and without any specific order from the board in charge of the department.[12]

Thus, councilmanic preoccupation with particularistic services enhances the tendency for budgetary growth. The services requested of city agencies for constituents require money; if a councilman is an obstructionist at budget time he may find that used against him when he goes to a city agency seeking prompt action on a constituent need. Nor is a councilman likely to act as fiscal conservative on other councilmanic pet projects; this could too easily backfire. So "in matters affecting his district, every councilman gets the automatic support of all the others." [13] Councilmanic particularism, combined with mayoral "powerlessness," leaves the door wide open for bureaucratic budget incrementalism.

Of course, Los Angeles is unique among the cities of Los Angeles County in that councilpersons are more like professional politicians than elsewhere. In smaller cities, there is a different pattern. City councilpersons tend to be volunteers, often elected at large, who are busy with full-time jobs elsewhere. In these cities, the city manager takes the initiative in budget preparation and execution. However, it is not clear that the city manager has an overwhelming incentive to keep budgets down. On the contrary, growing city budgets make it easier to solve organizational problems within a bureaucracy and to keep down troublesome labor problems that spoil a city manager's record, and they are an indicator of a city manager's growing responsibilities, status, and worth. Pasadena is an example of a city that has a dominant city manager, and there the city manager's responsibility for a growing electric power plant budget helps justify his high salary. Pasadena has also pursued a very aggressive policy of pursuing federal and state money. The result has been a rapidly expanding bureaucracy and budget. In the five years before Proposition 13,

Pasadena officials undertook more than sixty new programs accounting for $8.6 million in the local budget. Nor were these programs costless for the local taxpayer. While federal grants paid the initial capital costs of such projects as freeway landscaping and community centers, the fiscal impact of such projects "was to impose permanently higher maintenance and operating costs on the city's taxpayers." [14]

The result is that, whether they are strong councilmanic cities like Los Angeles or strong city manager cities like Pasadena, the old-line bureaucratic cities rely more and more heavily on the pooled, public resource base to provide public services. This is shown in table 3.2, which shows growth in expenditures as a proportion of assessments in old-line cities (as well as Lakewood Plan cities). These older cities not only taxed their resource bases more heavily than the newer cities, but the degree to which they taxed their bases increased dramatically in a single decade.

Is there a way to measure this supply-side push for governmental expansion? It would certainly seem to be necessary to attempt to include such a large factor in the analysis of municipal governmental expenditures. If we assume that the model estimated in table 3.1 is an accurate model of demand for public goods, we can take the residuals from the model estimation as being indicators of supply pressure. That is, a certain city with a

Table 3.2
Total Municipal Expenditures as a Percentage of Total Assessments 1960 and 1970

	0– 1.0%	1.0– 2.0%	2.0– 3.0%	3.0– 4.0%	4.0– 5.0%	5.0– 6.0%	6.0% +	Total
Prewar cities (1960)	0	1	6	20	17	1	0	45
Postwar cities (1960)	5	6	9	0	1	0	0	21
Prewar cities (1970)	0	1	3	6	17	8	10	45
Postwar cities (1970)	1	4	9	14	2	1	1	32

Source: *Financial Transactions Concerning Cities of California, 1970,* Table 19 (California State Controller, 1971).

given median tax share, median income, home ownership rate, and population will have a demand for expenditures at a certain level. Do supply factors cause a discrepancy above or below the level of demand?

If bureaucracies produce a gradual, "incremental" expansion of government budgets, then older cities should have budget levels beyond their demand levels, and younger cities should not. As it turns out, municipal age is the most important variable associated with the residuals from the demand model. Expenditures beyond those predicted by the demand model do increase with city age. The best fitting regression line, which explains over one-quarter of the variation, shows that expenditures increase an additional 7.4 percent beyond demand for every ten years of age (see figure 3.2[15]).

The gradual, incremental expansion of budgets that occurs when city councils tend to take preceding budget levels as a "base" and apportion out additional revenue as "increments" has been documented at the federal level and at the local level.[16] It further supports the contention that the older, more bureaucratic cities have a built-in tendency to expand the scale of governmental expenditure, and thus the extent to which services are provided redistributionally through a common pool of resources, rather than through individual choice based on the individual's budget constraint.

And in fact, spending in old-line, bureaucratic cities did increase faster than increases in assessments plus increases in new revenue sources such as the sales tax and government grants. As a result, property tax rates in most of these older cities showed the same tendency to rise incrementally. Tax rates went from $1.85 to $2.88 in Los Angeles between 1950 and 1977, and from $1.19 to $2.17 in Long Beach. In Pasadena, the municipal tax rate went from $1.11 to $2.11 in the same period. Except for some of the beach cities that were benefiting from a rapid increase in property assessments in the 1970s and some suburban cities that were explicitly keeping tax rates low to attract more development, 31 of the 45 prewar cities increased their tax rates from 1950 to 1977.

It is not possible to say a priori whether this expansionary impulse was good or bad. It is possible to say that it had its beneficiaries. The people who benefited from an increased reliance on public resource pools were the employees whose jobs were created by governmental growth and the low-

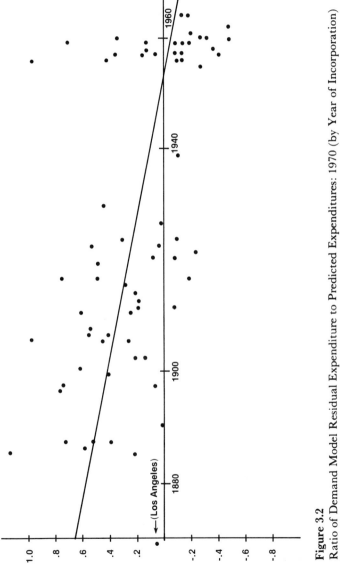

Figure 3.2
Ratio of Demand Model Residual Expenditure to Predicted Expenditures: 1970 (by Year of Incorporation)

income groups who received the benefits of the increasing number of local government programs at a tax price lower than the comparable market price.

The Redistributional Implications of the Lakewood Plan

While the increased expansion of the governmental scale of operation in bureaucratic cities benefited some, it certainly hurt those whose contributions to the shared resource pool were out of proportion to the benefits received from public activities. As a result, these individuals, who were to constitute the core of support for the Proposition 13 tax revolt, tended to lump bureaucrats and low-income groups together as the two groups against whom Proposition 13 was directed. While supporters of the initiative claimed that it was directed against bureaucratic waste and inefficiency, when pressed it became clear that redistributional services fell in that category. "Asked which services they would be willing to see government cut if necessary to implement Proposition 13, the overwhelming majority of Jarvis voters—69%—answered welfare." [17] The other services high on the list (parks and recreation was second with 33 percent, public transportation, third with 21 percent) were similarly oriented toward low-income groups.

This polarization between those who pay for and those who benefit from increased governmental activity is not limited to California. In a national poll, 78 percent of the respondents favored a constitutional amendment requiring a balanced budget. Asked which programs should be cut to balance the budget, 54 percent responded "welfare," while defense was a distant second with 29 percent. The rest of the respondents were split among Medicaid, education, and social security. Thus, budget cutters feel that budgets can be cut without hurt to themselves, if redistributional activity is limited or defense expenditures are cut.[18]

But if the dissatisfaction with the expanding use of pooled resources bases through taxation is not limited to California, neither is it limited to the 1970s. While many observers expressed surprise at the sudden articulation of taxpayer discontent in the 1970s, this does not mean that the discontent was absent before Jarvis-Gann provided the means of making it audible. Discontent was being expressed individually, rather than collectively, by the relocation of middle and upper-income taxpayers to Lakewood Plan cities with small-scale governments and low or no municipal taxes. It is the theme of this book that the primary motivation for Lakewood Plan cities was the creation of enclaves where taxpayers could escape from the redistributional patterns of old-line cities. If the new cities had sufficient resources apart from property taxation to supply an ample set of urban services, so much the better. If not, then incorporation with the promise of minimal services and no property taxation was preferable to annexation to an old-line city with its bureaucracy and redistributional programs financed by a shared resource pool.

Thus, for instance, Norwalk incorporated with a population of over 80,000, "with a campaign premised on an ability to operate the proposed city without a municipal property tax." In 1959, Lawndale escaped annexation to Hawthorne by incorporating with a platform that promised that "the new city would be operated without an increase in taxes and without municipal property taxes." Temple City, located near the inexorably annexing El Monte, incorporated in 1960 with the motto, "Representation without taxation." [19]

Indeed, public relations consultant Johnny Johnson asked the committees who invited him in to consider incorporation only two questions: whether it was possible to supply the minimum services without property taxation, and if so, if the citizens of the community were willing to set aside all other issues that might divide the community until after incorporation. Johnson thought that if the answer to both these questions was "yes," it would be possible to go ahead with a successful campaign. [20]

The main obstacle to incorporation would not be from people who did want expanded services through property taxation, but rather from people who felt that the incorporation of a new level of government necessarily meant a new level of property taxation. Consequently, it became a primary element of the incorporation campaign to demonstrate that the state supplied sufficient funds to make incorporation possible without taxation. The campaign literature emphasized the amount of money to be made available through statewide sales tax, state subventions, and fines and license taxes.

Johnson ran successful tax-avoidance campaigns in various low-resource incorporations. The communities of Paramount, Lawndale, Norwalk, and

Lomita all had very poor tax bases, especially compared with the cities that were willing to annex them (Long Beach, Hawthorne, and Torrance); yet these four communities were all willing and able to live within their meager sales tax revenue budgets in order to avoid property taxation and all that that implied in the way of redistribution through resource pooling. In all four, Johnson ran successful campaigns stressing the absence of property taxation.

Even more subtly, incorporation proponents were often able to promise an actual reduction in property tax rates as a result of incorporation. The basic reason for a reduction in rates was not an efficiency gain in service provision due to local control, but a redistribution of the cost of services. Many unincorporated areas had special district governments which provided single services, such as road districts, park districts, or lighting districts. These local services were paid for with local property taxes. However, upon incorporation, it was possible to dissolve these special districts, or withdraw from them, and allow the municipal governments to provide the services and pay for them through state subventions and sales tax revenue. The net effect of eliminating special district property taxes and adding a municipal government relying primarily on external sources of revenue was often to reduce local property tax rates, not only in comparison to those of annexing cities but also absolutely. Lakewood Plan citizens benefited through an "externalization" of the costs of local government.

The city of Lakewood was again the model for property tax reduction. As the city manager wrote in an article for the League of California Cities magazine in 1956,

It has been financially advantageous for Lakewood to incorporate rather than to remain as an unincorporated community. The property tax rate for all normal municipal functions is 22¢ less than it was in 1953, prior to incorporation. This reduction in property tax rates was accomplished by using other municipal revenues to pay the cost of our street lighting. Effecting an average reduction of 44¢ on the tax bills. The prospect for 1956 is a further reduction of at least 20¢ in the tax rate. This new advantage, of course, is a result of the uniform sales tax bill, which will net Lakewood $460,000 a year.[21]

Commerce's success in following this strategy has already been described in Chapter 2. Santa Fe Springs was also a follower of this pattern. A total special district tax rate of $1.15 was eliminated as the community withdrew from the county road and fire districts, and from the recreation and park district that it had belonged to along with Norwalk and La Mirada. It was replaced with a municipal tax rate of $.49.

That tax rates could actually be reduced through a combination of externalizing costs and eliminating social-welfare-type services became a major selling point as Lakewood and the county advertised the Lakewood Plan.

Because these communities were able to provide actual tax reductions, annexation was not necessarily a spur to incorporation. Palmdale incorporated with a zero municipal property tax rate despite the fact that it was separated from other cities in the county by the San Gabriel Mountains. The cities of Artesia and Dairy Valley (later Cerritos) incorporated with zero property tax rates, although they were midway between Whittier and Long Beach and relatively free from annexation by either city.

Except for these three cities, virtually every other incorporation in the 20 years after Lakewood occurred when the threat of annexation caused a reappraisal of the status of unincorporated communities. Because of the advantages just discussed, incorporation with a zero property tax rate looked better to most communities than annexation to a city with a large tax base and ample public services, but with large property tax rates as well.

The 13 cities whose names are in bold type in table 3.3 were those cities most vigorously engaged in annexation campaigns in the 1940s, 1950s, and 1960s. All were prewar cities except for Downey, the only postwar city to create its own bureaucratic agencies rather than adopt the Lakewood Plan. The Lakewood Plan cities that incorporated on the boundaries of these annexing cities (and in all cases as an explicit response to a specific annexation threat) are listed beneath. In every case, the new city incorporated with a much lower tax rate than that available in the city threatening annexation.

Except for Commerce and Santa Fe Springs, these communities had to pay a separate property tax rate of about $.60 during this period to the consolidated county fire district. (Commerce and Santa Fe Springs had withdrawn from the fire district.) Adding this $.60 tax rate on to the municipal tax rate, four cities had higher overall tax rates than the annexing cities. Even in these cities, however, the incorporation campaign was based

Table 3.3
Municipal Tax Rates for Annexing and Incorporating Cities:
Geographic Cluster

City	Year of Incorporation	1960 Tax Rate	1970 Tax Rate
Azusa	1898	1.45	1.45
Bradbury	1957	.97	.58
Duarte	1957	.16	None
Irwindale	1957	None	None
Bell	1927	1.43	1.29
Bell Gardens	1961	–	None
Cudahy	1960	–	None
Downey	1956	.29	.54
Commerce	1960	–	None
Norwalk	1957	None	None
El Monte	1912	.97	.87
Rosemead	1959	None	None
South El Monte	1958	None	None
Temple City	1960	–	None
Glendora	1911	1.38	1.38
San Dimas	1960	–	.60
Hawthorne	1922	1.00	.68
Lawndale	1959	None	None
Long Beach	1897	1.37	1.52
Bellflower	1957	None	None
Carson	1968	–	None
Hawaiian Gardens	1964	–	None
Lakewood	1954	.53	.08
Paramount	1957	.20	None
Los Angeles	1850	1.94	2.52
Hidden Hills	1961	–	.53
Montebello	1920	1.38	1.41
Pico Rivera	1958	.55	None

Table 3.3 (continued)

City	Year of Incorporation	1960 Tax Rate	1970 Tax Rate
Pasadena	1886	1.07	1.40
La Canada-Flintridge	1976	–	–
Torrance	1921	1.288	1.14
Lomita	1964	–	None
Rolling Hills	1957	1.00	1.00
Rolling Hills Estates	1957	.32	None
West Covina	1923	.93	1.03
Baldwin Park	1956	.13	1.31
Industry	1957	None	None
La Puente	1956	None	None
Walnut	1959	.64	.87
Whittier	1898	1.50	.82
La Mirada	1960	–	None
Santa Fe Springs	1957	.49	.49

Sources: *Financial Transactions Concerning Cities of California, 1960*, Table 19 (California State Controller, 1961) and *Financial Transactions Concerning Cities of California, 1970*, Table 19 (California State Controller, 1971).

on the issue of tax reduction. The Walnut incorporation leader made a case for the economic wisdom of incorporation by telling me that incorporation had increased property values by $4000 to $8000 and emphasized that the municipal tax rate was less than West Covina's. Property values also played a role in the incorporation of Rolling Hills and Bradbury (to be discussed in the next chapter). Norwalk's municipal incorporation campaign was explicitly based on the tax advantage of incorporation, and the promise of a zero property tax rate. With the exception of these four cities, the combined muncipal and fire district tax rates were less than the tax rate in the annexing city. Once again, this is especially important in understanding the low-resource communities who turned down annexation to high-resource, but high tax rate, old-line cities.

While other motivations for incorporation (like stricter regulation of land use) influenced at least the leaders in some incorporation movements, the most basic and pervasive common denominator for incorporation was the avoidance of high property taxation. It was explicitly used as the central theme in most incorporation campaigns, even in incorporations 20 years before the Jarvis Amendment. Where the leaders of an incorporation campaign were unable to convince the electorate that the city would not require a high property tax, the incorporation failed at the polls. This is true in the case of wealthy communities like Malibu in 1976, and in the case of the east Los Angeles ghetto in 1973.

The commitment to low property tax rates was maintained in a real, rather than symbolic, manner. In 1970, several years after the duel between incorporation and annexation had begun to subside, all but one of the 45 prewar cities still had sizeable property tax rates over $.50. But in the same year all but eight of the 32 new cities had tax rates less than that figure. Only two residential cities, one a high-income suburb and one a low-income suburb, had allowed the property tax rate to creep up to $1.00.

Expenditures in Lakewood Plan Cities

This does not mean that expenditures were always low in the postwar cities. In cities where a lot of revenue was generated automatically from sales tax or from federal or state grants, a great deal of money was spent. Industry spent over $2077 per capita on its several hundred inhabitants, without a property tax. But there were twelve cities which spent less than $49 per capita in fiscal year 1971: none of these cities raised any money through property taxation. If doing without property taxation meant spending $33 per capita, as in the elite suburb of Hidden Hills, or $39 per capita, as in the low-income city of Cudahy, then that is the amount of money that would be spent. Regardless of income class, the new cities' rule for expenditures was "spend everything you can get without a property tax."

Notice that this rule is more than simple price elasticity of demand, in which less is demanded as the price increases. A person who insists on near-zero property tax rates is like a consumer who will take everything that is free, but nothing that costs anything—a very severe form of price elasticity indeed.

The implication of this behavior for the study of local governments is very important. The only economic explanation for over half of the incorporations in Los Angeles County since 1954 is that there was a sizeable group of individuals who did not want to belong to local governments that would tax them in order to provide local services. So far as these individuals were concerned, Long Beach, Whittier, El Monte, and other old-line cities were supplying something they didn't want to buy. The issue was redistributional; since municipal services are essentially private goods, there is no reason for an individual taxpayer to purchase them from local governments unless it is cheaper to do so, that is, the market price is subsidized at someone else's expense through collective provision. But the middle-class and upper-class taxpayers knew that collective provision of public goods in these old-line, property-taxing cities would be at their expense. Incorporation into non-property-taxing cities was the alternative.

Lacking a redistributional advantage, there is no reason for essentially private goods to be supplied collectively. Police protection can be partially replaced by means of dogs, automatic alarms, fences, guns, and maintenance of a high-income neighborhood. Fire protection can be provided voluntarily (as it is in the most recent Lakewood Plan city, La Habra Heights) even if it means the lowest possible fire insurance rating (as it does in La Habra Heights). Parks and recreation can be provided by means of backyard tennis courts and swimming pools. Books can be purchased rather than taken from the library. The cities of Rolling Hills and Bradbury even rely on privately maintained roads, which incidentally help keep out the criminal element. The Lakewood Plan cities were created and are operated as "minimal cities," not for reasons of efficiency, but as a way out for property owners who didn't want to pay for the municipal provision of private or redistributional services.

Evidence for this interpretation can be garnered from a study of home ownership in Los Angeles municipalities. In 1960, all but one of the low-resource, "problem" incorporations were cities with a majority of homeowners. Between 1960 and 1970, home ownership in the county as a whole dropped dramatically, but homeowners continued to be attracted to the Lakewood Plan cities. By 1975, only 45 percent of the habitations in the cities with tax rates of over $1.00 were owner-occupied. But despite the suburban apartment boom of the late 1960s, owner-occupancy rates stayed at 60 percent in the low-tax-rate cities. Thus, as predicted by Tiebout, there was a gradual sorting out of the Los Angeles County population. Homeowners were a majority in the minimal, low-tax-rate suburbs, and renters were an increasing majority in the large-scale, high-tax-rate cities. The consequences of this sorting-out process will be further analyzed in Chapters 6 and 7.

In contrast to Tiebout's argument, however, the reason for this sorting out was not different tastes in public goods, but differences in attitude toward taxation and the scale of redistribution. The reason for creating or moving to a Lakewood Plan minimal city was not to signal something unique about one's demand for public goods, but to insulate one's property from the burden of supporting public services. Whether this type of "voting with your feet" results in gains in allocational efficiency or simply a different pattern of redistribution is discussed in Chapter 8.

4   Minimal Cities

The analysis in Chapter 3 makes it clear how middle-class and upper-class homeowners can develop an antibureaucratic, antiwelfare ideology. Homes are threatened by exorbitant taxes to pay for redistributional services and bureaucratic salaries. Long before this theme was being sounded by Howard Jarvis. it was being consciously articulated as the rationale for new jurisdictions, where the evils of bureaucracy could be forever exorcised.

The advantages of the Lakewood Plan for middle-class and upper-class home owners are obvious. First, the bureaucratic pressures for governmental expansion are cleanly eliminated by contracting. Contracting for services guarantees that there will never be a homegrown bureaucracy pushing for new services and the expansion of old ones. Secondly, by gaining control of the zoning function, Lakewood Plan cities can direct the makeup of the population to exclude service-demanding, low-income, or renting populations. Most importantly, permanent walls around local property can be erected to guarantee that high-tax-rate cities will not use local homes as a resource for governmental expansion.

Those cities that most clearly illustrate these tendencies are the half-dozen "minimal cities" that incorporated in low-density semirural areas to

keep out tract developments and bureaucracy. For the residents of exclusive residential suburbs, "development" and "bureaucracy" are indis-
solubly linked with the issue of "sprawl."

County Zoning and Planned Sprawl

When one invests a sizeable amount of money in a rural estate, one doesn't
like to see that investment threatened by ticky-tacky suburban developments, industry, cheap commercial establishments, or worst of all, apartment houses. Unincorporated communities in Los Angeles County are
supposedly protected by county zoning processes, but exclusive residential
communities have been unanimous in expressing dissatisfaction with the
way that the county board of supervisors has acted to protect (or not protect) the property values in these neighborhoods. Each of these communities has felt itself threatened by development projects that seem to leak
through the county zoning and planning apparatus as if it were a sieve.
And each of these communities has attempted to resolve the problem by
means of an incorporation which would guarantee local homeowner control over development, protect property values, and at the same time (it is
hoped) keep property taxes down. These incorporation efforts have been
successful in cases where the voters were convinced that property taxes
would, in fact, be kept down. They have failed when, as in Malibu, the
voters were convinced that incorporation would result in sizeable property
taxation.

Why should exclusive residential neighborhoods feel dissatisfied with
the county board of supervisors as zoners and planners? In an important
study of land-use politics, Mark Gottdiener[1] shows that three factors contributed to political subversion of the land-use planning system in suburban Long Island. First, the weak, local, political machines on Long Island
needed substantial contributions to ensure reelection. Second, the only
policy area over which these politicians had significant discretionary
power was land-use policy. Third, developers were highly interested in the
land-use decisions, which are often make-or-break factors in their firm's
success. Where these factors occurred together on Long Island, the local
political organizations obtained the essential campaign contributions, and
developers got their essential zoning variances, in a mutually beneficial

exchange. The only problem was that this subversion of the urban-planning process resulted in "planned sprawl."

The same three factors certainly occur together in parts of Los Angeles County as well. Since the Progressive Era, Los Angeles County has been notable for the weakness of its regular political organizations. This means that county supervisors must constantly look for support for their costly reelection campaigns, in which they must appeal to supervisorial district populations of almost one and one-half million each. Furthermore, developers are highly competitive, and especially anxious to develop the desirable coastal areas. The most lucrative of these coastal areas is the Palos Verdes Peninsula in southwest Los Angeles County. The pressure on the county board of supervisors to allow development in these areas has been immense, and the only source of opposition has been local homeowners' groups wishing to maintain the property values by fighting "sprawl." Incorporation has been the most effective weapon of the latter.

Rolling Hills and Rolling Hills Estates: Buy Your Own Dude Ranch

Several million years ago an event of minor geological and major political significance occurred. One of the rugged Channel Islands, moving slowly on its bit of earth crust, bumped into the southwest portion of the Los Angeles coastal basin, moving the mouth of the Los Angeles River over to what is now San Pedro and creating a hilly peninsula. The Palos Verdes Peninsula was, and is even to this day, difficult to reach, and even more difficult to cross. No freeways cross it, and the surface streets that span it are few and far between. While most of the Los Angeles basin was being bought, sold, and developed, the peninsula remained for the most part undeveloped; and for most of the twentieth century land values there were low compared to much of the rest of the basin. Most of the undeveloped land was owned by the Great Lakes Carbon Corporation.

One of the reasons land values stayed low, in addition to difficulty of access, was the hazard of building on the brushy, steep land. Fires remain a constant threat, and the topsoil is likely to slide away in a rain. However, beginning after World War I, rural living began to symbolize leisure and wealth, rather than poverty and hardship; land values on the peninsula began to respond to a new market for country living. This process was aided when the principal road to the peninsula (Palos Verdes Drive North) was constructed during the Depression by the hand labor of WPA work crews.

This minor project, sponsored by the newly emerging social welfare state, made possible the first upper-income housing development on the peninsula, which was to become a synonym for conservativism and wealth. As one of the early ads for this project suggested, the idea was to "Own your own Dude Ranch in Rancho Palos Verdes." [2] The development gradually evolved into a private, gated community called Rolling Hills. Restrictions were placed on the property, and in 1936 the Rolling Hills Community Association was established to enforce the restrictions.

As the Guide to Rolling Hills, put out by the Community Association, hints to prospective buyers, "Each property owner has a stake in preserving the simple, quiet, rural atmosphere of Rolling Hills." [3] The homeowners on the peninsula have been ever vigilant against threats to local property values in the form of neighboring tract developments, apartment houses, industry, and commercial development. In the postwar period these threats were embodied in the city of Torrance which lay at the foot of the peninsula's hills. As the city manager of Rolling Hills explained to me, Torrance was one of the largest cities in the county at the time—a diversified city with residential neighborhoods, commercial property, and industry. However, it lacked exclusive residential neighborhoods with high property values. Torrance's vigorous annexation program in the 1950s was designed to bring in that form of property, through annexation of the Rolling Hills community, or of similar developments on the peninsula.

The first community to respond to the threat from Torrance was not Rolling Hills, but its newer neighbor to the north of Palos Verdes Drive, Rolling Hills Estates. Serving as a buffer between Rolling Hills and Torrance, Rolling Hills Estates was a twin to Rolling Hills in most characteristics, although its roads were open to the public and it lacked an effective private homeowners' association to enforce building restrictions. Instead, it had over two dozen property owners' associations for as many tiny neighborhoods. With development less strictly controlled, it had already grown to twice the population of Rolling Hills (about 3,000) in the early 1950s when it felt itself threatened by tract developers. The homeowners of Rolling Hills estates soon became convinced that the county supervisors were unable or unwilling to restrict development to their satisfaction, a conviction that other residents of exclusive neighborhoods around the county came to share over the years. However, the homeowners found that threatening incorporation was an effective card in bargaining with the county and with the developers. Consequently, in the early 1950s, they twice filed boundary lines for an imaginary city of Rolling Hills Estates for strategic purposes only, with no intention of following through with incorporation.

However, the incorporation of the city of Lakewood in 1954 served to make the incorporation of Rolling Hills Estates more attractive. The final push to incorporate came when the city of Torrance began to make final plans for annexation of the area, and for drilling oil wells in the neighborhood. Rolling Hills Estates homeowners went down to the city offices to file a third set of boundary lines for a new city, only to find that the officials from the city of Torrance had arrived there ten minutes before them, making it impossible to follow through on the incorporation attempt until the issue of annexation was resolved.

A few days later, however, the county clerk, who had always been "quite friendly" to the Rolling Hills Estates people, called with word that Torrance's boundaries were inaccurately drawn and had been declared invalid. Rolling Hills Estates was free to proceed with incorporation.

They hired Johnny Johnson, the public relations consultant who had organized the incorporation attempts in Paramount, Norwalk, and Bellflower. Johnson, whose philosophy is that the most dangerous threat to an incorporation comes from internal dissension among advocates, immediately organized the two dozen homeowners' associations into a single federated association which could take action promptly.

The original boundaries for Rolling Hills Estates included most of a doughnut around the gated community of Rolling Hills. However, at a protest hearing before the board of supervisors, large landowners and homeowners on the less developed eastern and western sides of Rolling Hills protested against inclusion in the city. The board of supervisors once again held true to its normal prodevelopment position, and reduced the boundaries of the city to the Rolling Hills Estates development itself, between Rolling Hills and Torrance. To one Rolling Hills Estates organizer, it seemed as though the supervisors were trying to kill the whole incorporation by depriving it of any tax base whatsoever. It was obvious that the peninsula was going to become an economic plum for developers, and a political plum for county supervisors—incorporation by homeowners wishing to draw up the gangplank would spoil the whole thing.

Nevertheless, the proincorporation group formed an incorporation committee, and paid $9,500 for a feasibility study, doing much of the work on the study themselves, to keep the cost low. It took them 18 months to perform the study and proceed with the rest of the stages of incorporation before the election in September of 1957.

By way of comparison, the community of Rolling Hills already had the problem of organization solved, since it had an ongoing active community association which was accustomed to running the private road system and raising money. (It performed roughly the same function during incorporation proceedings that the local Chamber of Commerce performed in the cities of Pico Rivera, Paramount, Bellflower, and elsewhere.) Despite the fact that their incorporation proceedings were initiated after those in Rolling Hills Estates, they were able to go to election nine months earlier. Both incorporations were successful.

Not only were the incorporations successful, the cities were successful. Rolling Hills Estates, shortly after incorporating, was able to make two strip annexations to the southwest to pick up valuable commercial property. This made it possible, according to the individual who was mayor at that time, to provide ample services for the residential community at a low tax cost. Indeed, after the first few years, Rolling Hills Estates was able to abolish its property tax and subsist on the income of its commercial property and state subventions.

Since there was no danger of high property taxes, it was even more desirable to keep property values from being decreased by neighboring "incompatible" development. Again, the major threat seemed to come from Torrance's continued annexation campaign. The board of supervisors had kept the eastern slope of the peninsula from being part of the RHE incorporation, and so Torrance attempted to annex toward that property. To complete this "end run," however, required going through the old unincorporated community of Lomita, northeast of Rolling Hills Estates. Lomita, while not an exclusive residential community like Rolling Hills Estates, was similarly opposed to being annexed to the relatively high-tax-rate city of Torrance, and, in 1964, fought off the annexation attempt by the now tried and true method of incorporation. It has been without a municipal property tax for most of the time since then.

Rolling Hills Estates annexed up to the boundaries of Lomita, and the eastern slopes of Rancho Palos Verdes were effectively sealed off to Torrance.

Rolling Hills, too, was successful in its incorporation goals. While it did not annex a commercial tax base as Rolling Hills Estates did, its limited municipal activities, subventions, and contracting kept the tax rate low. And, as assessments increased, the city lowered its tax rate accordingly.

Rolling Hills is a unique example of the private use of public government. The city government is in many ways simply an extension of the private homeowners' association. The Community Association has rigid architectural control over its houses. In fact, one homeowner volunteered, "If there's any single issue that would be the biggest complaint it might be the building restrictions. They even tell you what shades of white paint you can use on your house." [4] (Colors other than white are not allowed.) While the Community Association is responsible for controlling the roads and maintaining the entrances, there is a city ordinance that threatens a $500 fine for outsiders who enter the city limits uninvited. The Community Association even levies a private property tax for maintaining the roads and recreation areas, based on the county assessment less personal property. Recreational facilities are owned by the city of Rolling Hills and leased by the Association. The city of Rolling Hills is responsible for contracting with the county sheriff for fire and police protection. While the Community Association and the city have separate five-person governing boards, the boards share administrative and legal staff.

The city government has maintained its homeowner, antidevelopmental attitude, and when more homeowners settled on the rest of the peninsula, the city of Rolling Hills furnished support for yet another antidevelopmental incorporation on the peninsula—that of Rancho Palos Verdes.

Rancho Palos Verdes: Save Our Coastline

The incorporation of Rolling Hills and Rolling Hills Estates, along with Palos Verdes Estates on the far western slopes of the peninsula, left the southern half of the peninsula unincorporated and mostly undeveloped. In the mid-1950s, Great Lakes Carbon Corporation began selling this land to builders under a county zoning plan that was intended to restrict development along the coast and keep housing densities down. However, once again the newly arriving homeowners began to experience unease as variances to the zoning plan were granted to the builders by the county board of supervisors. The homeowners began to anticipate the prospect of living in a hilly Long Beach instead of the exclusive residential area they had thought they were buying into. Between 1960 and 1968, 48 zoning variances were sought by developers, all of which were fought before the county board of supervisors by neighborhood homeowners' associations. The homeowners lost every fight. In 1965 the Palos Verdes Peninsula Advisory Council was created as a federation of neighborhood associations, in the hope that unity would give them more political strength before the county board. The council had no better luck with the board, but, with 80 percent of the developable land already developed, began to revise the 1955 plan, making concessions to developers' interest, but maintaining a commitment to the 1961 school board projections of a peninsulawide population of 92,000. This figure was 22,000 more than the 1969 population.

However, the developers secretly prepared an alternate plan, projecting a peninsulawide developed population of 140,000, double the 1969 population. The 70,000 additional people, according to this plan, would live primarily in multi-family dwellings in the remaining small fraction of developable land, mainly along the coast. When this secret plan was leaked to the public, the Palos Verdes Council began immediate plans for incorporation.

Realizing that it would be a long, highly political fight, they organized stringently to get the most out of their fundamentally weak political base. (The population of Palos Verdes constituted only a tiny fraction of the more than one million citizens in their county supervisorial district.) The organization consisted of a central cell of eight individuals, which was recruited for staying power. The individuals on the committee had to be willing to meet at any time, and stay on the committee until incorporation was successful. The committee planned strategy, controlled the flow of information so that crucial secrets would not be made available to the opponents, and raised money. In addition, there were up to 1100 active workers who obtained signatures, gleaned information about opposition strategy, helped to raise money, and performed the other menial tasks associated with a full-fledged political campaign.

Sufficient signatures were gathered for the incorporation petition within three weeks. At this point, the proponents of incorporation made their first, and perhaps last, significant strategic error of the two-and-one-half-year battle. They continued to gather signatures, rather than presenting the petition immediately, on the assumption that more names carried political weight, which was not the case. The problem with this strategy was that it allowed the opponents more time to organize.

In organizing, incorporation opponents began to circulate protest petitions. However, they too made a tactical error. Rather than keeping the petitions to themselves until sufficient signatures were circulated, they submitted them to the county as they were filled. This let the incorporationists forecast effectively when the opponents would get sufficient signatures, prepare for an attempt to disqualify the protest petitions because of unqualified signatures, and plan alternative strategies, including lawsuits.

The most important alternative strategy planned during this period was a lawsuit to challenge the constitutionality of the property-owner protest against incorporation, which allowed a minority of propertyowners with a majority of the property to veto incorporation. Ten minutes after the county board of supervisors certified the protest petitions at a September 17 lawsuit, they walked over to the county courthouse and filed suit.

As an indication of the degree of organization attained by the incorporationists, they had a backup alternative in case their court suit should fail. The state assemblyman for their district introduced a change in the state incorporation law that would have allowed a property owners' protest based on 51 percent of the value of property and improvements, rather than property alone. This simple change would have greatly decreased the efficacy of the property owners' veto, because the developers owned 38 percent of the property by value, but only 11 percent of the property and improvements by value. Because the change in the law would apply to Los

Angeles County alone, because it would be effective only for two years, and because it was introduced quietly so that the developers would never get wind of it, it passed easily in the winter-spring session of 1971. If a second incorporation petition had been necessary, this simple change would have greatly affected the nature of the ball game.

While they were waiting for a court decision, the incorporationists continued to fight zoning changes and development on the peninsula. Through a system of volunteers (that actually included temporary help for the developers and their lawyers), the proponents were kept informed of the actions planned by their opponents. This included information from volunteer watchers, at the La Mirada county office and downtown, about every building permit application from the peninsula developers. This network resulted in another court action when it discovered plans for condominium development in the heart of the peninsula that would have resulted in eight units to the acre. The incorporationists filed a lawsuit on procedural grounds, noting that the county board of supervisors had failed to hold the required public hearings on this violation of the general plan. This was successful.

In October 1972, two years after the original suit against the property-owners' protest, the California Supreme Court handed down a decision that was completely in the proponents' favor. In a decision that became a precedent for similar cases throughout the nation, the court held that the property-owner protest stage in incorporation proceedings was unconstitutional because it violated the one-man-one-vote principle, and it ordered the incorporation process to proceed to the boundary hearing stage.

At the subsequent boundary hearing, several county supervisors tried to terminate the incorporation altogether, arguing that the California Supreme Court had done a disservice to allow the incorporation proceeding to continue as if nothing had changed in the two years of law suits. However, the board limited its action to excluding the eastern section of the peninsula, called the San Pedro Hills area, from the proposed incorporation. This action guaranteed that one section of the peninsula would remain open to development for at least several more years, and this pleased landowners in this area who actually had filed a separate incorporation petition, feeling that their land could not be profitably developed in the Rancho Palos Verdes incorporation.

Because opposition to the incorporation was strongest in San Pedro Hills, the proponents were satisfied to see this middle-income area excluded. The result was a resounding victory for incorporationists, and a defeat for Palos Verdes developers.

Bradbury: Maintaining What We Have

In the land boom of the 1880s, numerous town sites were set out by land speculators. In April of 1887, one such promoter, Jonathan Slauson, located the town of Azusa "in a dry wash full of boulders." Reproached for planning his subdivision in such a spot, Slauson's answer was typical: "If it's not good for a town, it isn't good for anything."

By the 1950s, Azusa was still little known for anything besides a comedian's stock joke that linked it with Anaheim and Cucamonga. The 1950 census showed it having a little more than 11,000 in population, most of whom were in middle- and lower-income groups.

This latter reason alone was perhaps sufficient to make it unsuitable to the residents of a new, upper-class development when the subject of annexation arose in the mid-1950s. In addition, however, Azusa was, like many of the older cities, experiencing something of a fiscal crisis at that time. It was constantly having to expand its services as the postwar building boom hit, but its sales tax revenue was rather small, and its property tax base was relatively poor. It had had to increase its property tax rate from 1.50 in 1940–1941 to 1.96 a decade later, giving it the second highest property tax rate in the county at that time, after Santa Monica.

Consequently, the citizens of the elite residential development of Bradbury had a number of reasons to oppose annexation to Azusa. It would result in a high property tax to provide services through the municipal departments to a primarily middle-income and lower-income population. Furthermore, the citizens of Bradbury recognized that they could not expect the city council of Azusa to recognize the investment they had in their elite homes, but would be determined to encourage middle-class subdivisions and possibly even commercial and industrial development near their own exclusive neighborhood. Consequently, Bradbury incorporated as a separate municipality, under the Lakewood Plan.

In order to meet minimum population requirements, Bradbury had to

incorporate with one area of middle-class homes, an area that is still referred to as "awful" by one Bradbury founder.[5] The immediate effort,
however, was to isolate this small middle-class minority, and keep it an
ever smaller minority. Zoning practices were enacted to include a minimum lot size of half a commercial acre up to two acres, in various parts of
town. There is no low-income housing, no apartments, and no unemployment. With the exception of one family of blacks that has moved in since
1970, there is no racial diversity. The 1975 per capita income of $11,104 is
almost exactly twice that of the county's average. The mayor of Bradbury
views the job of the council as "maintaining what we have got." As one
councilman says, "We all want Bradbury to stay just the way it is. . . . A
person that came in and said that he wanted to make a big change would
be called a heretic and run out of town."[6]

"Maintaining what we have got" entails not only highly restrictive zoning to protect property levels and keep out "heretics"; it also means divert-
ing little of the private wealth of the community to collectively provided
services. As it is, the citizens of Bradbury get by with a minimum. In their
plush surroundings, they find it easy to do without city parks, city health
programs, and so forth. In fact, only two miles of road are publicly maintained; the rest are controlled by two controlled-access developments. As it
is not too difficult to keep crime down within a walled town, minimal law
enforcement is provided through a contract with the county sheriff. This is
sufficient to keep Bradbury one of the safest communities in the county. As
tiny as this expense is (less than $30,000 for fiscal year 1976) the contract
with the sheriff is still one of the few major expenses in the city budget, the
only other noticeable expenses being the salary of the three full-time employees, $10,000 for the maintenance of the two miles of public streets, and
$6,000 for the cost of the strict building regulation.

That these policies are advantageous to the citizens of Bradbury is demonstrated by the absence of any internal political conflict and the satisfaction expressed by all members of the city council with the status quo. The
city of Bradbury has, in effect, zoned out redistributional conflict by maintaining an income-homogeneous citizenry, and creating institutional
boundaries between itself and the relatively tumultuous politics of
neighboring Azusa. The battle which resulted in the creation of Bradbury
was the last political conflict with which Bradbury has had to deal.

As for Azusa, it continues to hope that its increases in tax base will out-strip the rise in demand for services. In the 1970s, this has been a losing battle. The increases in property evaluations seen in its assessment records were largely the result of inflation; in real terms, the per capita assessments dropped during the first seven years of the decade. At the same time, the drain on the tax base has increased. Expenditures were 3.6 percent of the tax base in 1960, 6.4 percent in 1970, and 6.7 percent in 1977. (For Brad-bury, these figures were 2.1 percent, 2.8 percent, and 3.3 percent.)

Summary

From the perspective of the homeowner, it is easy to see why the county zoning and planning process seemed a failure, and why incorporation of a "minimal city" seemed a viable alternative. County responsiveness to de-velopers' interests threatened valuable open land and property values. The American dream of home in a semirural suburb was at stake, just as Jarvis was to claim in the 1978 campaign over property taxation. The opponents were still the bureaucrats and low-income groups.

Yet it is possible to ask whether the incorporation of a series of tiny "minimal cities" was the right solution to inadequate county zoning. What happened to the developments that were kept from the low-density communities? Were they killed, or simply relocated elsewhere? To some extent both, and both alternatives represent an abnegation of effective land-use planning, rather than its fulfillment, as the incorporationists claimed.

To the extent that housing developments were simply killed in the mini-mal cities, the incorporation of the cities imposed a hidden cost on those low-income and middle-income families who have sought, and continue to seek, adequate housing in the Los Angeles County area. In *The Environmen-tal Protection Hustle*,[7] Bernard Frieden points out that the strong, localist no-growth movement in the San Francisco suburbs killed over 20,000 housing units surveyed in four case studies alone. Pointing out that many of the killed projects were in fact environmentally sound, Frieden argues that "many growth opponents use environmental arguments to mask other motives, such as fears of property tax increases or anxieties about keeping their community exclusive."[8] While no-growth policies are clearly of benefit to those individuals who have already gotten into the housing market and who can derive the benefits of soaring property values, they just as clearly pose as a threat to those who find themselves frozen out of that market.

To the extent that housing and other development is simply displaced, it probably goes to places that are less regulated, and likely to be farther from jobs and current commercial developments. This means that the individuals who will live in them simply burn more gas to get where they need to go. It is hard to imagine that creating these half-dozen small islands had a positive net effect on air pollution, open land, and urban sprawl in the Los Angeles area. While the incorporationists in these minimal communities are emphatic that "local control" is what is needed for better environmental planning, the case for local control as a substitute for regional planning has not been established. Frieden's remarks about the San Francisco environmental movement would seem to apply as well to the incorporation movement as a mode of land-use planning:

Building a logical argument in favor of the present system would be very hard. It would somehow have to justify benefiting existing suburban residents at the expense of potential newcomers, encouraging sprawling development in lightly regulated places, and charging young families and taxpayers in general for the benefits that go to selected suburbanites. Nobody has yet made a persuasive case justifying these results.[9]

While the creation of minimal cities is of doubtful value as a land-use planning strategy, it clearly benefits local homeowners in other ways. In particular, it guarantees that those population groups who demand welfare-type benefits will not be able to live within local boundaries. The absence of these groups maintains high home values, while ensuring that those high assessments will not be taxed for extensive local services such as are provided in Los Angeles, Long Beach, or Pasadena. The use of the zoning mechanism takes on significance as a natural aspect of the "quiet revolt" against property taxation.

Indeed, while Industry and Rolling Hills are strikingly different contract cities in almost every respect, they are strikingly similar when the most fundamental motivation for incorporation is analyzed. Both communities were incorporated to protect privately owned resources from property taxation while enhancing the private market value of those assets. In Industry, the private asset was prime industrial land; in the case of Rolling Hills, it was the elite home. In neither case was the efficient allocation of resources according to local tastes in public services the issue in incorporation. In both cases, the public benefit to be derived from that private asset was kept from a larger population to benefit a narrower population. The public rationales for these two incorporations, whether effective industrial planning or effective environmental protection, must not be taken at face value in either case.

5 Municipal Incorporation under LAFCO

In the light of the Tiebout argument, the incorporations discussed in the last few chapters would seem to be benign and desirable. Incorporations of minimal cities like Bradbury and Rolling Hills, and even industrial cities like Industry and Commerce, are seen in this light as having been "designed to provide public goods and services efficiently by articulating demand as small homogeneous units and purchasing goods and services from efficient producing organizations. Their incorporation served to prevent the imposition of political externalities by neighboring municipalities that wanted to acquire their relatively high tax bases for the financing of public goods and services of their own citizens." [1]

While these incorporations may be interpreted as "preventing the imposition of political externalities by neighboring municipalities," an alternative interpretation would be that they in fact imposed political externalities on their neighbors, by depriving them of a relatively high tax base that was capable of serving a broader population. Needless to say, this is the interpretation that the neighboring cities tend to place on the Lakewood incorporations. Still another, more neutral interpretation might be to visualize the incorporations as in fact the result of a zero-sum game between competitors for potential property and sales-tax revenue. This system of municipal incorporation has worked well for those cities that have either secured a high tax base, or have insulated themselves from crime and other urban problems that place a strain on a municipal tax base; but it is not clear that municipal competition is the best institutional framework for overall, long-run urban growth. The ease with which municipalities and special districts could be formed to service new developments has encouraged developers to use land in an extravagant way. Development has rushed outward from central Los Angeles along transportation routes toward the Orange and San Bernardino County lines, often on land that turned out to be in flooding zones, unsuitable for septic tanks, far from fire stations and other emergency services, or unable to handle increased traffic. Land that was viewed as unproductive of revenue was left out of municipal incorporations. This resulted in awkward islands of unincorporated territory, inefficiently and inadequately served by county agencies. With much of the taxable property located in municipalities that have no property taxation, the cost of municipal services falls all the harder on those jurisdictions that rely on property taxation of weaker tax bases to finance their municipal services.

These problems were magnified many times over throughout the state of California. As a result, in 1963, a major effort to reform institutional procedures for urban growth was made under Governor Pat Brown's administration. The avowed purpose was to put urban growth in a more comprehensive, less competitive governmental framework, and to attack the problem of disparities of tax levels and of urban services between municipalities that resulted from differing success in the competition for resources.

The Knox-Nisbet Act

As may be imagined, different political bodies took different positions on the problems of urban growth and municipal boundaries. In Los Angeles County, for instance, it was the county government which benefited most by the Lakewood Plan, which represented a peculiarly appropriate solution to the county's problem of maintaining demand for its services in an increasingly urban county. The county supervisors also had the most to lose, in that the current arrangements (before 1963) gave them final authority over municipal boundaries. The statewide lobbying organization for county agencies—the County Supervisors Association of California (CSAC)—reflected a recognition of the benefits of the status quo. They proposed the most conservative solutions to the problems of urban growth, suggesting a purely advisory state agency empowered to make technical studies of annexation and incorporation cases.

On the other hand, the old-line cities felt themselves most threatened by the Lakewood Plan, which constituted the only option to annexation in most cases, and which consequently deprived them of their best hope of improving their tax bases. Their proposal, with the support of the governor's administration, constituted the most radical proposal for the solution. It suggested a strong, state-level agency to rule on annexation and incorporation cases. They also suggested that cities be permitted to annex islands of unincorporated land without the approval of inhabitants, if it could be demonstrated that these areas could thus be served more economically. Cities also should be allowed to initiate annexation of inhabited areas, rather than relying on the inhabitants of the area to initiate proceedings by petition.

The cities' proposal calling for a strong state commission was offered as Assembly Bill 1662 by John Knox in the 1963 state legislative session. The position of the Supervisors' Association was articulated in the Senate by Eugene Nisbet, who proposed a county-level commission to review annexation, but not incorporation. This would have strengthened the county's ability to limit municipal annexation, rather than the cities' ability to limit procounty incorporation.

After Knox attempted to carry the procity position through the assembly, it became obvious that political pressure from county supervisors was sufficient to block the bill, and a compromise was sought. The compromise, known as the Knox-Nisbet Act, created multiple, county-level commissions rather than a single state commission, and thus conceded a major point to the county supervisors. The Local Agency Formation Commission (LAFCO) in each county would consist of five commissioners, two of which were to be county supervisors, thus guaranteeing strong representation of the county's attitudes regarding annexation and incorporation. The local agency commissions did represent a partial victory for the procity forces, because two more of the commissioners were to represent the cities, and the commissions were to have authority over incorporations as well as annexations. The fifth member of each LAFCO board was to be chosen by the other four members, and much of the ambiguity in the bill that made the compromise palatable to both sides rested on differing expectations about the political loyalties of the fifth member.

The compromise bill still had some powerful opposition, however, from Assemblyman Frank Lanterman of the unincorporated community of La Canada in Los Angeles County. He charged that the fifth member of the board would represent the cities, and that the bill represented the attempt by cities to "gobble up territory outside their limits." [2] As a leader of the Republicans in the assembly, he rallied his party to his position, and attempted last minute amendments on the floor of the assembly to make commission decisions advisory only. The final debate was dramatic, and the final vote was virtually along party lines, but the compromise Knox-Nisbet Bill was passed.

The LAFCO boards so created are empowered to approve or disapprove any petition for incorporation, special district formation, dissolution, or annexation. For municipal incorporation petitions, they may exclude territory from the proposed incorporation, but not include territory not mentioned on the petition. Any incorporations or annexations approved by LAFCO go on to the board of supervisors, who decide whether or not to grant a petition for an election in the proposed city or annexed territory, and in so doing, may also exclude territory from the incorporation. As before, the election finally decides the issue. The LAFCO boards do not do anything that was not previously done elsewhere; they simply represent a different balance of power by creating an extra review step in the incorporation process. The extra review step allows municipal governments a voice in a process that the county supervisors had performed virtually alone. Except for any extra planning done by the LAFCO staff, the creation of the LAFCO boards changed the process of municipal government formation in only a political way.

This was not lost to Lanterman, who continued to warn unincorporated areas about what he viewed as the LAFCO threat of annexation. Two months after the Knox-Nisbet Bill passed, the executive director of the

League of California Cities was complaining that incorporation movements had been started by communities which feared that they must either incorporate before the LAFCOs were actually formed, or be annexed afterwards. "Carpenter blamed Assemblyman Frank Lanterman (R-La Canada) for scaring many areas into a rush toward cityhood." [3] It was at this time that Lomita and Hawaiian Gardens incorporated in Los Angeles County; Lomita responded to an annexation threat from the city of Torrance, and Hawaiian Gardens to a double threat from Lakewood and Long Beach.

It is interesting to speculate as to whether or not the LAFCO boards have significantly changed the incorporation process along the lines Lanterman feared. Have these boards enhanced municipal annexation ambitions and retarded the spread of the Lakewood Plan to additional contract cities? The executive director of the Los Angeles County LAFCO board feels that her agency has indeed been responsible for stopping the rush to incorporation that began with the Bradley-Burns sales tax and the Lakewood Plan.[4] She also admits to the feeling that all unincorporated territory should sooner or later be added to one of the cities in the county. She is not only opposed to unincorporated communities; she also has an unfavorable view of low-resource incorporations, feeling that Hawaiian Gardens, for example, "should have been annexed to Lakewood because it is too small and too poor" to go it alone (despite the fact that this community has managed to keep its tax rates even lower than those in Lakewood).[5]

Furthermore, there is some evidence that LAFCO boards have actually changed annexation patterns. Table 5.1 shows incorporations and annexations in Los Angeles County before and after the Knox-Nisbet Bill went into effect in 1964. Although two cities were officially incorporated in early 1964, these were essentially the result of earlier procedure. It was not until 1968 that LAFCO allowed its first incorporation. On the other hand, annexations remained high. Most significantly, the average area of each annexation increased after 1964. This is important because, when the possibility of incorporation is real, an annexing city has to proceed with annexation warily, and in very small chunks, so as not to push the neighboring territory into incorporation proceedings. After 1964, cities were able to proceed with annexation more boldly, knowing that LAFCO served as a potential block to incorporation proceedings.

Table 5.1
Incorporations and Annexations in Los Angeles County, 1950 Through 1973

	Incorporations		Annexations			
Year	No.	Area square miles	No.	Area square miles	Total area incorporated and annexed	Average size of annexation*
1950	0	0	87	5.150	5.150	.059
1951	0	0	80	3.490	3.490	.044
1952	0	0	71	6.976	6.976	.098
1953	0	0	78	8.108	8.108	.104
1954	1	6.994	105	4.554	11.548	.043
1955	0	0	140	9.324	9.324	.067
1956	4	29.549	107	14.522	44.071	.136
1957	10	51.996	140	6.712	58.708	.048
1958	2	8.728	142	9.181	17.909	.065
1959	4	13.489	156	10.324	23.813	.067
1960	5	21.214	124	4.677	25.891	.038
1961	2	3.652	139	12.389	16.041	.089
1962	1	2.045	177	3.187	5.232	.018
1963	0	0	193	10.214	10.214	.053
1964	2	2.195	121	12.559	14.754	.104
1965	0	0	88	21.912	21.912	.249
1966	0	0	79	8.465	8.465	.107
1967	0	0	46	5.729	5.729	.125
1968	1	16.100	65	6.105	22.205	.094
1969	0	0	41	10.147	10.147	.025
1970	0	0	54	18.644	18.644	.345
1971	0	0	51	2.513	2.513	.049
1972	0	0	63	4.636	4.636	.074
1973	1	12.310	36	.584	12.894	.016

Source: County of Los Angeles, California, Regional Planning Commission, *Quarterly Bulletin*, No. 122, October 1, 1973, p. 6.
* Computed by author from Planning Commission data.

The hypothesis that LAFCO served the political interests of the old-line cities is further advanced by examining the history of the first city to incorporate after its creation.

Carson versus LAFCO

In the southern part of the county, Lakewood's incorporation was only the first in a series of deterrents to Long Beach's expansionary impulses. Paramount and Bellflower had incorporated in 1957, sealing Long Beach off forever from the economic boom in the southeastern part of the county. There was in fact only one further avenue of growth, the thirty-square-mile Carson-Dominguez area to the west. Bordered on the north by Compton and on the west by the Los Angeles "shoestring," the Carson-Dominguez area had undergone a significant amount of oil extraction and was developing into a major industrial center. In addition, it was located on major highway routes between the harbor and the central city. It is not surprising, then, that Long Beach became intensely interested in annexing part of the Carson area.

The first attempt was not long in coming. In 1958, Long Beach tried to annex the Dominguez area on its western border. It failed because of a technical problem with the definition of the boundaries. In 1960, Long Beach sought to get political support from the local inhabitants of this same area, but the proannexation movement died from lack of enthusiasm.

But these two attempts at annexation by Long Beach, along with a 1958 attempt by gambling interests to incorporate the heart of Carson as a gambling town, were enough to start serious incorporation efforts. In 1960, an insurance agency owner, backed by the Dominguez Chamber of Commerce and local businesses, attempted to incorporate the entire thirty-square-mile Carson-Dominguez area. This attempt quickly failed because of strong opposition from homeowners and a committee of 40 industrial leaders who feared higher tax rates and were not yet convinced that annexation by Long Beach was a serious threat.

A much smaller incorporation attempt was made in 1961. It involved only six square miles. This attempt failed when representatives of two organizations, the Carson Property Owners and the Industries Committee, charged that two signatures on the incorporation petitions were forgeries. The board of supervisors postponed the hearing because of the controversy surrounding the charge. This gave the property owners, who represented 51 percent of the property in the proposed incorporation area, time to sign a petition protesting the incorporation, which killed the proposal for another year.

In 1963, the debate over the LAFCO bill in Sacramento had ramifications in Carson. When Lanterman urged two unincorporated communities "to file for incorporation before the [LAFCO] commission came into effect, lest these areas be 'gobbled up' by nearby municipalities," the Carson incorporationists tried again.[6] This time they switched to a strategy of starting very small. They hoped to incorporate a tiny (less than two square miles) area without controversy, and then proceed with annexations. "The idea was mainly to eliminate practically all the larger landowners whose exclusions would bring the same failure as before."[7] Yet even this incorporation attempt failed, because of intense opposition organized by the Carson Homeowners Association, which insisted that the incorporation would bring higher taxes. Industrialists outside the tiny area of the proposal, fearing future annexations, still opposed the incorporation attempt—this time, ironically, charging that the city was too small, with too small a tax base, to be a viable city. Once again opposition petitions from property owners, representing over half of the assessable property, were presented to the board of supervisors.

Immediately after the 1963 failure of incorporation, Long Beach made its most daring annexation proposal—"a jagged dagger . . . aimed right at the heart of the Carson-Dominguez community. If successful, this attempt would have killed the community's chances of ever becoming a city."[8] This was especially potent, because the annexation proposal, though it actually did go all the way to the heart of Carson, followed a circuitous route so that technically it was an "uninhabited annexation," involving the residences of fewer than 12 persons and requiring little more than the approval of the major property owner, which happened to be a large land-development corporation. By protesting before the county board of supervisors, the incorporationists were able to stop this threat.

After this attempt, Long Beach's fears about Carson's incorporation, and Carson's fears about Long Beach's annexation, began to feed on each other more intensively. As Carson made more credible moves for incorporation, Long Beach launched more desperate annexation attempts. The result was to convince Carson homeowners and industrialists that they had no choice other than incorporation or annexation to Long Beach.

It was in this super-heated atmosphere that the new Local Agency Formation Commission for Los Angeles County was set up. The cities were allotted two seats. "The city selection committee had only one meeting at which city members were elected with little deliberation." [9] It is not surprising that one of the cities which volunteered to serve on the LAFCO board was Long Beach. Its representative was quoted shortly afterward in the Long Beach *Press Telegram* as saying that he would vote against the proposed city of Carson whenever that issue came before LAFCO. Furthermore, the fifth member of the board was the inheritor of a well-known Long Beach–based fortune.

At this time, the industrialists in Carson took their first serious look at incorporation. The incorporation attempt of the same year, 1964, was again a large incorporation proposal of 25.6 square miles. This time the Dominguez Industrial Council appointed a subcommittee with representatives of Shell Oil Company, the Watson Land Company, the Stauffer Chemical Company, the Southern California Gas Company, the Santa Fe Railroad, and the Dominguez Water Corporation. This subcommittee was to survey the proposed incorporation from the industrial perspective. It hired a consulting firm which concluded, in September of 1964, that no property tax would be necessary to operate the new city successfully, and consequently urged incorporation rather than annexation to Long Beach as the preferable alternative for the area's industry. However, the consultants suggested deferring the current incorporation attempt in order to build support for an incorporation filing in July 1965.

The Industrialists' Council hired two consulting firms to work on the issue of incorporation. One was Gold-Thompson, the same firm used by the industrialists in the incorporation of Commerce, and the other was George Voight, used by the incorporationists in South El Monte. The first set of consultants issued the Gold-Thompson Report, which concluded in September of 1964 that no property tax would be necessary, and urged incorporation as the preferable alternative for the area's industries. However, the report also suggested deferring the current incorporation attempt in order to build support for an incorporation filing in July of 1965.

In 1965 there was some opposition to incorporation because of delays in the county's program of major street improvements. "One industry spokesman said the new city could end up paying for all street improvements if incorporation were attempted at this time. This could mean a '25¢ per $100 valuation property tax to homeowners' it was pointed out." [10] By November, despite the fact that the consultants' report had led to greater proincorporation feeling than ever before among homeowners, industry decided that it would not support incorporation for one or two more years.

In 1966, Gordon Nesvig, executive secretary of LAFCO, proposed a one-year moratorium on any annexation or incorporation. The incorporationists violently opposed this proposal, feeling that they were on the verge of a successful conclusion, and feeling that LAFCO was not predisposed to Carson's incorporation. LAFCO received a $50,000 grant from the county to study the Carson problem, but the incorporationists, believing that "an adverse decision could have been the fatal blow that would stop all future incorporation attempts," [11] appealed successfully to the county board of supervisors to stop those funds from being delivered.

In a series of meetings a final agreement between homeowners and industry was worked out. Homeowners wanted local control over zoning and no property taxes; industry concurred heartily in the latter sentiment. In 1966 an incorporation proposal for over 29 square miles was filed, the largest incorporation proposal in the county's history.

In September of 1966, the crucial LAFCO hearing occurred. Gordon Nesvig, the executive secretary, proposed to deny the incorporation petition at that time; he was supported by the LAFCO board.

However, at the following meeting of the county board of supervisors, Supervisor Kenneth Hahn, representing the county district that included Carson (but not Long Beach), charged that the political influence of Long Beach had been felt at the Carson hearing.

I was shocked to find out that the [LAFCO] Commission by a three-to-two vote turned down the petition of the people in the Carson-Dominguez area. Now, the reason I am shocked is because I felt it was a stacked deck against them even before the meeting started. Of the five members there, our very able Chairman, Burton Chace, who was former mayor of Long

Beach, sat in as a substitute for Warren Dorn. Then they had a Council-man of Long Beach, Mr. Bond served, and then the Chairman of the Com-mittee, I think it is Mr. Hotchkiss, who has vast holdings representing the Bixby estate in Long Beach. So even before they appeared the citizens felt it was a stacked deck against them. They couldn't even get a fair hearing . . . they have been afraid that Long Beach, with all its power, was going to annex their uninhabited area, especially where the oil wells are.[12]

In 1967, the accelerating momentum of the Carson incorporation drive led to a rash of annexation proposals, not only by Long Beach, which filed three, but also by Los Angeles and Compton, which filed two each. In July 1967 a LAFCO hearing approved a staff recommendation that approved one annexation for each of these three cities, and resulted in further exclu-sions, totaling 45 percent of the proposed incorporation. The exclusions left a vacant corridor of land between Los Angeles and Carson on Carson's western border, and a large area of land between Long Beach and Compton on Carson's northeast corner. (Parts of the excluded land have subsequently been annexed by all of the cities involved.)

The opposition of LAFCO to Carson's incorporation and the granting of annexation proposals and exclusions that reduced Carson's territory by almost one-half resulted in deep-seated antagonism and distrust for LAFCO on the part of the local incorporationists. After all the frustrations of the previous attempts, including opposition by Long Beach, homeowner and industrial reluctance, and even charges of fraud, "it is almost certain that the majority of cityhood proponents would agree that the Local Agency Formation and Annexation Commission [sic] contributed the most in quantity and kind of frustration to their cause." [13]

The Carson incorporation is interesting for two reasons. First of all, it demonstrates that the LAFCO board, which was created in the hope of dealing with the political and economic problems generated by the "an-nexation and incorporation wars" of the preceding decade, was simply a continuation of that war by other means. The LAFCO handling of the Carson incorporation was dominated at every step by just the kind of po-litical conflict over resources that motivated the Knox-Nisbet Bill in the first place.

Further, the Carson incorporation suggests that the incorporations al-lowed under LAFCO were not necessarily different from pre-LAFCO incorporations. The debate over the Knox-Nisbet bill repeatedly cited "special interest incorporations" such as Industry and Commerce, with the implication that the new LAFCO machinery would not allow such incorporations. On the surface, at least, Carson was different from those cases: there seemed to be a great deal of citizen involvement, and there seemed to be some rationale for incorporation besides the simple calculus of property tax avoidance that had motivated Commerce and Industry. However, there is considerable evidence that the Carson incorporation was not significantly different from previous special interest incorporations. The history of the incorporation campaign, and the early history of the city itself, suggest that the most importance motivation for incorporation was once again the avoidance of property taxation; and it suggests that the same style of opportunistic, corruptible leadership that characterized the Commerce incorporation dominated the Carson incorporation as well.

After finally getting approval from LAFCO for the smaller version of the Carson incorporation, the incorporationists were free to turn their attention to the election. The first step, as in Commerce, was the selection of a professional public relations firm to organize and run the campaign. As in Commerce, the money for this came primarily from the Industrial Council, and the Industrial Council interviewed and hired George Voight. Voight had a hand in all the major decisions, from selection of the slate of candidates to be backed by the Industrial Council to selection of the major campaign issues.

There were two primary issues brought up in the incorporation campaign, after approval for the election had finally been received. These were land-use control and property taxes. The incorporation proponents argued in their literature that Carson was getting a reputation as "that area with all those junkyards and rubbish dumps" because the county supervisors were willing to allow those uses. In fact, there were 96 wrecking-yards in the Carson area at the time of incorporation, half of them illegal according to county ordinances. Proponents argued that only local control of zoning and zoning enforcement would "stop our area from being contaminated with junk yards, dumps, cemeteries, and any other unwanted and unsightly projects that [have] been shoved down our throats for years."

Ironically, however, the very individuals who ran for the city council on this land-use issue were discovered, almost immediately after incorporation, soliciting bribes to allow some of the very same obnoxious land uses to remain in the city. In 1969, one year after incorporation, John Junk (chairman of the incorporation committee) told a prospective builder that he could reverse the Planning Commission's action for $50,000 and a share in the building. Another councilman was brought into the deal, but a third, who had made a separate solicitation for a bribe from the same builder, was frozen out as an unnecessary vote. (This last councilman is still holding office in Carson.) The same coalition of councilmen asked for money, insurance, and tires from a refuse collection firm interested in a residential rubbish collection contract.

The next year, a fourth councilman was found soliciting bribes. This councilman, who was a former state and county prosecutor, was acting for a ring that included his brother (who was president of the Junior Chamber of Commerce), a parks and recreation commissioner, and an environmental commissioner. The object of the bribe solicitation in this case was a man who wished to develop a motorcycle park. This group also asked an Orange County developer for $100,000 to get zoning approval for a shopping center and an industrial park. These individuals were all sentenced and served time in county jail.[14]

This calls into doubt the sincerity of land-use controls as a campaign issue. And indeed, one of the consultants hired by the Carson Industrial Council reported that local control of land use was never brought up as an issue in the incorporation effort until after incorporation was decided on by the industrialists. For them, the primary concern was identical to the concern of the industrialists who sponsored the incorporation of Commerce and other industrial cities: minimization of taxation. It was this factor that the industrialists and homeowners could agree on, and the major promise of the election campaign was "services without the need for a property tax." The incorporationists won by a three-to-one majority; the minority were not those who felt that a property tax was desirable, but those who failed to accept the argument that a new layer of government could be created *without* property taxation.

Thus, the Carson incorporation was run by the Industrial Council–backed public relations firm, on issues chosen by that firm. While one of those was primarily a "front" issue for public consumption only, the Carson incorporation was very successful in maintaining the crucial goal of the industrialists, which was (as in Commerce) low tax rates. In fact, the city has been able to carry on without a property tax of any sort, one of 22 cities in the county to do so in 1971, one of only 5 in the year before Proposition 13.

Furthermore, Carson had one of the most successful records in growth of commercial and property tax base during the 1970s, a period in which most of the county's cities experienced a growth in assessable property per capita less than the rate of inflation. Carson, on the other hand, had a 5 percent increase in per capita assessments, even with inflation taken into account. Assessments rose from $3344 to $3863 in the first seven years of the 1970s.

Long Beach, on the other hand, for the first time in its history, experienced in the 1970s a decrease in its tax base. Its per capita assessments dropped from $2933 to $2747 in 1970 dollars (controlling for a change in assessment rates). To keep up services, it has had to increase its municipal tax rate from $1.52 to $2.17, a fact which may explain why its population has experienced its first significant drop, falling from over 358,000 in 1970 to a little over 341,000.

In sum, the Carson incorporation looks a great deal like the pre-LAFCO special-interest incorporations which captured prime development areas and insulated them from the principal population centers in the county. While the political influence of Long Beach could certainly be detected on the LAFCO board, that influence was not enough to change the outcome. While no other special-interest commercial incorporations have taken place under LAFCO, LAFCO cannot take any credit for that. All other prime industrial areas had already been incorporated.

La Canada-Flintridge is an example of another incorporation in which the influence of a large, diverse population center was felt on the LAFCO board, but was insufficient to change the outcome of the incorporation proceedings.

La Canada-Flintridge: Pressure from Pasadena

Like Long Beach, Pasadena is one of the larger suburbs of Los Angeles, with a population of diverse ethnic backgrounds and income levels. It has been one of the few outlets for blacks from central Los Angeles, who are seeking a place to live outside the central city. At the turn of the century it was, like Long Beach, a high-society tourist resort. It retains a significant population of wealthy older people, and at the same time it is building a larger population of lower-income minorities.

This diverse population was not represented in Pasadena politics, for the most part. As with most medium-sized and small California cities, Pasadena's politics were of the nonpartisan, consensual type which tends to result in a city council made up of white professional and businessmen and an active city manager working closely with these groups. The city government took a dim view of large numbers from low-income minorities entering the "City of Roses," but was unable to stop this trend altogether. And once in, the growing population required rising levels of services. Pasadena's budget almost doubled between 1960–1961 and 1970–1971, from $12.7 to $24 million. At the same time, its population actually decreased somewhat, and its tax base increased by less than a third. These trends continued into the 1970s, and the increased strain on the property tax base was seen in the property tax rate, which increased from 1.07 in 1960–1961, to 1.40 a decade later, and to 1.65 by 1975.

Unlike Long Beach, however, Pasadena had little opportunity for territorial expansion. It was surrounded on the south and east by smaller exclusive cities (San Marino, Arcadia, and Sierra Madre) which had used their zoning power to keep the population upper-class and white. On the north was Altadena, an unincorporated territory which had experienced the same influx of minority and lower-class population that Pasadena had. Pasadena's interest was centered on the two communities of Flintridge and La Canada on her western boundary.

La Canada, the larger of these two unincorporated communities, is an upper-middle-class community with low-density, single-family dwellings. This low density is protected by the lack of sewers, which makes multi-family developments impossible. The community had a long history of defending its unincorporated status. During the controversy over the Knox-Nisbet Bill in 1963, it was its representative, Assemblyman Frank Lanterman, who had led the opposition to the creation of LAFCOs and who had predicted that the new commissions "would discourage new incorporations adjacent to existing cities, because cities will have major influence over the commission and they dislike new cities on their bounda-

ries. Cities, as opposed to unincorporated areas, may wind up being represented by three of the commission's five members." [15]

Consequently, State Assemblyman Frank Lanterman and other La
Canada citizens kept a very close eye on Pasadena in the years after the
LAFCOs were created. Levels of service in unincorporated areas had improved during the postwar period, especially in affluent areas like La Canada; they felt no need to join Pasadena to procure better services. Furthermore, the county tax rate had tripled in the 30 years since 1943, from $1.30
to $3.90—there was no desire to add the Pasadena rate of $1.65 onto that.

The citizens of La Canada made one early attempt to ascertain the
threat of annexation when a local attorney and a local businessman accompanied Frank Lanterman to a meeting with the executive director of
LAFCO. At this meeting, which was described as "not very friendly," the
director assured Lanterman and the others that "there was no cause for
immediate alarm," although LAFCO was going to undertake a "sphere of
influence" study to determine whether La Canada and other unincorporated areas were logically linked to various incorporated cities. The others,
however, were not sure that inaction was safe and soon became convinced
that the sphere of influence study was involved in an annexation attempt.

The activists regarded as crucial the staff recommendation to LAFCO
on incorporation, because they felt that it carried a lot of weight with the
commissioners. According to the first mayor, the activists "did everything
we could to get a favorable staff recommendation." While relationships
with the LAFCO staff were not smooth to begin with, they became better
with time. Much of this improvement can be attributed to the influence of
Frank Lanterman. As Lanterman said in an interview: "it gradually sank
through to the staff that no one had done more to defend county government than 'Uncle Frank.' " [16] The staff no doubt realized that Lanterman
carried a good deal of weight with the county supervisors on the commission for that reason.

Both Pasadena and Glendale voiced objections to the incorporation. In
the words of a La Canada activist, they created an "obstructive kind of
situation." As an example, they claimed that La Canada was polluting
their water supply by not having sewers.

Lanterman's 1963 claim that the cities would have three representatives
on the LAFCO commission, because the public representative would side

with the cities' representatives, returned to haunt the incorporationists in 1976. The public representative at this time was the ex-city manager of the city of Pasadena, and the La Canada incorporationists claimed that he told them on one occasion that he would never vote for an incorporation of less than 100,000 population. At any rate, his opposition to La Canada was clear. He tried especially hard to keep the California Institute of Technology's Jet Propulsion Laboratory from being included in the incorporation's boundaries. In fact, one La Canada activist attributes the ultimate success of the incorporation to the public representative's blatant pro-Pasadena stance which he feels "backfired and cinched the deal in favor of us." [17]

Assemblyman Lanterman sheds more light on the vote of the LAFCO board. He claims that he threatened the board with a court suit based on the public representative's conflict of interest.[18] At the same time, Lanterman had been instrumental in getting LAFCO board member Schabarum appointed to the board of supervisors by Governor Reagan over the candidate of the City of Industry in 1972. At any rate, Lanterman gained the necessary votes, both for the incorporation approval and for the inclusion of the Jet Propulsion Laboratory within the boundaries.

After the LAFCO approval, the only opposition to worry about was internal. There was very little organized, but an eleventh-hour campaign was created by an inhabitant of the community of Flintridge, which had been included in the La Canada incorporation boundaries.

Flintridge was everything La Canada was, only more so. While La Canada was upper-middle-class, Flintridge was upperclass. While La Canada had low-density, one-half and one-acre lots, Flintridge had multi-acre lots. While La Canada had limited commercial property, Flintridge had no commercial property. The inhabitants of Flintridge attributed to the La Canada incorporationists the same motive that La Canada attributed to Pasadena: exploitation of a smaller community by a larger, resource-hungry one.

The internal opposition to incorporation was slow to recognize that the antiannexationists in La Canada had suddenly become proincorporationists, and even slower to organize a response to the threat. The opposition centered around a Flintridge resident and Pasadena businessman, named Carl Schulz. Schulz found a lot of latent support, but little active participation from the small Flintridge community, and he accurately perceived that the La Canada incorporation had effectively limited Flintridge's options. Nevertheless, Schulz waged an energetic eleventh-hour campaign against incorporation, and in the process provided one of the best grass-roots articulations of the antitax, limited-government movement in Los Angeles County.

As Schulz noted, the opponents of incorporation and its advocates shared similar goals; their differences were over means.[19] Both incorporationists and opponents wanted to maintain the rural character of La Canada-Flintridge and to protect the property owner from the large taxes and urban problems faced in Pasadena. The Flintridge opposition simply was not convinced that incorporation was the only way to avoid annexation. Said Schulz; "with respect to annexation, there is no law in existence this moment which makes annexation possible without a vote of property owners of the affected area. Neither is it conceivable in our judgement that there will be such a law in a free society like ours, because appropriation of private property without a vote is utterly repugnant to our way of life." [20] And if that was the case, then why incorporate? Pressure for incorporation had begun with the creation of LAFCO in 1964, when the previous case of incorporation hysteria struck and "the then proponents of incorporation predicted all hell would break loose—our schools would inadequately educate our children, adjoining cities would engulf us, etc. etc." [21] But, Schulz argued, it was only necessary to avoid panic in order to escape both incorporation and annexation.

It was true, Schulz admitted, that there was political pressure from the big cities:

We do know that many people are moving out of cities into suburban and semi-rural areas like ours in an effort to avoid exposure to crime, overcrowding and the increasingly heavy burden of city taxes resulting from costs of welfare and inflation. And as more people leave the cities—a trend which has been going on for some time—taxes levied upon those remaining in the cities inevitably had to rise. So it goes—one evil compounds another—and the net effect of this is pressure upon outlying areas like Flintridge.
. . . The straight-from-the-shoulder fact is the League of California Cities is doing its best in Sacramento to help bail out California cities from

their financial troubles. We would be downright unintelligent if we did not recognize that this poses a serious threat to a community like Flintridge. This threat is two-fold: cities need more tax revenue and more people want to move in to areas like ours as they seek to leave the cities. Both are highly undesirable aspects of a developing situation best typified by the danger to our community from both incorporation and annexation.[22]

While the incorporated, revenue-hungry cities were effectively organized under the League of California Cities, there was no similar organization for the unincorporated communities of the county and state. What was needed is a lobbying organization for these communities, not the panic-driven reaction of La Canada.

The special danger of La Canada's defensive incorporation was twofold, Schulz argued. First, it was a "pig-in-a-poke," and secondly, it is intended to exploit Flintridge. With regard to the first issue, Schulz acknowledged that the goal of the incorporationists was to avoid the problems of cityhood; but it is dangerous and even foolhardy to avoid the problems of cityhood by becoming a city. The "tragic fact about voters" is that they do not realize that by incorporating they are turning their property over to people they don't know, and giving them a first lien on their property. "That is the nub and substance of the cityhood issue."[23]

That is the danger in creating a new level of government, a danger felt by every property owner. But the special danger to Flintridge was that the incorporationists included Flintridge property to make the proposed city financially viable. Furthermore, the property in Flintridge might be even more attractive if it held a somewhat greater population. And, by downgrading the zoning in Flintridge to the level in La Canada, the purchasing power in Flintridge could be increased to support the commercial enterprises in La Canada.

Immediately after incorporation, Schulz claimed to see the beginning of the trend he was predicting, with the breakup of several pieces of property in the community: "We tried to build a wall around it, and failed."[24]

La Habra Heights and LAFCO: Our Enemies Are the Large Land Speculators and the Board of Supervisors

The cases of Carson and La Canada-Flintridge reveal the political influence on the LAFCO board of the cities, which are concerned about the creation of new cities on their boundaries. In cases where proposed incorporations are more distant from the boundaries of established cities, one is less likely to find opposition from cities to new incorporations. However, if the proposed incorporation is to be a minimal city, with the object of exclusionary zoning, then one might expect to find opposition from the county supervisors representing more lenient development practices.

The most recent incorporation is that of La Habra Heights. Located on the eastern boundary of the county between Whittier and Orange County, La Habra Heights is a semirural, residential area, consisting primarily of single-family homes on one-acre lots scattered among avocado groves and low timber. A minority of the population, however, live in a few densely populated developments on the urban fringe of Whittier. Whittier had excluded this area from its great East Whittier annexation of the early 1960s, because (unlike the rest of East Whittier) it had no commercial and little residential property tax base.

One-acre zoning was a matter of long-standing and intense conflict between the citizens of the affluent portion of the community and county officials. Several citizens remembered dozens of trips with busloads of homeowners to confront the County Regional Planning Commission or Board of Supervisors over a zoning variance. Unlike the homeowners of Rancho Palos Verdes, the citizens of the Heights reported fairly frequent successes before the county, despite what they perceived as the latent and low-key opposition of their own county supervisor, Pete Schabarum, himself a developer.

In order to institutionalize one-acre zoning, the inhabitants of the Heights approached the county government for a general plan. Schabarum gave them four planning-staff members, who worked with 100 volunteers from the Heights to help develop the plan. The 100 volunteers split 66 to 34 in favor of one-acre zoning. The majority found the staff members cooperative, but Schabarum hostile.

Schabarum had support from inside the Heights from landowners wishing to subdivide, and the homeowners in the few dense, middle-class developments on the fringe of the Heights, all of whom opposed one-acre zoning. At one dramatic moment in the negotiations over the plan, Schabarum sat the proponents of one-acre zoning down with the opponents, telling them to reach an acceptable compromise. The proponents walked out.

Instead of compromising on one-acre zoning, the proponents won a political victory by demonstrating, with a poll of the inhabitants, that 83 percent favored this strict zoning policy. The board of supervisors accepted the plan in 1975.

But the proponents of zoning, as in Rancho Palos Verdes, found that the plan was only as strong as its enforcement. The trips downtown continued, as numerous zoning variance battles were fought. The next year, in 1976, there was a prolonged fight over enforcement of the plan, and the proponents of one-acre zoning started incorporation petitions.

At the initial LAFCO hearing on the proposed incorporation, on June 22, 1977, the president of the Property Owners Association of La Habra Heights argued that incorporation was proposed by the horse-loving homeowners of the rural northern sections, whose primary purpose was to "restrict development and maintain a horse-oriented community." Rather than buying land for horse trails and parks, the horsey set wanted to get its recreation on the cheap by such restrictive zoning that landowners were forced to keep useful land undeveloped. Additional opponents from the more middle-class southern fringe of the Heights argued that incorporation would be at their expense, since the proponents of incorporation had no resources for providing services necessary in their more urban developments, and had expressed no intention of doing so.

Other opponents challenged the LAFCO staff report, which had said the city was financially viable. The staff report, which estimated annual expenditures for the city at over $763,000, had also estimated annual revenues of over $834,000. However, $530,000 of this estimated revenue came from revenue sharing, at $100 per person for $5300. The opponents pointed out that this was an entirely unreasonable figure; no city in the county received as much as $40 per capita in revenue sharing, and comparable cities received more like $5 a person, a figure which would leave an estimated annual deficit of over $400,000 or over half the budget. Opponents also claimed that the projected budget underestimated insurance costs.

The proponents then spoke for incorporation, without answering the charges regarding financial viability of the city. They said they lived in a rural area, growing avocados and raising animals, and wanted to preserve it as a natural area. Youth representatives, dressed in 4-H and Scout uniforms, asked LAFCO not to deny them the benefits of growing up in rural surroundings. The supporters of incorporation claimed that they could not maintain the one-acre minimum zoning as an unincorporated area. At this, County Supervisor Pete Schabarum, a LAFCO board member, defended the efficacy of county zoning; but incorporationists insisted on the necessity of incorporation.

The session was continued until July 27, at the request of County Supervisor Schabarum, in order to consider boundary changes. The LAFCO staff, faced with the embarassing problem of dealing with its drastically overestimated revenue-sharing figure for the new city, issued a revised report. The report mentioned the "difficulty" of calculating the revenue-sharing formula, but instead of lowering the estimate to a more reasonable figure, simply estimated revenue sharing for the new city as falling "between" $21,000 and $530,000. This of course was not an estimate at all, but a tacit admission of the LAFCO staff's inability or unwillingness to come up with the information necessary to resolve the issue of financial viability for the new city. The report also mentioned the possibility of a $1.00 tax rate, which would generate $268,000—still not enough to cover projected expenditures should revenue sharing turn out to be on the low side of the staff's "estimate." The report also recommended that three pieces of developed acreage along the Orange County line be excluded from the boundaries of the proposed incorporation, noting that they were "fully urbanized, developed with single-family residential units, have curbs, gutters, and street lights, and have little in common with the lifestyle of the rest of the La Habra Heights area."

At the July 27th hearing, persons from the urbanized areas mentioned in the revised report supported their exclusion, as did spokespersons from other, similar urbanized areas that had not contacted the LAFCO staff in the period of time between the meetings. Despite the fact that the rationale for excluding some urbanized neighborhoods would seem to apply as well to other urbanized neighborhoods, a motion to accept the staff report was passed. This meant that those urbanized areas which had contacted the LAFCO staff in time to be included in the staff report were successfully excluded, while those that had not contacted the staff were not.

In the brief discussion preceding the vote on the motion, the commissioners voiced doubts about the financial viability of the proposed new city, as well they might in the light of the highly ambiguous staff report. They also worried aloud about the fact that their exclusions created new "islands" of unincorporated territory along the county line that would be extremely costly for the county to service. Then, although these were the very concerns that the LAFCO board had been created to deal with, the board voted in favor of the exclusions and approved the incorporation election with the exclusions. The rationale voiced for ignoring the potential problems was that if the incorporation was in fact a bad idea, the community could vote it down. (This reasoning of course ignored the fact that their exclusions had increased the likelihood of a majority vote for incorporation by excluding the most vocal and organized opposition.)

At the meeting of the county board of supervisors, concerns about the financial viability of the city were once again expressed. However, the supervisors were told by their county counsel that they could not return the proposal to LAFCO for reconsideration, but only for boundary rehearings. By default, then, the election date was set for November 1978.

The residents of the excluded county "islands" were relieved to have avoided the incorporation and the municipal property tax that they were convinced would go with incorporation. However, they were still dissatisfied with the outcome, which placed them in an unincorporated no-man's-land between Los Angeles County and Orange County. County services had been poor, especially those provided by the sheriff's office, which seemed to have difficulty in locating addresses in the tiny urban neighborhood when called to deal with burglaries or other emergencies. The residents anticipated that services would be even worse now that the sheriff's office would be focussing attention on the contract city of La Habra Heights. Residents of these neighborhoods really wanted to secede from Los Angeles County and join Orange County, where the tax rates were lower and services better, but the difficulties in doing so seemed insurmountable.

Once the date for the election was set, prodevelopment forces had very little hope of stopping the incorporation. Exclusions of the urbanized neighborhoods had virtually guaranteed a majority in favor of one-acre zoning. The only other issue which could be used against incorporation was the financial infeasibility of the city. But here two things worked in the incorporationists' favor. The first was that, as discussed in Chapter 3, the inhabitants of areas like La Habra Heights, as middle-income and upper-income property owners, had very limited demands for services from local government. Thus, the opponents of incorporation missed the point when they charged that the city could provide inadequate services at best; the city was not intended to provide services, but to limit urban development and property taxes. And here the second factor worked to the incorporationists' advantage: the recent passage of Proposition 13 seemed to guarantee that the city could not raise property taxes without the vote of the population no matter how dire its financial plight. This served to reassure citizens who were worried about the city's financial viability that property taxation would not be the fall-back source of revenue.

In the election, approximately 60 percent of voters opted for incorporation. Of the remaining 40 percent, less than half opposed incorporation because they opposed one-acre zoning. The primary source of opposition was the belief that the revenue base was inadequate. In a sample of 62 voters, not one of the 22 anti-incorporation voters felt that the revenue base was adequate. But in the end, the incorporation vote was successful because a majority of the voters were convinced by the incorporation proponents that the revenue base was adequate to support a minimal-service, antidevelopment city.

It was energetic, active organization on the part of the proponents that convinced the voters, late in the campaign, that cityhood was feasible. The proincorporation group found a large group of "undecideds" as late as a few weeks before the election. Virtually every voter was contacted by mail, on the phone, and in person. All but one of the ten council candidates was actively in favor of the city, and all argued that the city could be run economically and protect the "rural" nature of the Heights. The leading vote-getter, Jean Good, sounded the theme of fiscal restraint and wise economic management: "I want to see a fiscally conservative, low-key government, one dedicated to maintaining our rural lifestyle." At the same time, she supported the fight for one-acre zoning. "Our adversaries are the large land speculators, the Los Angeles County Board of Supervisors and the County Regional Planning Commission." The citizens of La Habra Heights were in agreement.

LAFCO and Detachment Procedures:
El Monte versus Industry

In all three of the LAFCO-supervised incorporations discussed in this chapter, the politics of resource control is apparent. The question has been whether property is to be controlled by developers or by homeowners, by independent cities or by contract cities and the county. In fact, this question has been so dominant that the rational analysis of issues like sprawl, efficient service provision, and fiscal equity has been no more apparent than in the days before LAFCO.

These issues could have been addressed by LAFCO, if not during incorporation proceedings, then during annexation proceedings. Until January 1, 1979, state law allowed for one chink in the otherwise impenetrable walls that municipal incorporation erects around property. Under state law, one city could "detach" part of another city's territory without the second city's approval. This annexation required the approval of the voters in the area to be annexed, or of the property owners if the area was uninhabited, but with these conditions met, the city government previously "owning" the territory could not veto its transferral to another city.

This mechanism could have given LAFCO the opportunity to deal more vigorously with the problems that it was created to correct. If a boundary between two cities was inefficient in that it created a "knife" extending from one city into another, then LAFCO could allow that territory to be transferred from one municipality to another where it could be more effectively served. If the annexing city were resource-poor, and the other city were a special-interest city designed simply to serve a small clique of property owners, then all the more reason for allowing the transfer of property.

In 1978, the old-line city of El Monte proposed such an annexation of territory from the City of Industry. El Monte was a resource-poor city, with a large Chicano population, that had been hard hit by the recession of the 1970s and the Jarvis-Gann Amendment in early 1978. The border between Industry and El Monte consisted largely of the San Gabriel River, except in one place where the boundaries of Industry reached across the river toward the heart of El Monte. El Monte surrounded the 78 acres on three sides, and it was connected to Industry by a little arm of territory less than 1000 feet wide. El Monte proposed that this area be detached from Industry and annexed to El Monte. The detachment would not only regularize the boundary; it would bring El Monte's lighted sports complex into the city, and would reduce emergency response time for police and fire services, as El Monte had stations for these services close at hand.

El Monte had checked with the county registrar and found that the area had only one registered voter. It had checked with the property owners, and found that they were amenable to the change of boundary. They, therefore, informed Industry on August 10, 1978, that they were going to propose the detachment.

At the November 8 hearing before the LAFCO commissioners, the LAFCO staff presented its report and recommended approval of the detachment on the grounds that it would regularize the boundary and improve services for the area. However, at this meeting, Industry presented evidence that there was in fact more than one registered voter in the area in question; the city attorney argued that there were more than 12 registered voters, making it legally an "inhabited" annexation requiring the approval of the residents. Needless to say, Industry had petitions from several of these people opposing detachment.

In some confusion, the hearing was continued until November 22. At this time, the El Monte city attorney presented further evidence that eight of the registered voters mentioned by Industry's city attorney had in fact been registered to vote within two weeks after the August 10th meeting in which Industry first heard of the detachment. It was found that several of these people did not, in fact, live in the area, but merely had shops or work places there. An immigration officer presented evidence that several were illegal aliens, and several more had registered under names other than their legal names, and were in any case transients.

This November 22 hearing was the last opportunity for the annexation to take place before a change in law made the detachment impossible. The next LAFCO meeting was in December. Because of this, it was essential at that meeting to decide whether or not the annexation would proceed. Because several commissioners had planes to catch, there was only a small amount of time to hear the evidence and make what was in fact a crucial decision for the cities involved.

Two commissioners, one representing the cities and one representing the public, felt that there was ample evidence to find the area legally uninhabited and to approve annexation. The other city representative expressed uncertainty as to the evidence and voted against approval of the annexation, as did one of the county supervisors. Since three votes are necessary to pass a bill, and since one of the county supervisors was absent, the annexation failed. The absent county supervisor, representing Industry, later admitted to me that he had purposely avoided the meeting, because he couldn't bring himself to vote in favor of Industry, but he had need of Industry's approval for one of his county projects. Politics, once again, kept LAFCO from performing its nominal function of rationalizing the structure of local government.

LAFCO's Record: Incorporations That Make No Sense

That the LAFCO decisions are often made in the context of the political constraints on the board members is clear from the preceding cases. The interests of old-line cities are apparent in some instances, the interests of the county supervisors in others. In some cases, the two sets of interests clearly clash, as in one of the major problems facing LAFCO in the late 1970s—the question of county service areas. Urban services in municipalities are paid for by municipal taxes, while urban services in unincorporated areas are paid for by countywide taxes; incorporated areas, in effect, subsidize unincorporated areas by an amount up to $50 million annually. The creation of county service areas would shift the burden of urban services for unincorporated areas to those areas themselves. The county has opposed the creation of such service areas, which would encourage further incorporation of most of the remaining unincorporated territory; and LAFCO board votes have barely supported the county position—most recently by a surprise defection of a city representative from Palmdale, amidst charges of county politicking.

The clash of political influences has clearly limited the ability of the LAFCO board and staff to deal with the problems for which they were supposedly created—urban sprawl and fiscal inequities. In particular, one of the problems relating to both urban sprawl and fiscal inequities is the number of isolated islands of unincorporated territory, surrounded by cities. These areas often become havens for tacky or ill-considered development, they are difficult for county agencies to serve efficiently, and the residents of these areas often find as a result that they get very inadequate services for their tax dollars. Yet LAFCO decisions have often resulted in the creation of county islands as the easiest short-term solution to sticky political problems.

For instance, the 1967 proposed Carson incorporation would have left no county "islands." However, in deference to the annexationist ambitions of Long Beach and other cities, LAFCO found it expedient to create county islands on all sides of the proposed city. Now that they have been created, these islands pose serious problems with regard to the delivery of urban services. Some of these areas are not in the least coveted by any of the cities involved, including Carson, as they are residential areas with a poor ratio of expected tax benefit-to-service expenditure.

Baxter Ward, something of a "maverick" on the county board of supervisors, has pointed out another instance of LAFCO's allowing islands to continue. Sun Village is a postwar development for middle-class blacks, east of Palmdale. While Palmdale has annexed huge tracts of territory in the Antelope Valley, it has ignored Sun Village. As a result, it has deteriorated rapidly, with terrible roads and other urban services that are "incredibly bad." Although Ward suggested that annexations be stopped until the Sun Village problem is solved, LAFCO has allowed Palmdale to ignore Sun Village.

The La Habra Heights case, too, resulted in LAFCO-created islands, this time in an area along the county line with extremely difficult, inefficient access—again because this seemed the easiest way out of the political controversy posed by the incorporation proceedings. And, again, politics resulted in a blatant deviation of LAFCO's behavior from the goal of effective urban planning.

In the case of Rancho Palos Verdes, too, LAFCO did not object to the county's exclusion of territory from the eastern section of the proposed incorporation. As a result, the Palos Verdes peninsula was to have four odd-shaped cities and several difficult-to-serve county islands. One county supervisor regarded this as evidence of LAFCO's failure, and said so in no uncertain terms, comparing the creation of Rancho Palos Verdes to the notorious incorporation of Industry.

If anyone can figure out how you can have these islands and hobgoblin lines for essential services, and know where police and fire equipment should go or what city a person is in—it's unbelievable in 1973 we're still putting cities that look like this . . . I have talked about this for 15 years. And I was the one who brought in the motion [to support the creation of a LAFCO agency] when the City of Industry was formed which was six miles long and a thousand feet wide when they had less than 500 voters in it to create a city just for zoning. . . . and therefore the Local Formation Agency was created by the legislature to block [such incorporations]. But, I haven't really been impressed with their actions. They are still creating these monstrosities of designs of lines. I was hoping that they would come with uniform lines and uniform areas, and they have pretty well slowed it down, but they are still creating these incorporations that make no sense or logic or reason.[25]

LAFCO and the Politics of Resource Allocation

It is clear that if any leadership is to be found to carry out the functions originally designated for LAFCO, it will have to be found in the staff instead of the board. And indeed, the board has demonstrated a willingness to rely on staff recommendations in those instances in which it was not subject to strong political pressures. In fact, it is the opinion of LAFCO observers that, in the absence of political constraints, board members are happy to act simply as ratifiers of staff decisions. The reasons for this are widely agreed upon. The LAFCO board members are busy with other professions and responsibilities, and there is little status and no pay associated with sitting on the board. In 1973, County Commissioner Debs said, "I got off of LAFCO. That was the greatest thing that ever happened to me as far as I was concerned, but I had a tough time getting off. I had to wait for someone to get elected. . . . The newcomers get all the bad things, and I was a newcomer. I inherited it." [26]

The LAFCO members have no incentive to do their own research, but there is a sizeable cost attached to checking staff reports for accuracy. Consequently, unless a political constituent specifically asks for board member involvement, the tendency is to abdicate responsibility to the staff. Furthermore, the LAFCO members are very aware of being only an intermediate link in a long chain of administrative procedures for incorporation. Besides the county supervisors' hearing, there is always the possibility of passing the decision about the wisdom of an incorporation on to the voters, as the "democratic way." The obvious retort is that the election result can generally be determined by the geographic boundaries of the proposed incorporation; so that LAFCO decisions about geographic boundaries are responsibilities that can hardly be passed on to the electorate so simply. However, this point is never raised at LAFCO meetings.

For all these reasons, the board members have little reason to do anything besides ratify staff decisions in noncontroversial cases, or even in controversial cases where "staff expertise" is the easiest political solution to a touchy problem. As one observer said, "the Commission will always back the staff because she [executive director of LAFCO] is their mule, she does the work for them."

Since the staff has such a great responsibility, it is unfortunate that the staff resources are hardly commensurate. The staff consists of an executive director and an assistant. The director was previously mayor of one of the smaller towns in the county, and one of the original city representatives on the LAFCO board. She has no academic training in urban planning, although she does have a long history in local politics. Yet these two individuals are responsible for preparing reports and recommendations for the biweekly meetings, on often technical issues; they must provide information to all the local governments in the county which are contemplating an annexation or incorporation; they must undertake sphere of influence studies, again on the technical issues related to determining which unincorporated areas are most closely tied with which cities; they must deal with pending legislation, attend meetings of the Southern California Association of Governments and other multijurisdictional agencies, and respond to requests for interviews from academics, students, and newspaper reporters. In addition, the staff has been closely involved in the creation of the statewide association of LAFCO staff members and in the lobbying that this organization has done in Sacramento.

It is remarkable that any semblance of this schedule of activities can be maintained. The question becomes why more staff is not provided. One reason, of course, must lie with the fact that LAFCO board members find a weak LAFCO in their own self-interest. LAFCO is not the political power base of the board members, and a stronger LAFCO staff could only undermine the political discretion of the LAFCO board members.

A tacit recognition that LAFCO will never be able to perform the functions it was originally intended to perform, as long as it must rely on a competitive body for resources, is made in the recent legislation proposed by the state association of LAFCOs. This bill, Assembly Bill 287, introduced by Assemblyman Knox in early 1979, would provide the requisite independent resources for LAFCOs for reorganization studies of cities and special districts receiving property tax revenues. The bill provides that if these LAFCO reorganization studies, funded by state grants, demonstrate that cost savings could be achieved by realigning boundaries of local governments, the local governments involved must forward the proposal to voters for aproval or face the possibility of having their share of property tax money cut off.[27]

Thus, this bill represents a bid by the state's LAFCOs to perform effectively the job they were originally intended to do 16 years ago. Predictably, however, the reaction from the agencies other than LAFCOs themselves is overwhelmingly negative. County supervisors see this as a significant invasion of their power, and the cities feel that it is a violation of home rule and local autonomy. Chances for passage are very dim, as are chances that the postwar pattern of urban sprawl, inequities of service delivery, and segregation of races and income classes will be significantly altered by LAFCO.

I would suggest that the reason LAFCO has proven inadequate is that it has no power to change the basic problem which motivated the incorporation and annexation wars in the first place. This problem is that the "point of origin" nature of revenue generation gives municipalities a "property right" to all the resources they can squeeze into their corporate boundaries, while similarly benefiting all those cities that can squeeze out of their boundaries those groups of individuals who put a strain on municipal resources through their redistributional demands. As long as this system of revenue generation is in use, the politics of resource allocation must be the paramount consideration of the various political actors involved in incorporation and annexation proceedings, no matter what the institutional structure in which these proceedings take place.

6   Stratification of Social Classes

It is worthwhile, perhaps, to review the argument of the book thus far. The Lakewood Plan incorporations were motivated, for the most part, by different kinds of redistributional considerations. Some cities, like Industry and Commerce, were motivated by a zero-sum conflict over high property and sales tax bases. Other cities, among them, Rolling Hills and Bradbury, were motivated by the subtler redistributional considerations involving the creation of low tax rate havens within the metropolitan area, where opposition to welfare spending and bureaucratic growth has resulted in various kinds of "minimal cities" (meaning cities providing all the services that can be provided without resorting to property taxation). In both kinds of cities, the end result has been a repudiation of local property taxation similar to that embodied in the Jarvis-Gann initiative.

This outright or latent redistributional conflict creates a different kind of setting for thinking about the Tiebout argument than that which is generally used.[1] The normal application of the Tiebout argument pictures people in a metropolitan area as having different tastes for public service mixes: some prefer libraries to parks, for instance, while others prefer parks to libraries. The creation of two kinds of cities, one of which spends more on parks and one of which spends more on libraries, allows everyone to make himself better off. Bookish people improve their position by avoiding the cities which tax for parks, while the latter kind of city is sought out by outdoors types.

However, if there is a redistributional or class-linked dimension in the way that people choose among different cities, is it still true that metropolitan fragmentation makes everyone better off? In Los Angeles County, the major difference between different kinds of municipalities is high-tax, high-service-level cities, versus the newer low-tax, minimal cities. Does this kind of jurisdictional choice make both the tax avoiders and the service-seekers better off, as the analogous choice makes bookish people and outdoorsy people both better off? This question is addressed directly in Chapter 8. The intervening two chapters address two subsidiary questions. In this chapter, we ask, "Has the population of metropolitan Los Angeles, in fact, become increasingly sorted out into tax avoiders and service seekers?" Having answered this in the affirmative, Chapter 7 addresses the question, "Has the distribution of municipal resources been linked to the distribution of tax avoiders and service seekes in the metropolitan area?"

Segregation of Income Classes by Municipality

To what extent have the various income classes become increasingly sorted out and segregated by municipal boundaries? In order to answer this question, it is necessary to develop a measure of homogeneity for income class that can be applied to the county's municipalities at different points in time.

The county's population will be divided into three income classes, as equal in size as is possible, given census categories for family income. In 1950, for instance, 35.5 percent of all the county's families had an income of less than $3,000 and 33.9 percent had incomes greater than $4,500, leaving 30.6 percent between the two figures. These income figures will serve to divide the three income classes for that year.

If a city has a representative mix of income classes, roughly one-third of its population will be in each income class. The probability that any two of its citizens will be in the same income class will be approximately one-third, the same as for the county as a whole. But as a city becomes more homogeneously composed of one income class or another, the probability

Table 6.1
Examples of Increasing Homogeneity: 1950 to 1970

City	Year	% Lower-class	% Middle-class	% Upper-class	Homogeneity
Huntington Park	1950	32.6	31.0	36.4	.3349
	1970	47.1	32.0	20.9	.3679
Maywood	1950	31.2	34.3	34.5	.3343
	1970	46.0	34.6	19.4	.3691
Manhattan Beach	1950	24.7	32.8	42.5	.3496
	1970	15.3	30.0	54.7	.4122
Torrance	1950	27.8	42.4	29.1	.3417
	1970	16.3	32.9	50.8	.3926

Sources: Figures calculated from *Census of Population, 1950*, vol. 1, pt. 6, Table 37 (U.S. Bureau of the Census, 1951) and *Census of Population, 1970*, vol. 1, pt. 6, Tables 89, 107, 118 (U.S. Bureau of the Census, 1971).

that any two of its citizens will be from the same income class will approach the limit of one. This probability can be calculated as the sum of the squared proportions of each city's families in each income class (see table 6.1).[2]

As table 6.2 reveals, 25 of the 42 cities for which we have data were, in 1950, virtually indistinguishable from the completely heterogeneous case, with a measure of homogeneity of less than .340. By 1970, these same cities had shifted markedly away from this pole, with only nine left in this category, and more cities in every category of increasing homogeneity. Furthermore, only one of the 30 cities created in the intervening period was in the extremely heterogeneous category. The pattern of changing homogeneity is shown in table 6.3.

As one might imagine from the increased homogeneity within, and diversity among, municipalities, the distribution of poverty became increasingly concentrated. In 1950, those families and unrelated individuals with incomes of less than $500 constituted 9.4 percent of the county's population. This poorest "tenth" of the population was relatively equally distributed. San Marino had the smallest percentage in this income class, with 3.8 percent. El Segundo had 4.8 percent; and every other city had more than 5 percent.

Table 6.2
Frequency Distribution of Homogeneity Scores

	.333–.339	.340–.349	.350–.369	.370–.379	.400+	Total
1950	25	5	5	3	4	42
1970 (old cities)	9	13	11	4	5	42
1970 (cities with missing data in 1950)	2	0	0	0	1	3
1970 (new cities)	1	9	12	1	7	30
1970 (all cities)	12	22	23	5	13	75

Sources: Figures calculated from *Census of Population, 1950,* vol. 1, pt. 6, Table 37 (U.S. Bureau of the Census, 1951) and *Census of Population, 1970,* vol. 1. pt. 6, Tables 89, 107, 118 (U.S. Bureau of the Census, 1971).

By 1970, many more cities had successfully waged their own wars on poverty. The proportion of the county's population classified as having incomes below the poverty level was 10.9 percent. But nine of the older cities now had 5 percent or less in this class, with only 1.4 percent in Beverly Hills. In addition, seven of the newer cities had proportions of poor less than 5 percent. While some of the cities had come very close to eliminating poverty in their midst, other cities had very high concentrations of poverty (13 percent or more). These cities included Los Angeles and the older cities along Los Angeles's southeastern boundary.

Racial Segregation by Municipal Boundaries

As Los Angeles County was being suburbanized by the Lakewood Plan, blacks in Los Angeles were also undergoing their greatest degree of suburbanization. Between 1960 and 1970 alone, for instance, the number of blacks in suburban Los Angeles increased from 117,099 to 240,247. One might expect then, that many blacks were among those seeking the low-tax-rate Lakewood Plan cities. However, this was not the case. Instead, Los Angeles followed the national pattern in that black suburbanization constituted suburban reghettoization in a small number of jurisdictions.

The national pattern was that blacks settled in areas where housing was older and deteriorating.[3] These areas are poorer than white suburbs, with a lower quality of education available and greater unemployment.

In Los Angeles, the proportion of blacks increased from 5.5 percent in 1950 to 10.7 percent in 1970. However, most of this increase was concentrated in the older cities of Los Angeles, Pasadena, Inglewood, Pomona, and Compton. Compton became the first majority black city in the county with a 71 percent black population in 1970. In that year over 73 percent of the county's blacks lived in Los Angeles and Compton alone, although those cities represented only 41 percent of the county's total population.

While the county's blacks became concentrated in a few of the older cities, the proportion of the county's population living in racially exclusive cities actually increased. In 1950, there were 38 cities with less than 1 percent black populations; these cities contained 24 percent of the metropolitan area's population. In 1970, there were 58 cities with less than 1 percent black populations, containing 33 percent of the metropolitan area's population. Both the number of segregated cities and the population living in those cities had increased.

Of the 58 segregated cities, 31 were older cities which had successfully retained their antiblack housing patterns. (These included such upper-income cities as Arcadia, which went from .21 percent to .07 percent black.)

The other segregated cities were the new Lakewood Plan cities. Of the 32 created between 1950 and 1970, 28 contained less than 1 percent black populations. Thus, the Lakewood Plan cities were essentially white political movements. Further advancing this trend was the creation of the segregated cities of Rancho Palos Verdes, La Canada-Flintridge, and La Habra Heights, all incorporated since 1970 with almost totally white populations.

By comparison, the Spanish-speaking and Spanish-surnamed minority in Los Angeles is much more dispersed, perhaps because it is much less underprivileged, as a whole. The percent of the Spanish-speaking population living in poverty in 1970 was 14.7 percent, as compared to 24.0 percent for blacks (and 10.7 percent overall). Virtually every city in the county has a sizeable proportion of this minority.

However, as one might expect, poorer Spanish-speaking population was much more highly concentrated in certain cities, and virtually nonexistent

Table 6.3
Income Class Homogeneity in Los Angeles Cities: 1950 and 1970

1950	1970			
	Heterogeneous (homogeneity < .350)	Homogeneous lower-income	Homogeneous middle-income	Homogeneous upper-income
Heterogeneous (homogeneity < .350)	Alhambra Burbank El Monte Glendale Hawthorne Hermosa Beach Inglewood Long Beach Los Angeles Lynwood Monrovia Monterey Park Pasadena Pomona Redondo Beach Santa Monica South Gate	Bell Compton Huntington Park Maywood San Fernando Signal Hill		Covina Culver City Glendora Manhattan Beach Sierra Madre Torrance Whittier
Homogeneous lower-income	Gardena La Verne			Claremont

Homogeneous middle-income	Azusa			West Covina
Homogeneous upper-income	Montebello San Gabriel			Arcadia Beverly Hills El Segundo San Marino South Pasadena
No data in 1950	Avalon Vernon			Palos Verdes Estates
New cities since 1950	Artesia Bellflower Carson Duarte Lawndale Lomita Palmdale Pico Rivera Rosemead Temple City	Baldwin Park Bell Gardens Commerce Cudahy Hawaiian Gardens	Irwindale Norwalk La Puente Paramount San Dimas Santa Fe Springs South El Monte	Bradbury Cerritos Downey Lakewood La Mirada Rolling Hills Rolling Hills Estates Walnut

Sources: Figures calculated from Census of Population, 1950, vol. 1, pt. 6, Table 37 (U.S. Bureau of the Census, 1951) and Census of Population, 1970, vol. 1. pt. 6, Tables 89, 107, 118 (U.S. Bureau of the Census, 1971).

in others. While 2.66 percent of the county's population consisted of poor Spanish-speaking individuals, 23 cities[4] had less than 1 percent of their populations in this category. Poor Chicanos were concentrated in ten cities on the east side which had more than 5 percent each.

However, the greatest concentrations of poor Chicanos and poor blacks were not in any of the cities. Instead, they were in three unincorporated "islands" in the center of the county (see table 6.4). As all desirable areas of the county were incorporated or annexed, these three areas, each with high concentrations of poor and few municipal resources, became increasingly deteriorated under lax county zoning and building code enforcement.

Willowbrook had tried to incorporate in order to keep out blacks during the period when the county discouraged incorporations. Its attempt failed, and it became by 1970 the area with the greatest proportion of blacks in the county. Although it is bordered by Los Angeles, Compton, and Lynwood, none of these cities plans to annex the area.

Florence-Graham, too, is a heavily nonwhite area, with the least valuable housing stock in Los Angeles County. Los Angeles has also passed up the opportunity to annex this area, as have Huntington Park and South Gate.

East Los Angeles is the largest unincorporated community in California, with over 100,000 inhabitants. (Since it also has probably the largest concentration of illegal aliens in the country, no one knows its precise population.) It has a long history of attempted incorporations, including three since 1960. The most recent attempt took place in 1974. At that time proponents of incorporation argued that the county had been insensitive to the needs of the predominantly Chicano population. One proponent, an organizer for La Raza Unida, pointed out that 78.8 percent of its housing was dilapidated, and that "East Los Angeles has almost no health facilities, child-care centers or parks." He said that Chicanos had been the ones to suffer removal from past redevelopment projects, which included the stadium for the Los Angeles Dodgers, the Music Center in downtown Los Angeles, and the Bank of America complex, and that developers were now free to continue the same sort of activity in East Los Angeles, without any local control of land use. He argued that "an incorporated East Los Angeles could become a symbol for all poor people, as well as an exam-

Table 6.4
Inner City Unincorporated Areas: 1970

Unincorporated area	Population	% Black	% Spanish-speaking	% Poor	Per capita income	Median value of owner-occupied housing	% of housing over twenty years old
East Los Angeles	105,033	0.3	87.1	19.4	$2157	$19,100	72.5
Florence-Graham	42,895	55.6	38.5	30.9	1792	13,900	74.2
Willowbrook	28,705	82.3	14.9	25.5	1964	16,700	61.8
Los Angeles County	7,032,075	10.8	18.3	10.9	3884	24,300	44.7

Sources: *Census of Population, 1970*, vol. 1, pt. 6 (U.S. Bureau of the Census, 1971).

ple of what Chicanos can accomplish when they control their own community." [5]

His arguments focusing on special community needs, local pride, unresponsive government, and the necessity of local control of land use were the same that had been used in other, successful incorporations. However, in this case, the proponents of incorporation were not able to argue convincingly that incorporation could supply these benefits without requiring a substantial municipal property tax. Opposition centered in homeowner groups was able to defeat incorporation on this issue alone. "Can supporters of incorporation really believe that anybody will fall for a simple appeal to community and ethnic heritage—and forget everything else? . . . *Pride?* There is none in having the county's 12th largest city when you know it will be crippled by a low tax base." [6] The measure was defeated by a 58 percent majority, and proponents admitted that the fear of a municipal property tax was the major obstacle. [7]

The Relocation of Crime

As the metropolitan population of Los Angeles has sorted itself out on the basis of income and racial patterns, it is not surprising that this has had consequences for the distribution of crime in the county. The relationship between income, race, and crime has led one political scientist to explore the effects of suburbanization on the geographic distribution of crime. Wesley Skogan indicates that correlations between crime rates and various environmental factors such as population density have changed over time. [8] Most strikingly, the correlation between population density and crime has changed from sharply negative to sharply positive in the past quarter century. He examines the possibility that

the selective movement of people and jobs from the central city to the suburban fringe, and the impact of that movement on those left behind, may have produced the changes observed in this sample of communities. The middle class, reacting rationally to the availability of cheap, safe housing with handy connections to freeways, has acted to escape the taxes, politics, and litter which plague them. The opening of new ring highways plus the movement of white collar and skilled workers to the suburban fringe has pulled industrial and commercial development in the same direction. . . . As the suburbanization process sorts people on the basis of race and class and weakens the economic fabric of the central city, it leaves behind poverty, limited opportunity, despair, and physical deterioration, all of which contribute to crime at the individual level.[9]

Skogan shows that among the 32 largest cities in the United States, there is no correlation between the present crime rate and that right after the Second World War. However, there is an observable correlation between the exodus from the central city and the 1970 crime rate; in other words, those cities whose poulations shifted to the suburbs most rapidly during the period 1946 to 1970 are the cities which now have the highest crime rates.

While earlier social stratification and geographic segregation by race, class and culture were neighborhood-level processes, the massive flight of the white middle class beyond the jurisdictional grasp of the schools, courts, police, and governments of many central cities has turned city boundaries into the relevant lines of cleavage.[10]

This pattern is quite clear in Los Angeles County, as can be seen in table 6.5. The crime rate for this county as a whole is just over .07. However, many of the older cities in the county have crime rates significantly higher than that figure. These include Long Beach, Los Angeles, El Monte, Hawthorne, Pasadena, and Compton. Long Beach's crime rate is higher than that of any of the Lakewood Plan cities it failed to annex in the 1950s and 1960s: Lakewood, Bellflower, Paramount, and even the city of Carson, which has a high number of nonwhites and a lot of commercial property, both of which are often associated with crime. The only postwar cities with very high crime rates are the industrial cities of Commerce and Santa Fe Springs.

It is important to note that this variation in crime rate does not occur because the low-crime cities like Sierra Madre and Lakewood spend more per capita on law enforcement. Quite the contrary is true, of course. They tend to spend less, because less expense is required in homogeneous, middle-income cities, with low rates of poverty, unemployment, and rentership.

This is illustrated in table 6.6. The desirable positions in this table are on the upper left hand corner, with those cities that can maintain very low crime rates with very little expenditure. These include such Lakewood Plan cities as San Dimas and Temple City, both of which have very low crime rates and annual per capita police expenditures of only $19. At the other extreme are those cities with very high crime rates despite very high

Table 6.5
Distribution of Crime in Los Angeles County, 1977

Crime rate (per 100,000)	Prewar cities	Post-1954 cities
Less than 5,000	Bell (4,276) Burbank (4,446) Maywood (4,813) Monterey Park (4,129) Palos Verdes Estates (3,882) San Marino (3,372) Sierra Madre (2,266)	Cudahy (4,290) Lakewood (4,395) La Mirada (3,923) Lomita (4,862) Pico Rivera (4,272) Rosemead (4,813) San Dimas (4,742) Temple City (3,039)
5,000–7,000	Alhambra (6,139) Arcadia (5,750) Claremont (5,143) Covina (6,400) El Segundo (6,998) Gardena (6,525) Glendale (5,174) Glendora (5,458) Huntington Park (5,182) La Verne (5,512) Manhattan Beach (5,078) Montebello (6,586) Redondo Beach (6,997) San Gabriel (5,293) South Gate (5,391) South Pasadena (5,222) Torrance (5,011) West Covina (6,129) Whittier (5,388)	Artesia (5,575) Baldwin Park (5,950) Bellflower (6,396) Carson (6,506) Cerritos (6,359) Downey (5,386) Duarte (5,515) La Puente (6,150) Lawndale (6,437) Norwalk (5,814)
7,000–10,000	Azusa (9,601) Beverly Hills (7,285) El Monte (7,709) Hawthorne (8,564) Huntington Park (7,327) Long Beach (7,882) Los Angeles (7,939) Monrovia (7,010)	Bell Gardens (7,146) Palmdale (8,932) Paramount (7,752) South El Monte (8,827)

Table 6.5 (continued)

Crime rate (per 100,000)	Prewar cities	Post-1954 cities
	San Fernando (9,733) Santa Monica (9,518)	
More than 10,000	Compton (12,750) Culver City (11,451) Inglewood (10,780) Lynwood (11,338) Pasadena (10,481) Pomona (10,990)	Commerce (14,526) Santa Fe Springs (12,212)

Note: The numbers in parentheses are the numbers of crimes per 100,000 from the *FBI Uniform Crime Reports, 1977,* Table 6 (Washington, D.C.: U.S. Government Printing Office, 1978).

police expenditures. Again, with the exception of Commerce and Santa Fe Springs, these are the large, heterogeneous cities, for example, Long Beach, Pasadena, and Los Angeles, which spent in the neighborhood of $75 per capita on their police departments. These are the cities that are bearing the burden of the postwar relocation of crime in Los Angeles County.

Table 6.6
Crime Rates and Police Expenditures per Capita in Los Angeles Cities, 1977

Crime rate	< $30 (N = 14)	$30–40 (N = 15)	$40–50 (N = 15)	$50–60 (N = 5)	$60 + (N = 7)
≤ .05 (N = 15)	**Cudahy*** ($28) **Lakewood** ($24) **La Mirada** ($22) **Lomita** ($26) **Rosemead** ($25) **San Dimas** ($19) **Sierra Madre** ($29) **Temple City** ($19)	Maywood ($34) Monterey Park ($37) **Pico Rivera** ($30)	Bell ($48) Palos Verdes Estates ($41) San Marino ($48)		Burbank ($71)
.05–.07 (N = 28)	**Artesia** ($21) **Bellflower** ($27) **Cerritos** ($25) **Duarte** ($20) **La Puente** ($20) **Norwalk** ($24)	**Baldwin Park** ($38) Claremont ($31) Glendale ($35) Glendora ($36) **La Verne** ($33) **Lawndale** ($30) San Gabriel ($38) South Pasadena ($35) West Covina ($39)	Alhambra ($44) Arcadia ($40) **Carson** ($45) Covina ($41) **Hermosa Beach** ($47) Manhattan Beach ($40) Redondo Beach ($49)	**Downey** ($57) Montebello ($52) South Gate ($51)	El Segundo ($132) Gardena ($63) Torrance ($65)
.07–.10 (N = 13)		Huntington Park ($39) Monrovia ($39) Paramount ($39)	Azusa ($40) El Monte ($41) Hawthorne ($42) **Palmdale** ($41) South El Monte ($40)	**Bell Gardens** ($50) San Fernando ($56)	Beverly Hills ($112) Long Beach ($76) Los Angeles ($75)

.10 + (N = 9)	Lynwood	($38)	Compton	($49)	Santa Monica	($51)	Commerce	($149)
			Pomona	($49)			Culver City	($73)
							Inglewood	($101)
							Pasadena	($70)
							Santa Fe Springs	($68)

* Cities in bold type are those incorporated since 1954.

Sources: *FBI Uniform Crime Reports, 1977*, Table 6 (Washington, D.C.: U.S. Government Printing Office, 1978) and *Financial Transactions Concerning Cities of California, 1977*, Table 5 (California State Controller, 1978).

7

The Competition for Resources and Rational Fiscal Policy

In the last chapter, it was demonstrated that there has been a sorting out of the population of Los Angeles County on the basis of various social factors such as wealth and race. This process was interpreted as the result of a search such as Tiebout describes on the part of home owners and middle-income groups for those cities with appropriate fiscal patterns: that is, low taxes and a low level of redistribution.

It could be argued that the cities which undertake to provide little in the way of redistributional services are probably not active in the competition for municipal resources. If this were so, then those cities which do undertake expansion of services would be the most successful in attracting municipal resources, resulting in a beneficial pattern of resource distribution. Those cities with the highest concentrations of low-income groups (renters and illegal aliens, for example) would then be the cities that are most endowed with municipal resources, and most able to handle the burden imposed on them. It will be argued, however, that this is not the case. It takes resources like sales tax revenue and industrial activity to keep taxes low, just as it does to keep service levels high. Thus, the cities that appear most attractive to high-income taxpayers will be just as intensely interested in attracting resources within their boundaries as those that are dominated by bureaucrats and low-income groups. Furthermore, the former class of cities will be more successful in attracting many types of economic activity than the latter, because retail sales activity, high-income housing construction, and many kinds of businesses will rather locate among high-income groups than among the increasing concentrations of crime and blight in low-income jurisdictions.

Because of the recognized link between high-income individuals and revenue-producing municipal resources, high-income individuals themselves become the objects of competition among municipalities.

Indicators of Inequality

In a recent article, Richard Hill investigated municipal corporate boundaries as a form of institutionalized "social arrangements that generate and perpetuate intergenerational inequality in the distribution of scarce economic, political, and social resources." Hill's primary means of pursuing research was a multiple regression analysis of 127 metropolitan areas in 1960. Because indicators of fiscal resources and fiscal capacity have various meanings in different states and metropolitan areas, he chose as his indicator of fiscal capacity the median family income of a municipality. He defended his choice by pointing out that all municipal resources must come ultimately from personal income.[1]

While this is perhaps a useful first approximation of fiscal capacity, it is imperfect. While all taxes must ultimately be paid out of someone's income, it is not necessary for a municipality's revenue to come from the income of that municipality's own population. In many Los Angeles cities, there is no property tax and no direct taxation link between the municipality's revenue and the local population's income. These cities may rely on the sales tax, which taxes the income of anyone who purchases items in the municipality, and of course there is no guarantee that the shopping population will be the same as the municipality's population. Indeed, much municipal rivalry is generated as neighboring municipalities attempt to become regional trade centers.

Another increasingly important form of revenue for municipalities is intergovernmental grants from county, state, and federal agencies. These grants, even more than sales tax revenue, come from sources other than local pocketbooks.

For the purposes of this book, an even more serious problem with the use of median family income as an indicator of fiscal capacity is that it assumes the very relationship that is of central research interest. If, for instance, low-income families happen to cluster together in commercial areas with a high public resource base, then much of the reason for normative concern with municipal inequality is obviated: poor families living in resource-rich cities make for a favorable pattern of redistribution. However, if this is not the general tendency, then the pattern of poor families living in resource-poor cities raises serious questions about the efficacy of our current policies and institutions dealing with urban decay and social welfare.

For these reasons, a more direct measure of fiscal capacity, separated from family income, will be used. In 1970, the most discretionary source of income for municipal governments, and the only form of taxation that applied only to the inhabitants of the municipality directly, was the property tax. If all the taxable property in the 77 cities were divided up evenly among the more than six million inhabitants, there would be almost $2680 worth of property per capita. However, this property was not distributed evenly. In fact, it ranged from less than $1000 per person in some cities to almost $1 million per person in the small city of Vernon. In fact, Vernon, the smallest city in the county, had more taxable property than 63 of the larger cities in the county.

Those individuals in the property-poorest 16 cities make up about 10 percent of the population. Yet they have only about 4.9 percent of the taxable property. The individuals in the 19 richest cities make up about 10 percent of the population, yet these cities have about 16 percent of the property.

There are, of course, other sources of revenue, including, most importantly, those already mentioned: sales tax revenue and grants from state and federal agencies. These sources of revenue tend to be correlated with property per capita, however, and with each other. The result of this intercorrelation is that all other sources of revenue besides property tax also tend to be highly unequally distributed. For instance, Hidden Hills, a

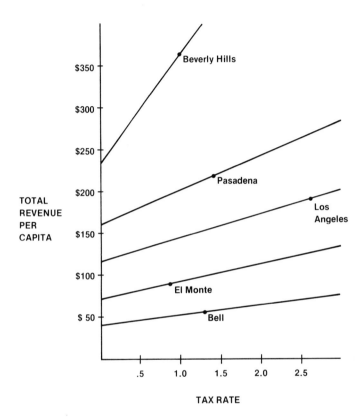

Figure 7.1
Total Revenue per Capita Generated by Alternative Tax Rates for Selected
Cities: 1970 (Dots Denote Actual Tax Rates)

small residential suburb with no commercial enterprises, obtained in 1970–1971 only $18 per capita in other sources of revenue, while Los Angeles ranked 59th from the bottom with $118 per capita. Vernon again had the most, with over $20,000 worth of other revenue per capita. There would have been approximately $110 per capita if all the sources of nonproperty tax revenue were distributed equally among the area's inhabitants.

Now, what governmental inequality fundamentally means is that certain cities have to tax their citizens harder to achieve the same revenue. Figure 7.1 illustrates this idea. Revenue per capita is shown on the y axis, and the tax rate on the x axis. Each line represents feasible combinations of tax rate and revenue per capita for each city, given that city's property valuation, other sources of revenue, and population. The y-intercept reveals the city's other revenue per capita, and the slope of each line is interpretable as the municipality's property per capita. This form of presentation strikingly depicts the most important fact about government inequality. Many cities simply cannot achieve the revenue per capita of, for instance, Los Angeles, at a politically feasible tax rate. Or alternatively, a uniform tax effort would result in very different levels of revenue for different cities, as a result of both of the differences in property valuations and other forms of revenue.

Residential Segregation and the Distribution of Municipal Resources

It is clear that municipal segregation based on income and race increased in Los Angeles County during the period from 1950 to 1970. However, I have not yet shown that poor, or blacks, or rich, or whites increasingly tend to live in those municipalities with the highest levels of taxable property per capita.

A first examination of this problem can be made by looking at those cities that were identified earlier as being most homogeneously rich, middle-income, or poor. As table 7.1 demonstrates, there does seem to be a relationship between property per capita and predominant income class for homogeneous cities, with almost all high-income and almost all low-income cities being rich and poor, respectively, in taxable property. The

major exceptions are Signal Hill and Commerce, low-income cities with
high levels of commercial activity.

Furthermore, the gap between the cities seems to be widening. While
most of the cities in the lower right-hand corner experienced increasing
assessments in the 1970s (even after inflation is taken into account) those
cities in the upper left-hand corner all experienced decreases in constant
dollar per capita assessments. The only low-income city to experience a
significant increase in per capita assessments was Signal Hill, part of whose
increase was due to a rapid reduction in population in the 1970s.

The growing disparity between rich and poor cities in revenue generating resources can be attributed to several factors. First of all is the relocation of manufacturing activity in Los Angeles County. The city of Los
Angeles began to experience a sharp reduction in manufacturing in the
mid-1960s. Between 1967 and 1972, the number of employees in manufacturing dipped from 310,000 to 281,000. The city experienced both an absolute and a relative decline in value added by manufacturing in this period.
In constant 1967 dollars, this figure went from $4.3 million to $3.8 million,
and its share of the county's manufacturing activity went from over 35
percent to less than 32 percent. By 1977, the *Los Angeles Times* reported
that the city was losing up to 50 firms a year to the suburbs and to Orange
County. The reason given was that the executives of these firms preferred
to live and work in these less smoggy, less crime-ridden areas. As one business executive said, "the problems of the city—crime, racial tension, and
poverty—are very uncomfortable things for the businessman to deal with.
Why stick around and fight trouble when you can move your company to
the suburbs and avoid it?" [2]

These problems also limited the industrial growth of such small,
poverty-ridden cities as Bell, Maywood, and Compton. In none of these
three cities did increases in value added by manufacturing keep up with
price increases over the decade 1963 to 1972. Increases in manufacturing
tended to be most rapid in the San Gabriel Valley and the eastern part of
the county, including such high-income cities as Arcadia and Covina.

A similar story can be told for retailing. The largest development in the
last few decades has been that of retail malls. And the competition for
these malls has been intense. A city which is not willing to subsidize a
developer is not likely to obtain a mall. In Pasadena, for instance, the

Table 7.1
Taxable Property per Capita for Homogeneous Cities: 1970
(homogeneity score greater than .35)

Predominant income class	Taxable property per capita		
	Less than $1500	$1500-$2500	$2500 +
Homogeneous low-income	Baldwin Park (−3.7%) Bell (−24.4%) Bell Gardens (−3.8%) Compton (−7.5%) Cudahy (−25.6%) Hawaiian Gardens (−8.5%) Maywood (−25.0%)	Huntington Park (−34.4%) San Fernando (1.0%)	Commerce (−24.9%) Signal Hill (59.5%)
Homogeneous middle-income	Norwalk (−5.4%) La Puente (−22.8%)	Paramount (9.6%) San Dimas (22.6%)	Irwindale (−12.7%) Santa Fe Springs (2.7%) South El Monte (−17.6%)
Homogeneous upper-income		Claremont (−1.2%) Glendora (7.0%) Lakewood (−22.7%) La Mirada (−16.9%) Sierra Madre (−24.0%) West Covina (−5.8%) Whittier (−7.9%)	Arcadia (−2.3%) Beverly Hills (9.4%) Bradbury (38.3%) Cerritos (−32.2%) Covina (−17.8%) Culver City (−14.2%) Downey (−19.2%) El Segundo (14.7%) Manhattan Beach (26.7%)

Palos Verdes Estates (26.1%)
Rolling Hills (17.8%)
Rolling Hills Estates (−18.7%)
San Marino (−6.1%)
South Pasadena (16.5%)
Torrance (6.2%)
Walnut (8.0%)

Sources: Calculated from *Financial Transactions Concerning Cities of California, 1970*, Tables 4, 5, 19 (California State Controller, 1971), and *Census of Population 1970*, vol. 1, pt. 6, Tables 89, 107, 118 (U.S. Bureau of the Census, 1971).

Note: Figures in parentheses are constant-dollar changes in assessments per capita between 1970 and 1977.

developer of the downtown retail mall got a subsidy worth more than $100 million in costs of land acquisition, clearing, and interest.

The cities that have been most successful in competing for malls have been those which can guarantee a good buying market. This necessarily means that high-income populations help attract the retail sales activity. The high-income cities of Arcadia, Cerritos, and Glendale were able to develop some of the largest, most successful retail malls, and this has shown up in retail sales volume. In 1977, these three cities had per capita retail sales levels of 53 percent, 91 percent, and 25 percent larger than the county average of $3700. Bell's retail sales were only 7 percent larger than the county average, while Compton's and Maywood's were 36 percent and 51 percent lower.

The most significant factor in the disparate expansion of high-income and low-income municipal resource bases was the increase in home values in the 1970s. Here again, the high-income cities seemed to have a natural advantage over low-income cities, since their housing values increased the fastest, especially in the high-income beach cities and high-income residential cities in the San Gabriel Valley. Between 1966 and 1976, assessed housing values increased between 98 percent and 107 percent in various parts of the Palos Verdes Peninsula, 132 percent in Arcadia in the San Gabriel Valley, and 165 percent in Lakewood, but only 52 percent in the low-income community of Cudahy.[3]

While all but four of the 23 high-income cities had some significant level of commercial tax base, even those four cities that were most exclusively residential (Walnut, Bradbury, Rolling Hills and Palos Verdes Estates) still experienced a strong growth in municipal resources, and were able to reduce taxes during the 1970s while keeping service levels up. Here again, the difference between low-income and high-income noncommercial cities is important. While Baldwin Park and Cudahy would get only $10 per capita in property tax revenue from a tax rate of $1.00 per hundred, Rolling Hills would get $66 per capita from an equal property tax rate and with an equally small level of commercial activity. Thus, lack of a commercial tax base means different things in low-income and high-income residential communities.

Since the more homogeneous low-income and high-income cities tend to be property poor and property rich, respectively, what can rich or poor individuals expect to get out of their municipalities? On the average, what amounts of taxable property are available to rich and poor individuals? An answer to this question can be found by calculating the expected value of property per capita for different groups of individuals, based on the municipal dispersion of those groups. This is done with the formula

$$EV_i = \Sigma_j(p_{ij} V_j),$$

where P_{ij} is the probability of being in jurisdiction j if you are a member of income class i; V_j is the value of some resource such as taxable property per capita; and EV_i is thus the expected value, or weighted mean, of taxable property available to a person of a certain income class.

Table 7.2 reveals the differences in expected value of property per capita for four different income groups and whites and blacks. As can be seen, the distributions of the lower- and middle-income groups are such that they can expect to live in municipalities with fairly similar levels of property per capita. The upper-income group, however, can expect more than $130 worth of assessments more per capita. The very highest income subgroup can expect even more taxable property per capita on the basis of its distribution among Los Angeles cities, averaging over $630 per capita more than the lower two-thirds of the population.

The difference between whites and blacks is equally notable. While whites can expect a level of taxable property per capita somewhere between the upper- and middle-income thirds, blacks can expect a level of taxable property per capita that is over $150 lower than that received by the lower-income third.

Competition for Resources and the Rational Fiscal Strategy

The fact that wealthy individuals and municipal resources go together is, of course, not a secret. It has led many cities that feel themselves to be in fierce competition for municipal resources to try to attract wealthy individuals at the same time that they try to attract other municipal resources like industry and shopping malls.

This is the "rational fiscal strategy for an individual city government," according to James Buchanan:

Table 7.2
Expected Values for Property per Capita for Different Population Groups: 1970

Overall	$2680
White	2710
Black	2480
Lower-income third	2635
Middle-income third	2650
Upper-income third	2780
Families with incomes greater than $50,000	3380

Sources: Calculated from *Financial Transactions Concerning Cities of California, 1970*, Tables 4, 5, 19 (California State Controller, 1971), and *Census of Population, 1970*, vol. 1, pt. 6, Tables 89, 107, 118 (U.S. Bureau of the Census, 1971).
Note: Figures for all 77 cities except Industry and Irwindale for which data was not available. Comparable data were not available in the same set of cities for the Spanish-speaking population.

The objective for rational fiscal strategy is the maximization of per capita fiscal dividend or surplus. This translates directly into the requirement that all persons who contribute positively to the generation of fiscal surplus be kept within the club. . . . If this is accepted, then the relative emphasis on retaining the high-income high-wealth residents becomes obvious. If low and middle income-wealth groups withdraw from the fiscal arrangements of the city, net effects on fiscal surplus may be positive rather than negative.[4]

In other words, Buchanan's argument is an application of the Tiebout hypothesis. Assuming that Tiebout is right, and that individuals will sort themselves out by finding those jurisdictions that cater to their demands, the trick for the city is to cater to the high-income people who benefit the city's budget. If this means that low-income groups leave the city, so much the better.

Buchanan is explicit about the kinds of inducements that are necessary for the long-run health of the jurisdiction:

We have found it useful analytically to assume that all persons secure equal quantities of consumption services provided collectively. This rule or institution can also be modified as one tool in an urban strategy kit. . . . This is observed to occur in special police details in high-income areas of cities, in better parks in some areas than in others, in better-equipped and better-staffed schools, etc.[5]

While such service differentials in favor of upper-income groups "may seem to violate traditional equity norms," and "may seem harmful to low-income consumers," this is necessary for "strategic considerations," for the long-term health of the city's fisc.

Like Tiebout, Buchanan is arguing that packages of public goods make a difference in where people choose to live. Unlike Tiebout, however, Buchanan claims that the major differences among jurisdictions are not the set of intrinsic "tastes" catered to, but the redistributional bias of various public goods packages. It is clear that, unlike Tiebout, Buchanan is not really concerned with achieving allocational efficiency by providing a wide assortment of public goods packages. Instead, Buchanan argues that competition must drive cities to provide the exact same public goods package: a package that is biased in favor of high-income groups. The irony is clear: Tiebout's argument, which was initially an argument about making everyone better off by operation of the "invisible hand," has become an apology for promoting a uniform bias in favor of upper income groups.

To what extent have cities followed this "rational fiscal policy"? Buchanan claims that the "fiscal plight of cities" around the country suggests that "optimal strategies have not been followed." [6] And of course Buchanan is correct in surmising that not all cities have pursued the rational fiscal policy. The reason is that it is not always politically expedient to be as casual about the needs and demands of low-income groups as Buchanan is. As was suggested in Chapter 3, there is in many older cities a strong political coalition between low-income groups and the politicians and bureaucrats who benefit from providing services to these groups. The recent rent control movement in Santa Monica, El Monte, and Pasadena is just one example of the political force of this coalition in many old-line cities. (How well this political force actually benefits low-income groups, as opposed to the bureaucrats and politicians who seek to represent them, is another question.)

For the most part, however, there does seem to be a healthy competition for upper-income groups among the cities of Los Angeles County, indicating that most of these jurisdictions are aware of the rationality of Buchanan's proposed strategy in a fragmented metropolis. Elements of Buchanan's strategy may be seen not only in the low tax rate policies of the Lakewood Plan cities, but also in the outright subsidization of high-income groups through housing plans and the "optimal" mix of public services.

Rational Fiscal Policy in Los Angeles County

Duarte, for instance, is a community that had a variety of housing mixes and a healthy tax base after World War II. When it incorporated, however, its high-income housing area incorporated separately as Bradbury, and its industrial tax base incorporated separately as Irwindale. (As Robert Warren puts it, "Incorporation allowed the industrial area of Irwindale and the estate-type community of Bradbury to differentiate themselves from one another and from the large residential population of Duarte." [7]) As a result, Duarte's new city government needed resources and a better housing mix. But, as Duarte's city manager noted, there was no way to attract or even retain high-income housing. "Duarte residents who wanted better housing had to move outside the city to places like Glendora or West Covina." [8]

This was true until Duarte became the first city in Southern California to take advantage of a new residential mortgage revenue bond program. Under this program, redevelopment agencies may sell tax-exempt bonds at low interest rates, and repay the bonds with mortgage loans at rates two or three points lower than conventional loans. Duarte sold $66 million to finance 720 middle-class home mortgage units. Now, the city manager finds that Duarte has a chance of keeping its upwardly mobile citizens. "Instead of losing these people, we're able to keep them here."

Redondo Beach used a similar program to build $100,000 to $175,000 beachfront condominiums, and was criticized by the head of the California State Housing Finance Agency of perpetrating "a waste of limited resources that should be used to meet the critical need for housing for low- and moderate-income Californians." [9]

The older cities of Pomona and Azusa have begun similar projects. Pomona's programs would finance 278 single-family homes ranging in price from $90,000 to $200,000. The Pomona community development director said, "This project represents the highest quality residential development package ever presented to the City of Pomona." [10] Pomona's tax base had been eroding rapidly; in this situation, a city which cultivates low-income housing instead of high-income housing cannot expect to survive, as Buchanan said.

The other side of the coin is not only cultivating high-income residents, but discouraging low-income residents. In this, the Los Angeles suburbs are aided by Article XXXIV of the California Constitution, which requires that any low-rent public housing project must be approved by the community. Similar provisions do not apply for middle- and upper-income housing; so the article was tested in the case of *James* v. *Valtierra*. The new Nixon court upheld the validity of the provision in 1971.

While Article XXXIV does not apply to Section 236 housing, which allows subsidized mortgage interest rates for private low-income developments, cities have used construction moratoriums to stop these projects as well. Within days after the *Valtierra* ruling, Torrance banned all construction in an effort to stop a proposed Section 236 housing project, something La Puente had done earlier. In 1970, Pomona's city council adopted a resolution declaring Section 236 housing unacceptable in that city.[11]

In some cases, the official bias in favor of wealthy citizens has amounted to outright "poor removal." Thus, we observe that redevelopment projects are used in Southern California, as elsewhere, for replacing low-income with high-income housing. (Between 1949 and 1974, the urban program nationwide demolished 300,000 more housing units than it produced, most of them poor homes.[12]) In Pasadena, one city councilman remembers that a major new interstate highway was used to the same effect.

Until the late 1950s, the city manager of Pasadena was a street engineer by training. He maintained the streets and the sewer system, and if you asked him about the growing problem of minorities in Pasadena he would say, "Don't raise that issue, we're going to build a freeway which will wipe out that section of town." [13]

The freeway did eventually replace three to six thousand low-income households in Pasadena, and redevelopment replaced another thousand. As Buchanan says, if rational fiscal strategies mean that low-income groups "withdraw from the fiscal arrangements of the city, net effects on fiscal surplus may be positive."

Given that high-income individuals are the object of intermunicipal competition, as are other resources, which cities have been most successful in this competition? Table 7.3 shows that the cities that had become ho-

Table 7.3
Increases in Per Capita Income in Income Homogeneous Cities

Predominant income class, 1970	Increases in per capita income, 1970–1975			
	< 30%	30–40%	40–50%	50% +
Homogeneous low-income	Bell Bell Gardens Cudahy Maywood	Baldwin Park Compton Huntington Park	Commerce Hawaiian Gardens San Fernando Signal Hill	
Homogeneous middle-income	Paramount	South El Monte	La Puente Norwalk	Irwindale San Dimas Santa Fe Springs
Homogeneous upper-income		Beverly Hills San Marino	Arcadia Bradbury Cerritos Claremont Covina Glendora La Mirada Palos Verdes Estates South Pasadena Torrance Walnut West Covina Whittier	Culver City Downey El Segundo Lakewood Manhattan Beach Rolling Hills Rolling Hills Estates Sierra Madre

Source: U.S. Department of Commerce, Bureau of the Census, *Population Estimates and Projections*, Current Population Reports Series P-25, no. 744 (Washington, D.C., January 1979), pp. 8–9.

mogeneously low-income by 1970 were less able to compete for new high-income groups than those cities which had become homogeneously high-income. Per capita income grew at less than the county average rate of 44.6 percent in every low-income city but Hawaiian Gardens, San Fernando, and Signal Hill. It grew faster than the county average in most of the upper-income cities. The municipal distribution of municipal income was thus tending to become even more marked. The end result was not only the fiscal success of some cities, but the fiscal failure of others.

Conclusion

The problems I see with Buchanan's "rational fiscal strategy" are four in number. First of all, for several cities, fiscal crisis may have proceeded to the point where it is impossible to muster enough free resources to provide the inducement to high-income residents to return. Compton may well be such an example, although Compton is attempting to follow just such a rational strategy in the wake of previous administrations' "irrational" catering to low-income needs and desires. (See the discussion of Compton in the next chapter.)

Second, even where it is financially possible to follow this strategy, it may be politically impossible in some cities, because of the mobilized influence of low-income groups.

Third, if some cities are unable or unwilling to undertake Buchanan's rational fiscal strategy while other cities pursue it, the result will be the creation of concentrations of low-income groups and inadequate resources in some jurisdictions, including suburban jurisdictions. Buchanan seems to dismiss this possibility in the following passage:

If the dominant majority should be from the upper income-wealth groups, and if this majority attempts to exploit other persons maximally, outmigration (of the low-income groups) might increase rather than reduce fiscal surplus. I can justify my neglect of this possibility empirically. What we observe is the outmigration of upper income persons and groups; we are not concerned about the formation of slum suburbs.[14]

However, on empirical grounds, this possibility cannot be dismissed. That old-line cities like Pasadena can drive out low-income groups is a very real possibility, and the creation of slum suburbs like Compton is the natural outcome of the use of rational fiscal strategy.

A fourth problem is a moral one. While Buchanan speaks sadly of the "fiscal frustration imposed by the apparent constraints of nonattainable and false ideals" (such as equality of treatment of different income groups), I believe it is neither politically nor ethically feasible to dismiss the needs of low-income groups with the argument that the long-run fiscal health of the cities in the Los Angeles basin requires low-income groups to become invisible.

Given current institutions of urban fiscal finance, however, Buchanan's argument describes quite accurately the dilemma of any urban officials who do have political or moral qualms about following the rational fiscal strategy. As Buchanan says, as long as high-income individuals can migrate from cities that do not cater to their redistributional perspective, "some such strategy must exist." [15] Ultimately, it is as pointless to condemn city officials for following the rational fiscal strategy, as it would be to condemn a high-income individual from taking advantage of the existence of a city which caters to his needs. Because cities must compete for high-income residents, as they do for business, these residents must be, along with business, the main beneficiaries of the competition for municipal resources in a fragmented governmental structure; and the low-income residents must find themselves a drag on the "market."

For anyone who sees ethical problems with Buchanan's strategy, the only course of action is to consider alternative institutional structures which do not create the incentives that make the rational fiscal strategy rational. Ultimately, this means changing the system of urban public finance so that local governments do not have to compete for high-income groups and fear low-income groups. One such change is considered in the appendix.

8

Is the "Invisible Hand" Biased?

Economists typically take for granted that since the creation of a market increases the individual's area of choice, it therefore leads to higher benefits.[1]

In this brief passage, Kenneth Arrow makes explicit, rather than implicit, the typical economic assumption about the superiority of exit over voice, of the "invisible hand" over political action as a means of adjusting the distribution of resources in society. Greater "area of choice" makes exit possible, and provides the opportunity for the invisible hand to work its magic. Greater range of choice "leads to higher benefits" because it may provide some individuals with an alternative that makes them better off, while those who find the extra alternatives unattractive are at least no worse off. As applied to metropolitan fragmentation, this perspective sees the creation of the Lakewood Cities as unambiguously beneficial because it allowed those individuals who preferred small-scale, low tax rate cities the chance to move to such a city; it could not have made other individuals worse off because they did not have to move there.

But is choice in fact unambiguously beneficial? For instance, does it necessarily lead to an efficient outcome? And whether or not it leads to efficiency gains, does it make everyone better off? The purpose of this chapter is to show that these two questions are in fact different, but that the answer to both questions is "No" in general, and "No" in the particular case of the Lakewood Plan as an extension of the range of individual choice.

Divide the Dollar Game

Imagine a situation in which two individuals are given the opportunity to play "divide the dollar." If they can agree on how to divide the dollar, they will each get the part of the dollar they agree on. If they fail to agree, each gets nothing. Two specific players submit the decision to an arbitrator in order to make sure that they reach agreement. The arbitrator, however, sets the division at 40 cents each. This outcome, while legal, is not efficient, because part of the dollar is lost to the two players of the game. Both players could have been made better off by dividing the dollar at (for instance) 55 and 45 cents. The arbitrator's allocation, however, seems to be the one they are stuck with. We will call this outcome the "no choice" outcome.

Now imagine, however, that each player is given two choices. Each may choose to agree to the arbitrator's allocation (this choice will be called A_1) or may choose not to abide by the allocation (A_2). If both choose to stick, they will in fact get the original allocation of 40 cents each. If one or both choose A_2, however, there is a totally new allocation.

Each player is told that no matter what the other player chooses, he will be better off by choosing A_2 than A_1. In game theory, such an alternative strategy that is always better for the player, regardless of the opponent's choice, is called the dominant strategy.[2] The predicted outcome of a game in which each player has a dominant strategy is the outcome associated with the dominant strategy choice for each player. However, does the introduction of a new and individually rational alternative into the choice set of each individual lead to an efficient outcome? And does it make everyone better off than with the original "no choice" outcome?

In Game I (see figure 8.1), the invisible hand works as advertised: both individuals, in employing their dominant strategies, are made better off. Although the outcome is not efficient, the introduction of the new alternatives represents an efficiency gain over the no-choice outcome.

In Game II, however, the widened choice range results in a new outcome which is worse for everyone; this is the so-called Prisoners' Dilemma game.

Figure 8.1
The Ambiguous Value of Choice

No-Choice Outcome

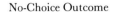

Jane
A_1

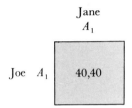

Joe A_1 | 40,40

The Effect of Giving Each Player A Choice of Alternatives

Game I:

The game with alternatives 1 and 2 available to both players leads to a new equilibrium outcome (lower right-hand corner) which is *better* for both players.

Joe	Jane A_1	Jane A_2
A_1	40,40	20,60
A_2	60,20	45,45

Game II (Prisoner's Dilemma):

The game with alternatives 1 and 3 available to both players leads to a new equilibrium outcome (lower right-hand corner) which is *worse* for both players.

Joe	Jane A_1	Jane A_3
A_1	40,40	20,60
A_3	60,20	30,30

Game III (Institutional Bias):

The game with alternatives 1 and 4 available to both players leads to a new equilibrium outcome (lower right-hand corner) which is better for one and worse for the other player.

Joe	Jane A_1	Jane A_4
A_1	40,40	30,50
A_4	80,0	50,20

Note: the first number is Joe's payoff, the second number is Jane's payoff.

[   ] Equilibrium outcomes.

While the new alternative is the rational, self-interested best choice for each player, the new equilibrium is worse for both players, and the outcome is even farther from Pareto efficiency than the original no-choice outcome. Both players would prefer that they not be given the choice of A_2; they would prefer to have no choice.

Game III, I believe, has not been generally recognized as an entirely distinct and politically interesting kind of game. The new outcome, in the lower right-hand corner, is indeed an equilibrium position for the new game; no one has an incentive to change his choice. Jane, for instance, would get nothing instead of 20 cents by choosing A_1 instead of A_4. But this differs from the other two games in that the two players are not in agreement about whether the increase in the range of choice is a good thing. One player would prefer an institutional contraction of the range of choice, while another would not. Such a situation may be called "institutionally biased," because extension or limitation of the range of individual choice is not universally beneficial. The decision to broaden or limit the range of individual choice is in this case an institutional question that masks a substantive reallocation of benefits.

The game of institutional bias is an essentially conflictual game, unlike the Prisoners' Dilemma game. In the latter game, cooperation can lead to real gains without side payments. In the game of institutional bias, there is no room for cooperation. Furthermore, the efficiency aspects of the game are totally irrelevant. The dynamics of the game are exactly the same whether the new equilibrium represents an efficiency gain or an efficiency loss (as in the example). In either case, the decision to broaden or narrow the range of individual choices will be made on redistributional and political grounds.

The linkages between this little model and the issue of metropolitan governance are fairly direct. A consolidated metropolitan government is a "no choice" institution, in which residents have effectively no opportunities to choose a different set of urban services. The creation of new suburban jurisdictions providing, for instance, a low-scale, low-tax-rate alternative, "increases the individual's area of choice," in Arrow's words. The question is whether the creation of this new alternative is unambiguously beneficial, unambiguously detrimental, or is biased in its results.

The traditional urban reform advocates have painted a Game II picture of metropolitan organization, in which the choice provided by numerous small but economically inefficient jurisdictions is a trap. By simply cooperating to consolidate urban government, everyone could benefit from the economies of scale to be achieved.

On the other hand, Tiebout and his followers have argued that metropolitan fragmentation is a Game I situation, in which the extension of individual choice of public service mixes allows everyone to choose his or her own "right" city (dominant strategy), and that efficiency gains are to be realized from this institutional setting. "A public economy composed of multiple jurisdictions is likely to be more efficient and responsive than a public economy organized as a single areawide monopoly." [3]

Both consolidationists and advocates of fragmentation use "efficiency" to bolster their side of the argument. However, it is the purpose of this chapter to argue that choice in the context of metropolitan fragmentation is a Game III situation; the extension of choice in the form of the incorporation of Lakewood Plan jurisdictions helped some people (middle-class property owners) and hurt others (the low-income inhabitants concentrated in low-resource jurisdictions). If this is so, then neither the proconsolidation nor profragmentation position is justified in relying on a Game I or Game II interpretation of jurisdictional choice. Metropolitan organization may be viewed in terms of alternative forms of "biased" extension or retraction of individual choice.

The rest of the chapter addresses three questions in the following order: (1) is fragmentation universally beneficial? (2) if not, is the end result efficient? (3) if the end result of increased fragmentation is not efficient in an absolute sense, does it result in an efficiency gain?

Preference Position and Conformity Cost

One assumption common to Tiebout and other public-choice defenders of fragmentation is that individuals have markedly different tastes for public goods, and that these tastes motivate mobility from one jurisdiction to another, or even the creation of new jurisdictions. For instance, Tiebout says

The consumer-voter moves to that community whose local government best satisfies his set of preferences. The greater the number of communities and the greater variance among them, the closer the consumer will come to fully realizing his preference position.[4]

This use of the expression "preference position" seems to suggest that an individual has some ideal level of demand for municipal goods which does not change with movement from community to community. Bish seems to make the same assumption, as in his observation that "families with similar tastes locate together." [5] Oates claims that individuals have a "desired level of consumption" of public goods, and that when the jurisdiction provides a level of service other than that level, the individual incurs a "welfare cost" that can be called the "conformity cost." [6] Total "conformity costs" are seen to be necessarily smaller in small, homogeneous jurisdictions than in a single heterogeneous jurisdiction, because at least some individuals will have the opportunity to influence the smaller governments to provide service levels that are closer to their ideal "preference positions." Tiebout's theory is, therefore, about individuals minimizing "conformity costs" by locating in the appropriate jurisdictions. Of course, conformity costs is a meaningful concept only if individuals do in fact have a preference position that is unchanging in various jurisdictions; a preference position that changes as an individual crosses jurisdictional boundaries would not allow meaningful comparisons of costs incurred in different jurisdictions.

In all of these instances, I believe, the public-choice theorists miss a fundamental and crucial point: the politically relevent phenomenon is not some immutable preference position based on an intrinsic set of "tastes" for public goods, but the quantity of a public good demanded by an individual in a given jurisdiction. And if the quantity demanded of a public good varies from jurisdiction to jurisdiction, then the idea that the individual chooses his jurisdiction by minimizing conformity costs (measured as distance from some unvarying preference position) is not useful or correct. Indeed, because expressed preference is a function of the opportunities and costs in a given jurisdiction, an individual may actually prefer to live in one jurisdiction, enduring conformity costs rather than live in another jurisdiction where the preferences he or she expresses are identical to the levels of public goods provided.

To show that an individual's preferences for a publicly provided good depend on what jurisdiction he or she is in, let us look at the following simple but not totally unrealistic example. We assume a jurisdiction J with a population N_J of individuals divided into three income classes of equal size. The individuals in the highest income class all have income $Y_i = Y$, while the individuals in the middle-income class and lower-income class have incomes equal to $.64Y$ and $.36Y$, respectively. There are two goods in the economy, one a private good, and one a good that is publicly provided. All individuals have identical utility functions of the form

$$u_i = z_i^\gamma Q_J^\beta,$$

where z_i is the individual's consumption of the privately supplied good, and Q_J is the per capita level of provision of the publicly provided good in jurisdiction J.

The budget constraint for each individual is given by

$$y_i = p_z z_i + t_i r Q_J N_J,$$

where P_z is the price of the privately supplied good (assumed equal to 1), r is the price of the publicly supplied good, and t_i is the proportion of the public expenditure for Q paid by the ith individual.

With these assumptions, the individual demand function for the publicly provided good is

$$Q_i^* = \left(\frac{\beta}{\beta + \gamma}\right) \left(\frac{y_i}{t_i r N_J}\right).$$

Thus, as in the normal economics literature, the quantity demanded or preference position of individual i (Q_i^*) is a function of income, tax share, and population; but two of these three arguments in the function vary with jurisdiction.

If we assume a regressive, budget-balancing tax share, for example,

$$t_i = \frac{\sqrt{y_i}}{\Sigma_{i \in J} \sqrt{y_i}},$$

the demand function represents a normal good, for which demand increases with income. (A progressive tax structure would have led to analogous conclusions about preference, conformity costs, and utility.) If we assume $\alpha = \beta = \frac{1}{2}$, and $N_J = 30$, divided equally into the three income groups, then each income group demands the amount listed in table 8.1. Since there is but one public good, with single-peaked preference orderings, the median voter's preference is the majority winning alternative. The quantity of Q supplied is that preferred by the middle-income class, and everyone else is out of consumer equilibrium, preferring more or less public good than is supplied.

Now we assume that two other jurisdictions are set up on the outskirts of the central jurisdiction, but within easy commuting distance of the original city, so that commuting costs can be neglected. The individuals in each jurisdiction obtain the benefits of only the public good supplied by that jurisdiction; so that externalties are internalized to the jurisdiction. Individuals are faced with a choice of jurisdictions. If Arrow is correct, then this choice can help those individuals who are unhappy in the old consolidated institutional framework, without hurting anyone.

This situation exactly fits that described by Tiebout, since there are an adequate number of municipalities now to satisfy the range of demands of the total population. We would predict, with Tiebout, that the residential equilibrium would result in perfect stratification of the population, with each municipality serving each income class perfectly, and with no conformity costs. But as can be seen in table 8.2, this does not mean that everyone is better off in the fragmented metropolitan area. On the contrary, the lower class is worse off, by a noticeable amount, in the fragmented institutional setting where its (new) preferences are exactly met, than in the consolidated framework suffering conformity costs. The minimization of conformity costs is not a sufficient normative rule for making decisions about institutionalization of local government.

The reason for this counterintuitive result is that, even though the consolidated metropolitan government had a radically regressive taxation system, the presence of the wealthy individuals was a "positive externality" for the lower-income classes, who benefited from their resources in the provision of the publicly provided good. Choice of communities, on the other hand, is a bane to the lower-income individuals in the example. Once the choice of municipalities is made freely available to the population, the fate of the lower class, in the form of decreased purchasing power, is sealed. If urban problems, such as crime, tend to concentrate in the lower-class juris-

Table 8.1
Individual Demand and Satisfaction under Consolidated Metropolitan Government

	Lower-income group	Middle-income group	Upper-income group
Size	10	10	10
U_i	$z_i^{1/2}Q_J^{1/2}$	$z_i^{1/2}Q_J^{1/2}$	$z_i^{1/2}Q_J^{1/2}$
y_i	$(.36)Y$	$(.64)Y$	Y
t_i	.025	.033	.042
Q demanded	$(.24)Y/r$	$(.32)Y/r$	$(.42)Y/r$
Q received	$(.32)Y/r$	$(.32)Y/r$	$(.32)Y/r$
Total cost of $Q_J = (9.6)Y$			
Tax total for each individual	$(.24)Y$	$(.32)Y$	$(.40)Y$
z_i	$(.12)Y$	$(.32)Y$	$(.60)Y$
U_i	$\dfrac{(.196)Y}{r^{1/2}}$	$\dfrac{(.32)Y}{r^{1/2}}$	$\dfrac{(.438)Y}{r^{1/2}}$

Table 8.2
Individual Demand and Satisfaction under Three Fragmented Metropolitan Governments

	Lower-income government	Middle-income government	Upper-income government
Size	10	10	10
U_i	$z_i^{1/2}Q_i^{1/2}$	$z_i^{1/2}Q_i^{1/2}$	$z_i^{1/2}Q_i^{1/2}$
y_i	$(.36)Y$	$(.64)Y$	Y
t_i	.100	.100	.100
Q demanded and Q received	$(.18)Y/r$	$(.32)Y/r$	$(.50)Y/r$
Tax total	$(.18)Y$	$(.32)Y$	$(.50)Y$
z_i	$(.18)Y$	$(.32)Y$	$(.50)Y$
U_i	$\dfrac{(.18)Y}{r^{1/2}}$	$\dfrac{(.32)Y}{r^{1/2}}$	$\dfrac{(.50)Y}{r^{1/2}}$

diction, then the deleterious effect of fragmentation on lower classes is exacerbated. But, neglecting exclusionary zoning, the individuals all have free choice. Why couldn't the lower-class individuals make themselves better off by moving into the upper-class jurisdiction?

Certainly, the poor individual has the right to move to either the middle-class or upper-class jurisdiction. But paying for the much higher level of publicly provided good on a limited income would leave the poor individual even worse off. Even without exclusionary zoning, the stratified fragmented framework is indeed an equilibrium position, in which no one has any incentive to move to a different jurisdiction populated by a different income class.

The example just presented suggests the possibility that externalities imposed by residential choices of different income class members may actually make lower-income groups worse off in a fragmented metropolis. That this possibility has actually occurred can be seen by summarizing the evidence of the past two chapters in a few case histories, in which the stratification by income classes resulted in decreased collective "purchasing power" for the low-income cities.

The Mixed Benefits of Metropolitan Fragmentation

During the period 1950 to 1970, municipal boundaries increasingly served to separate races and income classes in the Los Angeles area. The city of Los Angeles and some of its larger, older suburbs remained heterogeneous, but with increasingly large concentrations of poor and blacks. The smaller and newer suburbs were overwhelmingly white, and tended to be identifiably homogeneous for some income-class level.

At the same time, taxable municipal property became more unequally distributed. This trend, combined with segregation of income and racial groups, created a situation in which the poor, blacks, and middle class could expect to get less return for a given property tax rate. On the other hand, a large number of middle- and upper-class whites escaped the property tax burden altogether in the new homogeneous cities of the Lakewood Plan. In 1970, 22 cities representing over $1.6 billion worth of taxable property had no municipal property tax. At the modest tax rate of $1.00, this represented $16 million in potential municipal revenue.

What does this brief historical overview tell us about the benefits of metropolitan fragmentation in Los Angeles County? It seems to be true that
the improved municipal choice set in Los Angeles County benefited certain segments of the population. Those 875,000 people who lived in the
cities created under the Lakewood Plan (only 1.4 percent of whom were
black) were able, by and large, to live in low-crime areas, with few dilapidated neighborhoods, with little or no property tax, but with the opportunity to provide themselves with a pattern of expenditures that fit their
particular brand of needs, and with the power to zone to exclude people
who they think wouldn't fit in.

But some of the older cities as well as the Lakewood Plan cities benefited
from the general sorting out of individuals that occurred during the period
from 1950 to 1970. The city of Arcadia, for instance, reduced its proportions of poor and black populations, achieved one of the lowest violence
and property crime rates in the country, at the same time decreasing its
property tax rate. Yet in real dollar terms, the decreased property tax rate
is yielding more property tax revenue per capita than in 1950, because of
increased valuation per capita (see table 8.3).

But while the Lakewood Plan cities were protecting their municipal resources, and while other cities were following Arcadia's pattern of increased homogeneity, decreased tax rates, and increased property tax
yield, other cities were acquiring increasing concentrations of poor and
minority residents. The city of Los Angeles, for instance, often regarded as
one of the healthy sunbelt cities, markedly increased its population of low-
income citizens and of blacks. By 1977, the proportion of Anglos in Los
Angeles had dropped to 51.4 percent, from 60.2 percent at the 1970 census.
Eighteen percent of the Hispanics and 31.1 percent of the blacks were on
welfare.[7] The number of robbery and aggravated assault arrests jumped
from 250 to 1,037 per 100,000 from 1950 to 1970. Yet the resources to deal
with these problems did not grow at an equal rate (see table 8.4).

Between 1967 and 1972 the number of employees in the city's manufacturing firms actually decreased in the areas of food and paper products,
printing, and machinery manufacturing. Overall the number of manufacturing employees decreased from 309,600 to 281,200. In constant 1967 dollars, the value added by manufacturing establishments in the city of Los
Angeles decreased from $4260 million to $3843, a decrease of almost ten

Table 8.3
Profile of the City of Arcadia: 1950–1970

	1950	1970
Population	23,066	45,138
% high-income families	50.8	50.1
% middle-income families	23.6	32.1
% low-income families	25.6	17.8
% poor	8.1	4.4
% black	0.21	0.07
Income homogeneity	0.380	0.385
Robbery and aggravated assault per 100,000 pop.	MI	160
Property crime per 100,000 pop.	MI	2,867
Taxable property per capita (based upon 1970 $)	$2657	$3296
Property tax rate	$ 1.18	$ 1.00
Property tax revenue per capita (based upon 1970 $)	$ 31.26	$ 31.48
Total revenue per capita (based upon 1970 $)	$ 98.54	$ 116.50

Sources: Income and racial data from *Census of Population, 1950,* vol. 1, pt. 6, Table 37 (U.S. Bureau of the Census, 1951) and *Census of Population, 1970,* vol. 1, pt. 6, Tables 89, 107, 118 (U.S. Bureau of the Census, 1971); crime statistics from U.S. Federal Bureau of Investigation, *Uniform Crime Reports for 1950 and 1970*; revenue and tax data from California State Controller, *Financial Transactions Concerning Cities of California,* 1950 and 1970.

Table 8.4
Profile of the City of Los Angeles: 1950–1970

	1950	1970
Population	1,970,358	2,811,801
% High-income families	33.7	34.9
% Middle-income families	28.5	29.8
% Low-income families	37.7	35.3
% Poor	10.7	13.3
% Black	8.2	17.9
Income homogeneity	0.3373	0.3354
Robbery and aggravated assault per 100,000 pop.	250	1037
Property crime per 100,000 pop.	1388	5154
Taxable property per capita (based upon 1970 $)	$2039	$2500
Property tax rate	$ 1.85	$ 2.52
Property tax revenue per capita (based upon 1970 $)	$ 36.39	$ 63.24
Total revenue per capita (Based upon 1970 $)	$ 226.16	$ 181.50

Sources: Income and racial data from *Census of Population, 1950,* vol. 1, pt. 6, Table 37 (U.S. Bureau of the Census, 1951) and *Census of Population, 1970,* vol. 1, pt. 6, Tables 89, 107, 118 (U.S. Bureau of the Census, 1971); crime statistics from U.S. Federal Bureau of Investigation, *Uniform Crime Reports for 1950 and 1970*; revenue and tax data from California State Controller, *Financial Transactions Concerning Cities of California,* 1950 and 1970.

percent.[8] Major manufacturing firms continued to relocate from Los Angeles to the suburbs of Orange County and elsewhere at a rate of 50 or 60 firms a year.

This erosion of the city's resource base shows up in its budget. The property tax rate increased from 1.85 in 1950 to 2.52 per hundred in 1970, but the total revenue per capita decreased from $226 (in real 1970 dollars) to $181.50. There was $242 of debt in 1950 (1970 dollars) for every individual in the city of Los Angeles. By 1970, this figure had almost doubled to $490. Fiscal and economic deterioration were at an even more advanced state in some of the smaller cities, such as Compton.

Compton: The Issue Was Survival, When It Should Have Been Progress

Compton, being slightly over half-way from downtown Los Angeles toward the port area of Long Beach, was in an excellent position to grow during the 1940s. The population climbed in that decade from 16,000 to almost 47,000. There was a healthy mixture of people in the city, including many blue-collar workers employed in the shipyards of Long Beach and San Pedro. In fact, the distribution of income groups in the city almost exactly paralleled that of the county as a whole, with one-third of the families earning more than $4500, just as in the county. If anything, there was a slight underweighting of low-income families and a larger-than-average proportion of middle-income families. The population was white, but not exclusively white: 4.8 percent were nonwhite. Without Long Beach's industrial base, the property tax base was relatively weak at $810 per capita. To provide services for the growing population, the municipal tax rate had reached a level of 1.4407 by the end of the decade, which was fairly high, but not significantly higher than other residential communities in the county; that is, not until Lakewood was incorporated in 1954.

While scoffers asked who was going to buy the 17,000 tract homes being put up by Louis Boyar and Ben Weingart in Lakewood, the young, white homeowners in Compton must have been watching the new homes going up on their way from work. Besides being a shorter commute to the shipyards of Long Beach, the homes were undoubtedly attractive for other reasons. They were newer than housing in Compton, they were in a more rural, less developed area, and they were inexpensive. The new neighbors in Lakewood would be other young, white homeowners. Furthermore, the tax rates would be much lower in Lakewood than in Compton, especially after the danger of annexation to Long Beach was averted. The crime rate was lower, and the ocean recreation areas were closer. The same kind of homeowner who preferred the incorporation of Lakewood to annexation by wealthy Long Beach would certainly prefer migration to Lakewood rather than remaining in Compton (see table 8.5).

Not all of the white homeowners in Compton moved to Lakewood, but some did. Those who didn't move to Lakewood had opportunities to move to a low-crime, low-tax white community when Paramount, Santa Fe Springs, and Bellflower were incorporated in 1957, along with Artesia in 1959. By 1960, the proportion of blacks in Compton had jumped to 40 percent, and that simply added another reason for white homeowners to leave.

While the first stream of individuals moving into Compton tended to be middle-income blacks, these groups soon found a more desirable location. The city of Carson, incorporated in 1968, began drawing off the black property owners from Los Angeles and Compton, who, like white property owners, were interested in low property tax rates in desirable, low-crime neighborhoods. Carson, with high levels of municipal resources and no property tax, fit the needs of these individuals, and consequently a layer of middle-income blacks was added to Carson's previous level of lower-income whites. As a result, Carson became one of the few areas in the country where blacks were of a higher status ranking than whites. In 1970, Carson's black median family income was $13,471, and the figure for whites was $11,623. Both blacks and whites in Carson agreed to oppose "increased density, apartments, or housing for low-income groups, and blockbusting." [9] These policies served to further isolate low-income blacks in Compton.

In the early 1970s, the city of Compton continued to keep a relatively open door for in-migrants, as indicated by the decision in the late 1970s to become involved in the federal Section 8 rent subsidy program for low-income renters. This decision further accentuated the differences between Compton and the neighboring Lakewood Plan cities, which avoided such rent subsidy programs, and resulted in further concentration of low-

Table 8.5
Profile of the City of Compton: 1950–1970

	1950	1970
Population	47,991	78,547
% High-income families	33.0	20.0
% Middle-income families	38.0	36.3
% Low-income families	29.0	43.7
% Poor	5.7	19.1
% Black	19.1	71.0
Income homogeneity	0.338	0.363
Robbery and aggravated assault per 100,000 pop.	92	2405
Property crime per 100,000 pop.	1167	10,710
Taxable property per capita (based upon 1970 $)	$1322	$1428
Property tax rate	$ 1.44	$ 1.59
Property tax revenue per capita (based upon 1970 $)	$ 18.93	$ 22.04
Total revenue per capita (based upon 1970 $)	$ 63.37	$ 108.93

Sources: Income and racial data from *Census of Population, 1950,* vol. 1, pt. 6, Table 37 (U.S. Bureau of the Census, 1951) and *Census of Population, 1970,* vol. 1, pt. 6, Tables 89, 107, 118 (U.S. Bureau of the Census, 1971); crime statistics from U.S. Federal Bureau of Investigation, *Uniform Crime Reports for 1950 and 1970*; revenue and tax data from California State Controller, *Financial Transactions Concerning Cities of California,* 1950 and 1970.

income blacks in Compton in the 1970s, until Compton became almost entirely black, and unemployment rose to even higher levels.

The tax base continued to follow the middle-income families out of Compton and into the new contract cities. The auto dealers who had been so important to Compton relocated in Lakewood, along with much of the retail business. Sales tax revenue failed to keep up with inflation, going from $16.92 per capita in 1960 to $17.90 in 1970. Compton dropped from 26th place in sales tax revenue (second only to Los Angeles) to 47th place among the cities of the county. In property tax revenue it dropped to 70th place.[10]

Yet, while Compton's tax base deteriorated, its need for public services drastically increased. With the concentration of unemployment went a concentration of crime: Compton had the highest rate of homicide, rape, robbery, burglary, assault, and auto theft in the county. To deal with this problem, the citizens had to tax themselves at ever higher rates. By 1970, its property tax had climbed to $1.59 per hundred, and by 1977–1978 it was to climb to $2.00, as property values continued to lag behind inflation and increasing problems of crime and decay.

In sum, by the mid-1970s, it was apparent that the choice offered by the Lakewood Plan incorporations had not benefited the citizens of Compton. It had resulted in a concentration of urban problems and a drain of resources. The sorting out of people that accompanied the incorporation of the Lakewood Plan cities was not a neutral process in which people with different tastes found each other under sympathetic local governments, but a political process in which resources were redistributed. The costs for the citizens of Compton were not trivial; by the mid-1970s, as the mayor of Compton told me, "the issue became survival, when it should have been progress."[11]

The problem developed because Compton's policies were friendly toward lower income groups and therefore unlike the policies of the Lakewood Plan cities. According to Tiebout, this variation in local government policies promotes efficiency. But ironically, the effects of the Tiebout process of "voting with your feet" were so bad for Compton that Compton was driven to imitating the policies of its Lakewood Plan cities. This occurred with the election of Lionel Cade, a black accountant, to the mayor's office in 1977. The new administration attempted to turn Compton's financial trends around, and it did so by running the city on businesslike terms: emphasizing the basic services, cutting back on inessential social services, and attracting the "right" kind of businesses and residents to the city.

The first thing the city did was run an audit to discover the extent of the financial crisis. They discovered a $2 million debt. The new administration eliminated that large deficit in one year by putting budgetary restraints on everyone in the city government.

The new administration actively sought federal money, which provided such things as a new communications system and burglary unit for the police department. While this money helped, it was found that some basic services were neglected and some inessentials were funded, simply because of the categories of grant money available through the federal government. The unconstrained revenue-sharing money was actively sought by all the departments, but was awarded to the police department.

The deteriorating tax base was supported by several means. The city sought to save the remaining auto dealers by relocating them in an auto mall. Tax-increment bonds were issued to initiate a redevelopment project for the downtown area, which is still underway as of this writing.

The attractive, unincorporated industrial land lying between Compton, Carson, and Long Beach had long been a subject for dispute. The city of Compton had objected to the incorporation of Carson along with Long Beach, but after incorporation had proposed that the remaining vacant land be split in roughly three equal pieces, for annexation by the three cities. Although this political compromise was opposed by Carson, it was the one eventually adopted by LAFCO in its sphere of influence study in 1972.

Carson continued, however, to oppose any annexations by Compton through its county supervisor, who, as county alternate, had a vote on LAFCO whenever another supervisor deferred to his preferences and was absent. As a result, Compton was unsuccessful in annexing any land in this area through 1977. In 1978, Compton proposed to annex ten acres on its south side. It had gained the support of the property owners for this industrial annexation by promising several hundred thousand dollars of street work. It was land in its own sphere of influence, by LAFCO decision. Carson requested a revision of the sphere of influence study, and managed to postpone the annexation temporarily, but it was finally approved late in 1978.

There is also some contiguous unincorporated land on Compton's north and west. The western area is industrial, and the northern area is Willowbrook, a very densely populated black ghetto. Compton officials say they are willing to take Willowbrook, although they don't really want it, as long as they also acquire the industrial property to support the burden of services for the Willowbrook area. They claim that the city of Los Angeles is attempting to get the industrial property for itself while leaving the Willowbrook area to Compton.

With respect to housing, the policy of the new administration was to wage an aggressive campaign for middle-income residents. The basic resource in this campaign was the inexpensive single-family houses themselves, since the spiraling inflation had made inexpensive homes a scarce commodity for middle-income families attempting to break into the housing market. As for new housing developments, Compton was unsuccessful in attracting private developers; so the city took the initiative with a four block middle-income single-family housing development.

As for low-income families and the rent-subsidy program, "one of our problems was that historically we went overboard," according to the mayor.[12] Consequently, Compton has decreased its commitment to the rent-subsidy program, and is trying to encourage the people on its waiting list for Section 8 rent-subsidy funds to apply with the Los Angeles County Housing Authority.

It is ironic that the competitive structure of financing local governments finally forced the only majority black city in Los Angeles County toward the same anti-low-income policies that the more successful cities adopted years ago.

Compton was one of three cities in the county to vote against Proposition 13, and the only one to do so by a sizeable majority. It had concentrations of the minorities (blacks, renters, low-income) who felt they had little to gain by property tax relief, and much to lose by cutbacks in government employment and social services.

The austerity program initiated by the new administration had already eliminated all the fat in Compton's budget. Consequently, the cuts in property tax revenues caused by the passage of Proposition 13 meant that every position lost would hurt. More employees were laid off in Compton than in any other city government except Long Beach: 200 employees were dropped from a total of 800. Although the administration tried to protect the fire and police departments, cuts had to be made even there—the police force was cut by 20.

The sorting out of the county's population that had occurred in the quarter century since the conception of the Lakewood Plan meant that some cities would be more hurt than others by property tax reform. Proposition 13, which was supported by the same middle-class homeowner who had moved to the Lakewood Plan cities, had its hardest impact on those cities which had already been hurt by the suburbanization of the middle class.

For low-income cities like Compton, the factor that must be included in any analysis of the benefits of fragmentation is the distribution of resources. While fragmentation may promote multiple, responsive, small-scale demand-revealing mechanisms for homogeneous neighborhoods, it may also result in increased income and racial segregation. And if income and racial segregation are empirically associated with either the concentration of resources, or the concentration of resource-draining problems like crime, then fragmentation may actually work against the welfare of the individuals in the low-income and minority jurisdictions, contrary to the original Tiebout expectation.

Because the distribution of consumers is linked with the distribution of resources, low-income cities have also been low-resource cities; the sorting out of metropolitan population by income class has been detrimental to low-income individuals. This is a counter example to the assumption which began this chapter: that increasing the range of individual choice necessarily makes no one worse off. On the contrary, the existence of individual choice is, in fact, a strategic variable, which can help some at the expense of others. As Edwin Mills and Wallace Oates have written:

Once we recognize that the demand for public services is systematically related to income, we see that the Tiebout model implies powerful tendencies toward segregation by income level. . . . The change from the typical prewar situation, in which most metropolitan residents lived in central cities, to the postwar situation, in which many high-income residents live in exclusionary suburbs, has tended to deprive the poor of most of the redistributive benefits accruing to the poor, while conferring benefits on upper-income households both in terms of reduced transfers through the local public sector and an enhanced efficiency in the local services they consume.[13]

At the very least, it is possible to conclude that the benefits of metropolitan fragmentation have not been universally distributed. While the homogeneous upper-income cities have benefited from effective demand articulation mechanisms and from strong resource bases, homogeneous low-income cities have been increasingly unable to meet demands for municipal services adequately.

Is the Tiebout Mechanism Efficient?

Even though the Tiebout mechanism can result in gains for some individuals and losses for others, the result could be justified on the grounds of efficiency. For instance, in figure 8.2, there is a loss to Jane and a gain to Joe, but many economists would have little doubt about justifying the gain on the grounds of Pareto efficiency: the initial position was inefficient, the final position was one in which the entire dollar was being used up. It is this same reasoning and the same norm of Pareto efficiency which is used to promote airline deregulation, which hurts smaller cities, or to advocate the deregulation of natural gas, which may increase heating costs for some groups in society.

Similarly, if metropolitan fragmentation does result in an efficient, market-like allocation of resources, then perhaps the problems of Compton must simply be ignored or dealt with separately in order to realize these efficiency benefits.

However, an economist named Hamilton has demonstrated that Tiebout was incorrect in arguing that revelation of demand for public goods by choice of jurisdictions was sufficient to provide market-like efficiency for public goods.[14] While a multiplicity of municipalities does guarantee a market-like choice, market-like choice is not sufficient to guarantee market-like efficiency; "choice among consumption bundles is not sufficient to obtain Pareto efficiency. We need prices in order to ensure that consumption decisions are made with proper regard for scarcity. . . . For if the mechanism for financing local public goods does not have the char-

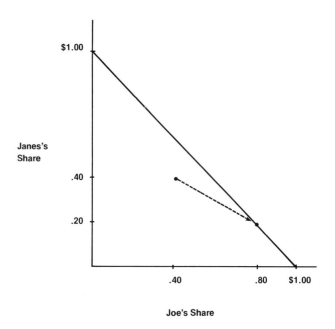

Figure 8.2
Alternative Outcomes in Divide-the-Dollar Game

acteristics of a price, then it is impossible to make the case that the local public economy is an efficient market analogue." [15] In other words, the efficiency of the marketplace operates by a combination of individual rel-evation of demand and a pricing mechanism that equilibrates individual demand and supply conditions through a rationing process. While the Tiebout model allows for individual relevation of demand, it does not in-troduce an analogous pricing mechanism that will ration goods efficiently. The Tiebout argument for efficiency of fragmentation is incorrect. It is not possible in general to justify the increased fragmentation of metropolitan areas on the grounds that the end result will be an efficient distribution of resources.

However, Hamilton has argued that it is possible to introduce an effi-cient pricing mechanism into a system of fragmented metropolitan gov-ernment. The pricing mechanism he suggests is based on property tax-ation, but on a special form. Normal property taxation would result in an efficiency loss by inhibiting property consumption. But if a system of exclusionary zoning is used that results in a set of jurisdictions each with a different, homogeneous level of home values, then every household in a given jurisdiction will pay the same amount of property tax. This system guarantees that the property tax will have the effect of a head tax and will not be considered a part of the price of housing, and that there will be no efficiency loss in the housing market. Because each household in a given city pays the same amount of property tax, there is no income redistribution within any city, and the property tax is simply a price for the public goods within that city. It performs the same rationing function that prices do in a private marketplace, and just as efficiently.

In such a system based on exclusionary zoning to insure homogeneous jurisdictions, a Pareto efficient distribution of public goods is guaranteed; in fact, it is the same Pareto efficient distribution that would obtain under a market solution.

Thus, it is possible to reconcile a system of choice among municipalities with a Pareto efficient allocation of resources. But there are two paradoxes associated with Hamilton's solution to the problem. The first of these is that this solution, unlike Tiebout's proposed solution, is not an invisible hand solution. Instead of letting the invisible hand operate through unrestricted individual choice, it is necessary to legislate a system of zoning in each municipality that effectively restricts individual choice; an individual who cannot afford a certain level of housing may not choose to live in the municipalities that require that level of housing. In fact, the restrictions on individual choice increase as one's income decreases: the very poorest individual can live in only that municipality with the weakest property requirements. This is necessary, in Hamilton's solution, in order to forestall the redistribution within the jurisdiction that keeps tax prices from acting as efficient rationers of public services.

Thus, the final analysis of the Tiebout mechanism seems to be that it can be made to work efficiently only by depriving it of its libertarian free choice character. Only by constraining individuals to sort themselves out by income is the provision of public goods in a fragmented setting secured with market-like efficiency. Once again, the invisible hand seems to be inoperative in the realm of public goods.

But the question then becomes, if income segregation is necessary to make fragmentation efficient, then perhaps it is possible to justify the Lakewood Plan on those grounds. However, a second paradox seems to eliminate that basis for arguing that the Lakewood Plan has increased efficiency. Michelle White has shown that while exclusionary zoning may be necessary to make fragmentation efficient, it is a certain kind of exclusionary zoning that cities are not likely to engage in.[16]

In order to work as in the Hamilton model, each municipality must zone to maintain its average income at a stable level. This means that each new entrant who buys a new house in the jurisdiction, will pay an equal share of the cost of the public services in that jurisdiction. But what is to keep a jurisdiction from zoning in such a way that every individual who wishes to join the jurisdiction must "buy in" with a greater than average level of property ownership? By doing so, the jurisdiction can require subsidization of the older residents by incoming residents as the "price" of their unique package of public goods. This would result in redistribution from the incoming to the older residents, but most importantly, it will result in property tax "prices" that are not equivalent to head taxes, that impose efficiency losses on the housing market, and that do not guarantee efficient market-like rationing of public services. In other words, while "fiscal zoning," as it is called, provides a mechanism by which efficiency can be achieved, the incentives for local governments are to use zoning to achieve a redistribution from incoming residents rather than efficiency.

And indeed, there is evidence that cities in Los Angeles do engage in fiscal zoning to achieve a subsidization of established citizens. The cities in the upper right-hand corner of table 6.3 (Covina, Culver City, Glendora, Manhattan Beach, Sierra Madre, Torrance, and Whittier) all became homogeneously upper-income cities during the 20 years from 1950 to 1970. They did this largely by sponsoring a fiscal zoning campaign that limited multi-family dwellings and required a higher than average level of property ownership from incoming residents.

Sierra Madre, for instance, is a small, older city in the San Gabriel Valley. Says the city manager, "This city is sort of dedicated to residential quality." Of the city's 4500 dwellings, over 80 percent are single-family dwellings, and most of the multi-family dwellings are smaller, older apartments. The city's "limited growth" plan keeps down the number of large, multi-family dwellings. The city manager regards this requirement of property ownership on the part of incoming residents as noncontroversial: "There is no known opposition." And the amount of property ownership is nontrivial. The minimum lot size is 7500 square feet the city over, with some of 9, 11, and 15 thousand square feet. While there are 90 units per acre in parts of neighboring Pasadena, nowhere in Sierra Madre are there more than 15 units per acre on developing land. This policy has been sufficient to guarantee that Sierra Madre's per capita income increases with incoming residents. While the county's per capita income increased 44.6 percent from 1969–1975, Sierra Madre's per capita income rose 56.7 percent.

In a city that has been highly dependent on property tax revenue, this zoning policy has also guaranteed that incoming high-income residents, buying one of the increasingly expensive homes that developers build on 1100-square-foot lots, subsidize the long-term residents. And once again, this subsidization means that market efficiency is not guaranteed.

Efficiency, Bias, and the Possibility of Compensation

There are theoretical and empirical reasons to suspect that the people of low-income, low-resource communities such as Compton have been made worse off by the presence of the Lakewood Plan alternatives that improved the lives of the middle class who moved to these new cities. It is worth reiterating that there is no theoretical reason to justify this change on the grounds that the final outcome was an efficient outcome. But it is still possible that the change in distribution of resources, while not resulting in a perfectly efficient outcome, did help the middle-class more than it hurt the low-income inhabitants of Compton, and that the change was therefore justified in some sense.

For instance, the change from (40,40) to (55,30) is one in which one person gains more than another loses. However, I would maintain that such a change is not ethically unambiguous, despite the efficiency gains, unless compensation is guaranteed to the individual who is called on to make the sacrifices for the sake of efficiency. In other words, I would maintain that efficiency is not a sufficient normative basis for making policy recommendations regarding metropolitan organization, despite the fact that that is the only normative criterion that is specifically mentioned by Tiebout himself, and by most of his followers. Oates's claim that "it is always preferable to provide Pareto-efficient levels of consumption for subsets of a group than for the group as a whole" rests on an inadequate normative basis.[17]

One alternative normative basis, for instance, might be a "minimum standards" criterion. For instance, we might argue that each individual in the divide-the-dollar game should get at least $.25 for taking the trouble to participate in the game. That would eliminate a move such as that drawn in figure 8.2 from consideration, despite the fact that it would allow efficiency gains. Furthermore, we might develop a minimum standards requirement for urban politics, which says that every individual should live in a jurisdiction that has sufficient standards to guarantee him or her a minimum degree of physical safety, minimum housing quality, and minimum public health and education services. Several of the jurisdictions in Los Angeles County would fail to meet moderate standards of this sort.

It might be objected that the rich would be willing to pay compensation payments to those who have suffered from the fragmented metropolitan institutions that have benefited them, and that they, in fact, do so in the form of federal subsidies to poor communities. I feel that explicit Kaldor-Hicks compensation payments from rich to poor for the privilege of living in rich homogeneous communities would be a possible solution to the problems associated with fragmentation. However, I don't believe that federal subsidies qualify as compensation payments. This is because the rich in a large, heterogenous central city like Los Angeles have to pay the same federal income taxes as the rich living in tiny, walled suburbs like Rolling Hills. Further, I don't believe that benefits from federal revenue sharing, for example, go to the low-income cities in proportion to the need generated by metropolitan fragmentation. Nor are the absolute levels of federal subsidies sufficient to compensate the impacted urban poor for the effects of fragmentation.

For example, two of the wealthiest, high-income cities in the county, Culver City and El Segundo, got $12 and $28 per capita, respectively, from federal revenue sharing in 1976, while two of the poorest, low-income cities, Bell and Bell Gardens, received $5 and $9, respectively. When added together with other federal grants, Culver City and El Segundo got $19 and $52, while Bell and Bell Gardens received $28 and $15 per capita.

Bell Gardens was taxing itself at $1.99 per $100, and spending only $123 per capita. El Segundo was taxing itself at $.44 and spending at $841 per capita. Thus, the federal subsidies do not meet the requirements of compensation payments in terms of who pays, who benefits, or the scale of payment.

This raises the related question: even if compensation payments are not now being made at the federal level, isn't this the level at which redistribution should take place, if metropolitan fragmentation causes problems of fiscal disparity? This is of course theoretically correct, since those who are able to avoid the burden of a redistributive local policy by relocation will do so.

However, from a political perspective, it is pointless to ask those who are actively interested in redistributional questions to divorce themselves from local governmental issues because redistributional policy "should" come from the federal government. If questions such as the organization of metropolitan organization have predictable redistributional effects, the relevant political question is not whether or not to engage in redistribution at the local level, but rather in which direction should the redistribution take place. If the benefits of fragmentation fall primarily on homogeneous white middle- and upper-class suburbs, then the question of economic efficiency is politically less important than the issues of distribution of benefits and mobilization of bias.

The years since 1954 have seen Los Angeles County become an example of a

spatially differentiated metropolis in which blacks are separated from whites, the poor from the more affluent, the disadvantaged from economic and educational opportunity, and local jurisdictions with the greatest public needs from communities which possess the greatest share of the public resources.[18]

No existing theory can justify this transformation simply by reference to the Tiebout argument and the norm of allocational efficiency.

9

From Exit to Voice:
The Deepening
Conflict

In the mid-1970s, several things happened to the housing market. The first was a pause in the building boom that occurred with the recession of 1974–1975. At the same time, the babies born in the postwar baby boom had married, begun to have children of their own, and were looking for homes to buy. This caused an imbalance in supply and demand that was exacerbated by the growing number of two-salary families, who increasingly sought to buy their own homes. The result was a rise in housing prices, especially in the sunbelt, and most especially in Southern California, where the number of jobs continued to grow. In 1974 home prices averaged $37,800 in both Southern California and in the rest of the United States, but an enormous differential in housing prices rapidly appeared. By April of 1978, the average home price in the country as a whole had risen to $56,100, while in Southern California it had risen to $83,200; a differential of $27,100 had appeared in four years.[1]

The burden of increasing tax rate assessments chafed most heavily on those groups already most sensitized to property taxation—white homeowners. A study in 1978 showed that, based on current trends, it was white homeowners who were reaping both the benefits and burden of increasing home values: median housing value of homes in white areas was approaching twice that of homes in black areas.[2] This enhanced the tendency for the property tax revolt to be largely a white movement.

Although assessments did not automatically keep up with the rapidly changing market value, every year some part of the county was reassessed, and individual property taxes rose in distressing jumps. This was true even in cities which had incorporated to maintain low tax rates, or in communities which had never incorporated. Furthermore, the tax rate applied to those assessments continued to rise. The county tax rate had not been much of a burden in 1954, when Lakewood was incorporated. But it had risen from $1.92 in that year to $4.25 in 1977, and school property tax rates had increased similarly. In the El Monte school district, the total tax rate in the property rich Lakewood Plan city of South El Monte was still significantly lower than in the older city of El Monte ($10.71 compared to $12.64), but the smaller figure still seemed large enough to the inhabitants of a city that had successfully avoided a municipal property tax for 20 years, especially when new assessments showed jumps of up to 130 percent. In the unincorporated community of Diamond Bar, a warehouse manager's house was reassessed from $29,100 to $54,600, an increase of 88 percent. The owner said, "I'm upset and I know a lot of neighbors are too. I'd really like to see a tax revolution. It's time people got together and didn't pay the taxes." [3]

The key phrase was "get together." For more than two decades previously, homeowners had been voting with their feet for low taxes, but this was essentially a quiet protest with virtually invisible political effects. With the increase in countywide redistributional programs, it was becoming more difficult to follow the exit strategy and feel that one's action was effective.

"No Exit" Brings Tax Revolt

It could be done, of course. One way was by moving to middle-class Orange County. To some extent, the Los Angeles-Orange County metropolitan area was being sorted out by income class in the 1960s and 1970s in much the same way that Los Angeles municipalities were being sorted out in the 1950s and 1960s. While Los Angeles County experienced a population decline between 1970 and 1976, Orange County experienced a 23.5

percent population increase. While Los Angeles County was becoming increasingly nonwhite, Orange County was remaining essentially white. In 1970, 9.8 percent of the housing units in Los Angeles County were occupied by blacks, while only 0.6 percent of the housing units in Orange County were occupied by blacks. Furthermore, while the per capita income in 1970 was almost identical for the two counties ($3870), Orange County's income per capita increased 52.6 percent to Los Angeles County's 44.6 percent by 1975. The difference in tenure also reflected the sorting process. By 1970, Los Angeles County was a majority-renter county, and becoming more so; whereas Orange County homes were almost 65 percent owner occupied.

And once again, the demographic differences were matched by differences in expenditure patterns. Like many of the wealthier cities within Los Angeles County, Orange County had a better property tax base and fewer redistributional drains on those resources. Orange County had $5801 worth of property per capita at the time of the Jarvis Amendment, compared with $4770 for Los Angeles County. That property tax base was taxed at $1.33 per hundred in Orange County, to $4.25 in Los Angeles County. Per capita public assistance expenditures amounted to $189 in Los Angeles County, but only $64 in Orange County, and total health and sanitation expenditures were $72 per capita in Los Angeles County, but $27 in Orange County. Orange County performed the same function for middle-class taxpayers that the Lakewood Plan cities were originally intended to perform, but it performed that function more effectively.

However, migration to Orange County was not possible for every middle-income homeowner in Los Angeles County. But, with the meaning of the Lakewood incorporations very clear, one solution was proposed that was unmistakably in the same vein: the secession of various homogeneous suburban areas from Los Angeles County. This would serve the same purpose of insulating upper-income groups from the burden of taxation imposed by the growing county bureaucracy. Thus, on the same ballot with the Jarvis Amendment were two proposals for new counties to be created out of the affluent southwestern section of Los Angeles County.

One of the proposed county secessions was South Bay County, which included the beach cities of El Segundo, Manhattan Beach, Hermosa Beach, Torrance, Redondo Beach and Palos Verdes Estates. The proposed county would have had a median family income of $16,600, compared to Los Angeles County's $13,500. Virtually none of its population would have had incomes below poverty level. The 1970 census showed a total of 351 blacks living in the six cities, approximately one-tenth of one percent of all residents. While the advantages of living in the new county would have been felt primarily by upper-income whites, the benefits were clear. The taxable property per capita was $6680, as compared to $4578 for Los Angeles County. In addition, there would have been substantially less drain in the new county for welfare services.

Much the same was true for the other proposed county on the June 6 ballot. This county, Peninsula County, would have consisted of the three Lakewood Plan cities of Rancho Palos Verdes, Rolling Hills, and Rolling Hills Estates. Its citizens had a median family income of $28,400, over twice that of Los Angeles County's. The 1970 census showed 6 blacks in Rolling Hills and 14 in Rolling Hills Estates. Rancho Palos Verdes had fewer than 30. The taxable property per capita was $5771.

The Los Angeles County Economy and Efficiency Commission studied the two proposals, and urged defeat of both measures. "New county formation would reorganize the county into a central county on which the surrounding suburbs would depend for jobs and associated government services, but to which they would no longer contribute except through federal and state income-transfer programs. . . . Residents would abdicate responsibility under our current taxing system for supporting those in the lower economic strata of metropolitan society, while still receiving the benefits of a metropolis." [4] The proponents argued that "the county's problem is it's just too big and the way to solve it is to make it smaller. . . . This would make it more responsive by reducing the amount of hassle and red tape involved in reaching the supervisors." [5] However, the Los Angeles County Commission argued that in order for the white, upper-class citizens of the proposed counties to get the benefits of smallness and responsiveness, the rest of the county would suffer. Virtually the same set of services would have to be provided with more than a 2 percent reduction in tax base. "Eventually, the central area will collapse financially, as New York City has, and the economic base of the entire region will decline." [6]

The widespread support for the county formations in the proposed new counties tells us several things about the recent municipal incorporations in the same area, most notably the Rancho Palos Verdes incorporation. These incorporations were supposedly undertaken only for the purpose of gaining local autonomy over development and zoning for the purpose of environmental protection. In this they were successful; after incorporation, the Los Angeles County government ceased to have any influence on zoning in Rancho Palos Verdes or the other cities in the proposed new counties. However, even with environmental protection no longer an issue, the formation of Peninsula County was supported for the reasons that I have argued were most fundamental for the Lakewood Plan incorporations: it erected financial barriers between the tax base on the peninsula and the tax base of the low-income and minority groups of the central city. Even with environmental protection guaranteed, the demand on the part of the wealthy peninsula homeowners for institutional barriers between themselves and the rest of the county seemed as strong as ever. Environmental protection must be regarded as an unnecessary, secondary motivation for the minimal cities.

However, while the issues involved in the new county formations resembled those that motivated the Lakewood Plan incorporations, the institutional procedures for settling the conflict were different. The formation of a new county, unlike that of a new city, requires the majority approval of the inhabitants outside the new jurisdiction. For this reason, the new county formations never really had a chance, suggesting that a similar fate would have met many of the Lakewood Plan incorporations if they had required majority approval of all the individuals affected by the incorporation, rather than just the population of the proposed city. While South Bay County inhabitants voted 77 percent for the secession of that county, and while Peninsula inhabitants voted for the new county by an overwhelming 80 percent majority, the rest of the county voted down the county proposals by a three-to-one majority.

Thus, the exit opportunities for middle-income and upper-income homeowners faced with rising county and school district property tax payments were extremely limited at best. As assessments continued to climb, more and more protest was heard. The inhabitants of Rolling Hills, Bradbury, Rancho Palos Verdes, and other exclusive cities had been successful in maintaining property values by zoning, and were beginning to feel the harmful effects. As Bernard Friedan points out in *The Environmental Protection Hustle,*[7] it is ironic that the rapid rise in property values was due, in part, to limitations in housing expansion brought about by the exclusive zoning practices of many of the suburbs which had the only available vacant land. The problem then for middle-income and upper-income homeowners was to make it possible to live in homes that were rapidly increasing in value without facing proportional increases in property taxation. The Jarvis-Gann Amendment of 1978 filled the bill. Homeowners were forced to switch from exit to voice in their protests against welfare, bureaucracy, and property taxation.

The voice of homeowner discontent had much the same effect as homeowner protest by means of exit: it weakened the ability of the large, redistributional governments to provide the services that were regarded as beneficial by low-income groups and by the bureaucrats whose jobs were dependent on these services. While a $4 billion state bail-out of local government came with conditions attached to guarantee that education, fire protection, and police protection would be maintained at nearly the pre-Jarvis levels, the remaining cuts necessarily took place in the "welfare"-type services, and primarily in the old-line cities.

For instance, the cities that had avoided annexation to Long Beach over 20 years before were relatively unhurt by the Jarvis Amendment. Bellflower, Norwalk, Paramount, and Carson felt no effects—they had to increase no fees or taxes, institute no reduction in services, and make no layoffs. The only effect for Lakewood was a reduction in library hours. On the other hand, Long Beach, which had suffered significant deterioration in its financial position since the early 1950s, when it was known as "the town with too much money," had both to increase fees and reduce services. There were cutbacks in medical services, social services, library services, animal control, recreation programs, provision of crossing guards, and contributions to community social organizations. Three hundred seventy-five employees were laid off by October 1978. Compton, the other full-service community in the area, had already cut back on social services before Proposition 13; it had to cut back on police and fire services, and street-sweeping as well.

The pattern holds in other parts of the county, where a new, high-income city feels no effects of Proposition 13, and a low-income city has to impose higher fees or taxes to provide more limited services. The pattern held with La Canada-Flintridge and Pasadena, the second of which increased health service fees and reduced health and social services, while firing 63 municipal employees. Downey, the lone example of a postwar city which created its own municipal service agencies rather than becoming a contract city, and whose attempt to annex Commerce's industrial land spurred that city's incorporation fifteen years before, was the only postwar city to have to cut back significantly on services; Commerce was unaffected by Proposition 13 (see table 9.1).

The same pattern held with El Monte and South El Monte; Glendora and San Dimas; Azusa and Bradbury; and the old-line city of West Covina and its residential offspring, Walnut. The effects of Proposition 13 had been determined in the pattern of unsuccessful annexations and successful incorporations of a quarter-century earlier.

Furthermore, the effects of Proposition 13 would seem to reinforce a major theme of this book: that the creation of the Lakewood Plan cities benefited middle- and upper-income groups at the expense of those low-income individuals who were increasingly concentrated in low-resource cities. The advantage of living in high-resource or low-demand minimal cities is still being felt in the differential impact of Proposition 13.

Proposition 13 revealed in bolder outlines the subtle redistributional conflict involved in the earlier incorporation movement. Both Proposition 13 and the incorporation of the Lakewood Plan cities allowed homeowners to enjoy the benefits of increasing property valuation without suffering the proportionally increasing cost of property taxation. And the costs were paid by low-income groups and minorities.

Conclusion: The Politics of Metropolitan Resource Distribution

This book has sought not only to describe the fragmentation of the Los Angeles metropolitan area under the Lakewood Plan, but also to present and analyze one theory which has served as the basis for a vigorous defense of metropolitan fragmentation. That defense, based on the Tiebout hypothesis and supported by the empirical evidence of the Lakewood Plan cities, demonstrated once and for all that fragmentation did not necessarily imply a fundamental inability to supply services effectively to an urban area. Nothing in this book should be interpreted as an attack on that contribution.

However, the more thoughtful of the defenders of fragmentation acknowledged that the defense was only partial. As Robert Warren notes, despite the advantages of the Lakewood Plan, "there are other things presumed to be desirable in metropolitan organization which do not result from this arrangement. . . . Except in the case of special districts, income redistribution cannot be achieved within the framework of the Lakewood Plan. Control over land use remains fractionated." [8] This book has touched on the latter deficiency and focused on the former. It has made the case that fragmented government introduces an explicit bias in favor of upper-income groups who move to favorable jurisdictions, and it has tried to do so in terms of the microeconomic analysis used by the defenders of fragmentation.

The problem is that an increasing tendency to overlook the redistributional deficiencies of fragmentation has appeared in latter defenses, along with a normative orientation that suggests that these problems are a not-too-bitter pill that must be swallowed in order to derive the glorious effects of market-like efficiency in urban government. Bruce Hamilton, for instance, pointed out that while the Tiebout mechanism does not guarantee efficiency by itself, the extra element of income stratification among the metropolitan area's population will provide that efficiency.[9] That this efficiency, achieved by the government enforced zoning and separation of income classes, is a departure from the original invisible hand, libertarian efficiency of Tiebout is not discussed, any more than the redistributional implications (see Chapter 8).

Buchanan goes Hamilton a step further (see Chapter 7). He frankly realizes that upper-income groups are linked to the resource potential of a jurisdiction, and suggests that cities should bias their public goods packages in favor of upper-income groups, or else fail in the competition for those groups. Instead of regarding homogeneous low-income cities as among the necessary elements in an efficient metropolitan political economy, as Hamilton does, he regards these failures as evidences of economic irrationality: they did not follow the implications of the only possible objective of urban governments, which is the "maximization of per capita fiscal dividend." Rather than accepting income diversity, as Hamilton

Table 9.1
Effect of Proposition 13 on Los Angeles County Cities Incorporated
before and after 1954

		New cities	Old cities
No effect	No new or increased fees or taxes. No reduction in services. No layoffs.	Artesia Bellflower Carson Commerce Hidden Hills La Canada-Flintridge La Mirada La Puente Lomita Norwalk Paramount Pico Rivera Rolling Hills Rolling Hills Estates Rosemead South El Monte Walnut	Avalon San Fernando Vernon
Minimal effect	Increase in fees or taxes.	Baldwin Park Duarte Hawaiian Gardens Industry Irwindale Palmdale Rancho Palos Verdes San Dimas Santa Fe Springs Temple City	Culver City Gardena Montebello
	Reduction in services.	Lakewood Lancaster	Hawthorne Hermosa Beach Maywood
Significant effect	Increase in fees or taxes with reduction in services. No layoffs.	Cerritos Cudahy Lawndale	Arcadia Azusa Beverly Hills Claremont El Segundo

Table 9.1 (continued)

		New cities	Old cities
			Glendora
			La Verne
			Los Angeles
			Palos Verdes
			Signal Hill
			Torrance
			Whittier
	Layoffs. No increase in fees or taxes.	Bell Gardens (4)* Bradbury (15)	Compton (160) Covina (28) Huntington Park (8) Pomona (60)
Maximal effect	Layoffs with increase in fees or taxes.	Downey (80)	Alhambra (23) Bell (6) Burbank (18) El Monte (3) Glendale (26) Inglewood (54) Long Beach (375) Lynwood (26) Manhattan Beach (1) Monrovia (4) Monterey Park (4) Pasadena (63) Redondo Beach (38) San Gabriel (10) San Marino (35) Santa Monica (11) Sierra Madre (5) South Gate (25) South Pasadena (17) West Covina (56)

Source: *Los Angeles Times,* 1 October 1978, and interviews.
* The number of full-time employees laid off is shown in parentheses.

does, he prescribes a uniform set of urban public goods packages, all biased in favor of upper-income groups.[10]

Finally, Robert Bish, too, picks up on the Tiebout theme that people are mobile and will respond to favorable public goods packages. His argument is that local governments are disqualified from engaging in redistributional programs (or at least redistributional programs that are intended to favor low-income groups), because so many low-income groups would move to jurisdictions that do engage in those programs that they would no longer have the resources to do so. Tiebout is thus the basis for the "rationale behind the limited income redistribution that takes place within and between local government units in metropolitan areas." [11]

Bish recognizes, however, that even with limited income redistribution, there are "wealthier" and "poorer" political units, a situation to which he gives the aseptic name "fiscal diversity." Fiscal diversity "has been viewed as a problem by many individuals," [12] especially "those who have high demands for income redistribution and wish to impose their own social welfare functions." [13] Bish answers these pushy people by pointing out that "if fiscal diversity per se does result in economic problems, it appears that an effective demand for income redistribution exercised through national policies would yield the most efficient solutions." [14] But there is a catch: "effective demand" is measured by the

amount of resources . . . one is willing to pay for achieving a particular income distribution. The demands of low-income individuals for an increased share of resources without any sacrifice are regarded as noneconomic or noneffective demands (like any "demand" of something for nothing), and satisfaction of these demands does not increase economic efficiency in its broadest sense. Demands of this type, if imposed on other individuals, are political externalities imposed through the political process on the individuals from whom resources are taken.[15]

We can expect redistribution, only to the extent that high-income individuals think that they might derive some benefit from alleviating poverty, or to the extent that they are altruistic. Bish concedes: "Many high-income individuals act as if they benefit from raising the consumption of low-income families." [16] But low-income demand for redistribution is irrelevant.

Put together, these three arguments, based on Tiebout's thesis, constitute a disturbing defense of the distributional status quo. The separation of income classes is defended on grounds of efficiency. Governmental bias in favor of upper-income classes is promoted as a policy on grounds of rationality. Lower-income groups are informed that local redistributional programs are inefficient, and their demands for federal redistributional programs irrelevant because they have nothing to give in exchange.

In sum, these arguments constitute a self-satisfied acquiescence in lower-class isolation, neglect, and impotence. Such a position is, of course, very much in tune with the times, in light of Supreme Court decisions defending exclusionary zoning and mass movements defending the social nonresponsibility of property owners.

Furthermore, the arguments are absolutely correct, in the context of the economic view of the world. As long as "the objective for rational fiscal strategy is the maximization of per capita fiscal dividend," cities which respond to lower-income demands are irrational. As long as "effective demand" is defined as that demand backed by a willingness to trade, the demands of those with no economic goods to trade must be dismissed as ineffective.

However, the problem with this analysis is that it is incomplete: it leaves out the political dimension. For the politician, lower-income demands are not ineffective simply because they are not backed by market power. While Bish is correct in stating that "the satisfaction of these (noneconomic) demands does not increase economic efficiency in its broadest sense," politics has very little to do with economic efficiency, and has a great deal to do with demands of "something for nothing." Policy recommendations should not be made without consulting this dimension.

At the heart of politics are noneconomic demands of something for nothing, which, as Bish notes, "if imposed on other individuals, are political externalities imposed through the political process on the individuals from whom resources are taken." There are numerous recorded instances of millionaires who benefit from governmental activities and yet pay no federal income tax. It is not unreasonable for lower-income groups to have the same kinds of demands.

It makes perfect sense to dismiss ineffective demand for an automobile, because an automobile is purchased in the marketplace only by individuals with something to trade. However, redistributional programs (like subsidies to failing automobile manufacturing firms) are often given away in the political arena. The political arena, unlike the marketplace, works through collective decisions instead of through trades among individuals, and the strongest truths we know about collective decisions are related to their fundamental unpredictability, inefficiency, and irrationality.[17] Indeed, it was shown early in the 1960s that collective redistributional decisions are not only unpredictable; they can cycle to any outcome including grossly inefficient ones.[18]

If redistribution is different from allocational efficiency in a "market" for local public goods, then it is unnecessary to accept at face value the Tiebout-based "rationale behind the limited income redistribution that takes place within and between local government units in metropolitan areas."[19] Rather, if fragmented government is shown to evince a bias against the needs of lower-income groups, then metropolitan governance should be addressed and analyzed as was the Jarvis-Gann tax revolt—as a fundamentally political, redistributional issue (despite the apparent difference of the use of exit in one case, and voice in the other, by discontented property owners). Until the political nature of the Lakewood Plan movement is not recognized, the connection between that movement and the Jarvis movement will be hidden, and the Tiebout argument will be misused to defend the present distribution of resources in the name of "economic efficiency."

Appendix   The Centralization of
                               Revenue Generation

At one time, metropolitan reformers criticized metropolitan fragmentation on the grounds that small local governments could not realize economies of scale in the provision of municipal services, and, therefore, could
not be efficient. Vincent Ostrom and others quite accurately pointed out
the fallacy in this argument, which is that small governments must necessarily supply themselves with municipal services by means of their own
small, bureaucratic agencies.[1] As Ostrom showed, there is nothing to prevent small local governments, acting as collective consumption units, from
contracting with the county or any other producer for services that exhibit
economies of scale. By clarifying the difference between the local government as collective consumption unit and as service producer, Ostrom was
able to show that the production of services may be centralized without
hurting the capacity of the local government to act as collective consumption unit.

   The purpose of this appendix is to make an analogous argument with
respect to a different function: revenue generation. Centralization of this
function would eliminate the competition for resources that seems to ne-
cessitate a neglect of lower-income group demands,[2] without reducing
whatever benefits derive from the existence of small collective consump-

tion units. That is, "revelation of demand" characteristics of metropolitan fragmentation postulated by Tiebout derive from decentralization of the demand articulation function alone, and not from decentralization of revenue generation or of actual service delivery. The central redistributional disadvantages of metropolitan fragmentation derive fundamentally from decentralization of the revenue generation function. It is theoretically possible, therefore, to have a just and efficient organization of metropolitan government by eliminating local control over the revenue generation function.

Competition for Revenue Resources in a Fragmented Metropolis

Historically, one of the functions of local government has always been the raising of revenue from a set of resources that are in some sense "located" within the boundaries of the individual jurisdiction, and to which a kind of "property right" has been assigned by the state government. This system of revenue allocation is in contrast to other feasible revenue allocation systems in which, for instance, revenue is raised directly by the state government and allocated among the local governments according to some formula set by the state legislature.

One of the consequences of this decentralized local control of revenue resources has been an intense competition for the retail shopper, for industry, for high-income residents, and for other resources. There has been an equally intense effort, on the part of some municipalities, to exclude low-income, resource-draining residents through slum removal, selective annexation of residential developments, bans on multi-family dwellings, and zoning.

In Los Angeles, for instance, the conflict over resources was most obvious during the period of intense annexation and incorporation from 1954 to 1964, in which over 240 square miles of land, worth literally billions of dollars, was the center of much controversy. As middle-income and upper-income families flocked to the newly created Lakewood Plan cities with their low tax-rates, they drew many of the most desirable revenue resources with them. With the high-income residential developments went the lucrative regional shopping malls, the central offices for many large firms, and much of the desirable (low polluting) industry. On the other hand, many old-line cities became increasingly low-income in population and often experienced actual deterioration in their revenue resources. This resulted in the redistributional problem noted earlier: the jurisdictions with the most intense urban problems increasingly have the fewest resources to deal with them.

Does this competition for local resources serve any useful purpose? As already noted, metropolitan fragmentation has been defended because it provides multiple, small-scale, arguably more responsive local governments. However, this advantage depends only on the existence of multiple service-providing jurisdictions. It does not require that those small-scale jurisdictions actually raise their own revenue from local shoppers, homeowners, and industry. To be precise, is there any advantage to making local governments raise their own revenue from these resources?

The one defense of this system that has been mentioned to me by local officials is that it encourages local governments to "go after business." And this is certainly the case. Local governments have gone after business by keeping tax rates low, by providing the infrastructure for industrial plants, and by providing outright subsidies. For instance, the city of Torrance lured a major department store "by providing a prime site at a discount." Pasadena provided a large subsidy to the private developer of its downtown retail mall by clearing the land, building the parking garage, and leasing the garage at a low cost to the developer. Such "sweetheart deals" seem to be necessary to lure the developers to Pasadena. And the reason that developers are in such an enviable position is the competitiveness among local governments for revenue resources. The prime beneficiaries of this competition are businessmen.

These examples of competition for business are all drawn from the vast number of redevelopment projects sponsored by local governments, which have become the primary means by which cities seek a competitive edge over each other in luring beneficial business within their borders. But according to two attorneys who specialize in these projects, redevelopment "doesn't attract new development to the county so much as determine where it will locate—in this city or that." [3]

In other words, there is little or no net benefit to the county when Torrance lures a department store away from Redondo Beach. But the subsidization of business that results from the competition for revenue resources does impose costs. Since these projects are paid for out of tax-increment financing, the cost has become very large in terms of foregone tax revenue, not only for the cities which sponsor the projects, but also for school districts and the county as a whole. By 1977, foregone tax revenue resulting from tax increment financing amounted to $80 million out of county taxpayers' pockets.

Having argued that competition for revenue resources results in very real costs for the taxpayer, the question becomes, what are the benefits of decentralized, competitive revenue generation. The primary advantage of fragmentation, it has been argued, comes from improved revelation of individual demand for public goods, as citizens "vote with their feet" for public goods packages in different cities. In the next section, it will be argued that revelation of demand is improved, rather than hindered, by centralization of the revenue generation function.

Revelation of Demand in a Fragmented Metropolis

It was argued in Chapter 8 that there are two necessary requirements for efficient allocation of resources for public goods. One is a mechanism for inducing accurate revelation of individual demand for those goods, and the other is a price mechanism for rationing resources according to that individual demand. Tiebout's proposal satisfied the demand revelation mechanism by allowing individuals to "vote with their feet" for different packages of public goods in different jurisdictions; however, as Hamilton demonstrated, demand revelation without a price mechanism is insufficient to guarantee efficiency.

However, the demand revelation qualities of metropolitan fragmentation should not be ignored. It is the purpose of this final section to demonstrate that centralization of the revenue function would not destroy the demand revelation qualities of metropolitan fragmentation, but instead would enhance them.

That is, imagine a system in which some level of government, such as the state, raises revenue which is distributed among local governments on the basis of a (possibly universalistic) formula. The local governments then have perfect autonomy over how that revenue will be used, but not over the size of the budget. The budget can be spent on a variety of local services or it can even be distributed among the members of the municipality in the form of a rebate. Such a system of metropolitan fragmentation would induce better revelation of demand than the present centralized system. In the present system, one of the main reasons why an individual might choose one municipality over another is the resource advantage: in El Segundo, an individual can get better services in all categories for a lower tax price than in neighboring Compton because of the differences in resources in the two cities. This resource advantage could easily swamp any preferences the individual has over relative mixes of public services in the two cities.

To see this, let us imagine a situation in which there is one public good and one private good. The public good Q is provided by any of a series of local jurisdictions. The individual's budget (y_i) goes toward his tax on the public good and toward consumption of the private good. His tax share is given by the proportion of property that he owns divided by the total property in the jurisdiction. His budget constraint in jurisdiction J is

$$y_i = p_z z_i + (h_i/H_J) r Q_J N_J,$$

where

p_z = price of the private good Z
r = price of the public good Q (assumed constant throughout the metropolitan area)
h_i = the property for which the individual z is taxed
Q_J = the amount of public good per capita in jurisdiction J
N_J = the population of jurisdiction J
H_J = total property assessments in jurisdiction J.

The slope of the individual's budget constraint in J is given by

$$- (h_i/H_J) N_J (r/p_z).$$

Now suppose the individual is considering purchasing a home in either of two municipalities, say Santa Fe Springs and Maywood in Los Angeles County (see figure A.1). The municipalities are close together, they have similar populations, and the homes are similarly priced. The difference is that Santa Fe Springs has roughly nine times the taxable property per

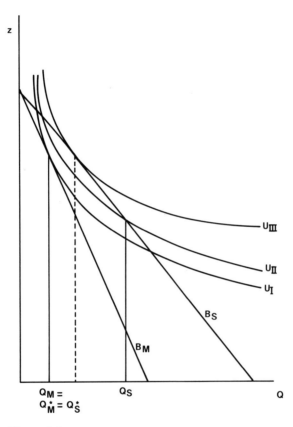

Figure A.1
The Effect of Different Budget Constraints on Individual Demand

capita, and provides Q_S of the public good, while Maywood provides the smaller level Q_M. Because budget constraint would be different in the two cities, preferences for the public good would also be different. The flatter budget constraint in Santa Fe Springs acts as a price decrease, so he prefers Q_S^* in that city, and Q_M^* in Maywood. Now let us suppose that Q_M^* is equal to the actual level of provision of the public good in Maywood (Q_M). He endures no conformity cost whatsoever in that municipality. He does in fact endure a large conformity cost in Santa Fe Springs, represented by the difference between U_{II} and U_{III}. But he will choose to live in that municipality which does not match his preferences rather than the one which does, because $U_{II} > U_I$. It is difficult to see how the Tiebout efficiency effect is operative in this case, since discrepancies in resources force individuals to reveal preferences for governmental output far removed from their true preferences. What is revealed is a taste for resource-rich communities over poor ones, a taste that is, no doubt, generally shared. The unique, important information about the individual's preference structure (indifference curves) is swamped by the effect of differential resources. The value of individual choice among jurisdictions as a demand-revealing mechanism is lost because of jurisdictional differences in resource bases.

On the other hand, if the county were to raise revenue by means of a uniform levy on the total county assessments, then every individual in the county would have budget constraints with exactly equal slope. The individual's demand would be determined only by the individual's own income and preference structure. When differences in resources among jurisdictions are controlled in this way, the ability of the system of metropolitan fragmentation to induce accurate demand revelation is improved. Paradoxically, the centralization of one function of local governments improves the ability of a system of small collective consumption units to induce individual revelation of demand.

Would Centralization of the Revenue Function Be More Equitable?

I have proposed that a decentralized system of revenue generation based on "point of origin" produces an intergovernmental competition for resources, promotes sprawl, encourages discrimination against low-income groups and minorities, and requires costly subsidization of businesses, industry, and high-income housing. As a solution, I have only vaguely proposed "centralization" of the revenue generation function.

It would certainly be possible to state a specific formula by which a state legislature could distribute revenues to local governments; and it would not be hard to come up with a formula that would be more equitable than the present system. But the more interesting and crucial question is, what might we expect if the state government takes over the distribution of local government revenue? Is the state government likely to come up with a formula that is more equitable than the "point of origin" system?

There is a well-developed theoretical explanation, based on the work of Kenneth Arrow,[4] for the short-run instability of redistributional issues such as these. This work demonstrates that, at certain times, there may be no alternative that can be considered by a legislative body that will win a majority against every other alternative. Subsequently, work by Benjamin Ward [5] demonstrated that redistributional questions always fall into this class of unstable issues—no distribution of state aid can win a majority against every other alternative. The outcome at any given time is determined by such extrademocratic parameters as the agenda under which alternative distribution schemes are considered. Any outcome is possible with the right agenda, including the most inequitable.

However, recent work by Morris Fiorina[6] has shown that if legislators are unwilling to take the chance of being hurt by a distribution scheme that may be inequitable they may collectively agree, in the long run, to change the rules of the game. As Fiorina points out, in the U.S. Congress the rules of the game are universalistic; they require that everyone get a share of the benefits being distributed. The operation of this norm in Congress has been noted by numerous observers.[7]

Likewise, there is evidence of universalistic norms among the Los Angeles County Board of Supervisors. For example, when faced with a recent $735,000 grant for juvenile justice programs, the board created a blue-ribbon panel to decide how the money should be allocated. The chairman of the advisory panel, District Attorney John Van de Kamp, reported a plan based on the merit of the applying programs; unfortunately this plan would have given much less money to some supervisorial districts than to others, and therefore violated the long-standing "rule of five" that requires that each supervisorial district receive approximately equal shares of money in park and recreation funds, in street-building funds, in capital development projects, and, apparently, in juvenile justice funds. When Van de Kamp stressed to the board that the recommendations were based on merit, Supervisor Schabarum replied, "John, the bottom line is that nobody cares about merit. . . . So go back. Redo it. Divide by five, and then determine on merit. That's what the members of the board are doing." And that was the outcome of the case.[8]

Such a universalistic norm cannot easily be defended on a priori or theoretical grounds. However, the existence of universalism in legislatures at all levels of government suggests that the long-range redistribution of funds to local governments by a state legislature could be more equitable than the current system based on competition for resources among cities for "property rights" in revenue resources. It could hardly be less equitable.

Summary

The passage of Proposition 13 has forced California's state government to undertake a reexamination of local government funding. It has driven home the previously hidden fact that the traditional decentralized means of allocating revenue, based on the assignment of "property rights" in local resources, is not unalterable. It has given the state government the opportunity to deal with the implications for local government generally of the 1976 decision of *Serrano* v. *Priest,* in which the state supreme court held that it was unconstitutional for a child to receive a lower-quality education because of inequities in school district property values.[9] It has given the state the opportunity to face the parallel question of whether it is any more constitutional for a citizen to receive lower-quality police services for the same reason.

The first state bail-out bill for local governments, passed immediately after Jarvis, gave no indication that the state would deal directly with such issues. The state aid simply had the intent of partially reimbursing municipalities for lost property tax revenue, and therefore maintained the previous inequities by failing to transcend the concept that local governments have a "right" to whatever property they can attract to their borders.

However, in the second year after Jarvis, state legislators are considering more radical alterations in the system. One plan, proposed by the League of California Cities, would allocate a share of the statewide sales tax to local governments, on the basis of population rather than point of origin. This would result in a major redistribution of revenue resources for local governments.

With a population-based formula for redistribution of revenue, it would no longer be necessary for local governments to engage in a war of subsidies to lure shopping malls and other sources of economic activity away from their neighbors. Perhaps even more important, it would no longer be a fiscal disadvantage to have low-income residents within the borders of a municipality; nor would it be necessary to maintain a public service bias against these groups to encourage them to locate elsewhere. The fiscal institutions that make such a bias the "rational fiscal strategy" are not unchangeable,[10] and the reevaluation of local public finance that has followed Proposition 13 make such changes politically feasible.

Symbols

Individual Variables

y_i Individual's income

t_i Individual's tax share

h_i Individual's home value

z_i Individual's consumption of private good

u_i Individual's utility level

Q_i^* Individual's most preferred level of public good

Jurisdictional Variables

Q_J Jurisdiction's per capita level of public good

N_J Jurisdiction's population

H_J Jurisdiction's total property assessments

Parameters

r The per unit price of the public good

p_z The per unit price of the private good

Y The income level of the upper income group

Notes

Introduction

1. Alfred O. Hirschman, *Exit, Voice and Loyalty* (Cambridge, Mass.: Harvard University Press, 1970).

2. E. E. Schattschneider, *The Semi-Sovereign People: A Realist's View of Democracy in America* (New York: Holt, Rinehart and Winston, 1960), p. 30.

3. *Los Angeles Times*, April 21, 1978, I:3.

4. *Los Angeles Times*, June 7, 1978, I:1.

5. Quoted in Gary Hoban, "The Untold Golden State Story: Aftermath of Proposition 13," *Phi Delta Kappan* (September 1979): 18.

6. Hirschman, *Exit*, p. 15.

7. Ibid., p. 16.

8. Adam Smith, *An Inquiry into the Nature and Causes of the Wealth of Nations* (Chicago: Encyclopaedia Britannica, 1952), p. 300.

9. Ibid., p. 194.

10. For a simple discussion of the welfare aspects of competitive markets see F. M. Bator, "The Simple Analytics of Welfare Maximization," *American Economic Review*, 47 (March 1957).

11. See Mancur Olson, *The Logic of Collective Action: Public Goods and the Theory of Groups* (New York: Schocken Books, 1965), esp. Chapter 2.

12. Milton Friedman, *Capitalism and Freedom* (Chicago: University of Chicago Press, 1962), p. 91.

13. Charles Tiebout, "A Pure Theory of Local Expenditures," *Journal of Political Economy* 64 (October 1956): 416–424.

14. See, for example, Committee for Economic Development, *Modernizing Local Government to Secure a Balanced Federalism* (New York: Committee for Economic Development, 1966).

15. Vincent Ostrom, Charles Tiebout, and Robert Warren, "The Organization of Government in Metropolitan Areas," *American Political Science Review*, 55 (December 1961): 831–842.

16. Robert L. Bish and Vincent Ostrom, *Understanding Urban Government: Metropolitan Reform Reconsidered* (Washington, D.C.: The Enterprise Institute for Public Policy Research, 1973).

17. Robert Bish, *The Public Economy of Metropolitan Areas* (Chicago: Rand McNally, 1971).

18. On the same theme, Aaron Wildavsky has argued that simple applications of the concept of economic efficiency to problems of public administration are apt to be simpleminded, because politics dominates and distorts other considerations. Aaron Wildavsky, *The Politics of the Budgetary Process,* 2d ed. (Boston: Little, Brown, and Co., 1974), pp. 189–194.

Chapter 1

1. Robert Fogelson, *The Fragmented Metropolis: Los Angeles, 1850–1930* (Cambridge: Harvard University Press, 1967), p. 64.

2. Quoted in William G. Bonelli, *Billion Dollar Blackjack: The Story of Corruption and the Los Angeles Times* (Beverly Hills: Civic Research Press, 1954), p. 82.

3. Winston W. Crouch and Beatrice Dinerman, *Southern California Metropolis: A Study in Development of Government for a Metropolitan Area* (Berkeley: University of California Press, 1964), p. 246.

4. John Anson Ford, *Thirty Explosive Years in Los Angeles County* (San Marino: Huntington Library, 1961), pp. 19–20.

5. Richard Bigger and James P. Kitchen, *How the Cities Grew* (Los Angeles: Bureau of Government Research, 1952), p. 88.

6. Ibid., p. 91.

7. Ibid., p. 93.

8. John Todd, "A History of Lakewood: 1949–1954" (unpublished manuscript available at Lakewood City Library), pp. 3–4.

9. Ibid., p. 36.

10. *Saturday Evening Post,* January 12, 1952, p. 32.

11. Todd, "A History," p. 19.

12. Ibid.

13. Ibid., p. 29.

14. Ibid.

15. Crouch and Dinerman, *Southern California Metropolis,* p. 201.

16. Richard M. Cion, "Accommodation *Par Excellence:* The Lakewood Plan," in Michael N. Danielson, ed., *Metropolitan Politics: A Reader* (Boston: Little, Brown and Co., 1966), p. 277.

17. Traffic law enforcement was procured by a separate agreement on a per car cost basis, since it was not a normal function of the county sheriff in unincorporated areas.

18. Sidney Sonenblum, John J. Kirlin, and John C. Ries, *How Cities Provide Services: An Evaluation of Alternative Delivery Structures* (Cambridge, Mass.: Ballinger Publishing Co., 1977), p. 90.

19. John J. Kirlin, "Impact of Contract Service Arrangements upon the Los Angeles Sheriff's Department and Law Enforcement Services in Los Angeles County," *Public Policy* 21 (1973): 558.

20. Interview with Milton Farrell, July 25, 1979.

21. Ford, *Thirty Explosive Years,* p. 19.

22. Interview with Johnny Johnson, June 27, 1979.

23. Sonenblum et al., *How Cities Provide Services,* p. 21.

24. See the discussion of public goods and the free rider problem in the Introduction and in Mancur Olson, *The Logic of Collective Action* (New York: Schocken Books, 1965).

Chapter 2

1. Robert L. Bish, *The Public Economy of Metropolitan Areas* (Chicago: Rand McNally, 1971), p. 88.

2. Ibid., p. 31.

3. Interview with E. W. Giddings, June 21, 1979.

4. Ibid.

5. Ibid.

6. Stanley Scott, *Annexation? Incorporation? A Guide for Community Action* (Berkeley: Bureau of Public Administration, 1953).

7. Interview with Warren Bedell, June 4, 1979.

8. Interview with E. W. Giddings.

9. *Southeast News,* August 20, 1959.

10. Interview with E. W. Giddings.

11. Interview with Warren Bedell.

12. *Daily Signal,* July 8, 1960.

13. Interview with Warren Bedell.

14. Valdds Pavlovskis, "The Economic and Fiscal Impact of the City of Industry on the Surrounding Communities" (Master's Thesis, California State Polytechnic University, 1973), p. 26.

15. Ibid., p. 37.

16. Ibid., p. 106.

17. Ibid., p. 57.

18. Ibid., p. 107.

19. Ibid.

20. *San Gabriel Valley Tribune,* May 11, 1977.

21. Ibid.

22. Interview with Frank Stiles, May 19, 1978.

23. Interview with Max Shapiro, May 19, 1978.

24. *Los Angeles Times,* February 19, 1978.

25. Ibid.

26. *Whittier Daily News,* January 23, 1979.

27. Ibid., January 22, 1979.

Chapter 3

1. John Ferejohn and Morris Fiorina, "The Paradox of Not Voting: A Decision-Theoretic Analysis," *American Political Science Review* 68 (June 1974): 525–536.

2. Theodore Bergstrom and Robert Goodman, "Private Demand for Public Goods," *American Economic Review* 63 (June 1973): 280–296.

3. When voters have single-peaked preferences along a single dimension, the median voter's preference is the voting equilibrium. For a proof, see Duncan Black, *The Theory of Committees and Elections* (Cambridge: Cambridge University Press, 1958); for a generalization, see Amartya K. Sen *Collective Choice and Social Welfare* (San Francisco: Holden-Day, 1970).

4. The major source of variation in functional responsibility among the cities in the sample was that some cities had no responsibility for fire protection, since they

belonged to the county fire district. To control for this variation, a regression was run for all municipal expenditures except fire protection. The results were almost identical to the results reported for total municipal expenditures in table 3.1. Income elasticity was .87 (.17 was the standard error); tax share elasticity, −.77 (.07); population elasticity, .40 (.08); home ownership elasticity, −.49 (.14). The F statistic was 212.2.

5. For a good discussion of fiscal illusion, see Charles J. Goetz, "Fiscal Illusion in State and Local Finance," in *Budgets and Bureaucrats,* ed. Thomas E. Borcherding (Durham: Duke University Press, 1977), pp. 176–187.

6. "Principles of Urban Fiscal Strategy," *Public Choice* 11 (Fall 1971): 1–14.

7. Robert Spann, "Collective Consumption of Private Goods," *Public Choice* 20 (Winter 1974): 63–81.

8. Robert Dahl, *Who Governs? Democracy and Power in an American City* (New Haven: Yale University Press, 1961), pp. 282–303.

9. *Los Angeles Times,* October 18, 1979.

10. C. E. Trygg, "Police and Fire Departments Re-established After Signal Hill Tries Contract Services," *Western City* 37 (January 1961): 17–18.

11. *Los Angeles Times,* April 2, 1979.

12. Edward C. Banfield, *Big City Politics* (New York: Random House, 1965), pp. 83–84.

13. Ibid., p. 86.

14. Joel Balbien, "Jarvis-Gann and the Politics of Budgetary Reduction in the City of Pasadena" (California Institute of Technology Social Science Working Paper #254, 1979).

15. Standard error for this estimate is 1.5 percent. The F ratio for the regression of municipal age with the ratio of actual to expected expenditures is 25.7.

16. At the federal level, see Aaron Wildavsky, *The Politics of the Budgetary Process,* 2nd ed. (Boston: Little, Brown, 1974); at the local level, see John Crecine, *Governmental Problem Solving: A Computer Simulation of Municipal Budgeting* (Chicago: Rand McNally, 1969).

17. *Los Angeles Times,* July 7, 1978.

18. Ibid., February 25, 1979.

19. Robert O. Warren, *Government in Metropolitan Regions* (Davis: University of California Institute of Governmental Affairs, 1966), pp. 175, 177.

20. Interview with Johnny Johnson, June 27, 1979.

21. Robert T. Anderson, "Portrait of Lakewood After Two Years of Incorporation," *Western City* 32 (1956): 39–41.

Chapter 4

1. Mark Gottdiener, *Planned Sprawl: Private and Public Interests in Suburbia* (Beverly Hills: Sage Publications, 1977).

2. Beverly Menze, *A Guide to the Rural City of Rolling Hills* (City of Rolling Hills, 1977).

3. Ibid.

4. *Los Angeles Times,* February 11, 1979.

5. Ibid., April 24, 1977.

6. Ibid.

7. Bernard Frieden, *The Environmental Protection Hustle* (Cambridge, Mass.: MIT Press, 1979), p. 140.

8. Ibid., p. 8.

9. Ibid., p. 178.

Chapter 5

1. Robert L. Bish, *The Public Economy of Metropolitan Areas* (Chicago: Rand McNally/Markham, 1971), p. 89.

2. *Los Angeles Times,* August 25, 1963.

3. Ibid.

4. Interview with Ruth Benell, July 21, 1977.

5. Ibid.

6. John Goldbach, "Local Formation Commissions: California's Struggle over Municipal Incorporations" in *Public Administration Review* 25 (September 1965): 216.

7. Jack E. Jerrills, *The History of a City . . . Carson, California* (City of Carson, 1972), p. 110.

8. Ibid., p. 115.

9. Goldbach, "Local Formation Commissions," p. 216.

10. Jerrills, *History of a City,* p. 121.

11. Ibid., p. 123.

12. Los Angeles County Board of Supervisors, "In the Matter of Requesting the Local Agency Formation Commission to Permit Proponents of Carson-Dominguez Incorporation to Refile Their Proposal" (transcript of September 27, 1966, board meeting), p. 2.

13. Jerrills, *History of a City,* p. 113.

14. *Los Angeles Times,* November 23, 1971.

15. Ibid., August 29, 1963.

16. Interview with Frank Lanterman, June 9, 1979.

17. Interview with George Parrish, July 29, 1977.

18. Interview with Frank Lanterman.

19. Interview with Carl Schulz, August 26, 1977.

20. Carl Schulz, "Flintridge in Trouble" (address before La Canada Thursday Club, August 8, 1976), p. 3.

21. Ibid, p. 8.

22. Ibid, pp. 3–4.

23. Interview with Carl Schulz.

24. Ibid.

25. Los Angeles County Board of Supervisors, "In the Matter of Ranchos Palos Verdes" (transcript of the board meeting March 29, 1973), pp. 46–47.

26. Ibid, p. 9.

27. Ruth Benell, "MORGA: Something New Has Been Added," *Western City* 54 (1978): 27, 48.

Chapter 6

1. For a more complete discussion of the Tiebout argument, see the Introduction.

2. This measure of income homogeneity was suggested by Rae's measure of fractionalization; see Douglas W. Rae, *The Political Consequences of Electoral Laws* (New Haven: Yale University Press, 1967), p. 56.

3. Phillip L. Clay, "The Process of Black Suburbanization," *Urban Affairs Quarterly* 14 (1979).

4. Data were not available on those cities with less then 10,000 population.

5. *Los Angeles Times,* October 30, 1974.

6. Ibid.

7. *Los Angeles Times,* November 7, 1974.

8. Wesley Skogan, "The Changing Distribution of Big-City Crime," *Urban Affairs Quarterly* 13 (September, 1977): 33–48.

9. Ibid., pp. 43–44.

10. Ibid., p. 47.

Chapter 7

1. Richard Child Hill, "Separate and Unequal: Governmental Inequality in the Metropolis," *American Political Science Review* 68 (1974): 1557–1568.

2. *Los Angeles Times,* July 14, 1977.

3. Ibid., August 1, 1976.

4. James M. Buchanan, "Principles of Urban Fiscal Strategy," *Public Choice* 11 (1971): p. 13.

5. Ibid., p. 15.

6. Ibid., p. 16.

7. Robert O. Warren, *Government in Metropolitan Regions: A Reappraisal of Fractionated Political Organization* (Davis: University of California Institute of Government, 1966), p. 197.

8. *Los Angeles Times,* June 24, 1979.

9. Ibid., July 5, 1979.

10. Ibid.

11. Michael N. Danielson, *The Politics of Exclusion* (New York: Columbia University Press, 1976), p. 99.

12. Chester Hartman, *Yerba Buena: Land Grab and Community Resistance in San Francisco* (San Francisco: Glide Publications, 1974), p. 9.

13. Robert Oliver, "Perspectives on Pasadena" (unpublished manuscript available in California Institute of Technology library).

14. Buchanan, "Principles of Urban Fiscal Strategy," p. 13.

15. Ibid.

Chapter 8

1. Kenneth Arrow, "Gifts and Exchanges," *Philosophy and Public Affairs* (Summer, 1972): 349–350.

2. For a discussion of dominant strategy and other aspects of game theory, see R. Duncan Luce and Howard Faiffa, *Games and Decisions* (New York: John Wiley and Sons, 1957); and William H. Riker and Peter C. Ordeshook, *An Introduction to Positive Political Theory* (Englewood Cliffs: Prentice-Hall, 1973).

3. Robert Bish and Vincent Ostrom, *Understanding Urban Government* (Washington, D.C.: American Enterprise Institute for Public Policy Research, 1973), p. 2.

4. Charles Tiebout, "A Pure Theory of Local Expenditures," *Journal of Political Economy,* 64 (October 1956): 418.

5. Robert Bish, *The Public Economy of Metropolitan Areas* (Chicago: Rand McNally/Markham, 1971), p. 137.

6. Wallace Oates, *Fiscal Federalism* (New York: Harcourt Press, 1972), p. 41.

7. *Los Angeles Times,* April 9, 1979.

8. U.S. Bureau of the Census, *Census of Manufacturing*, 1972 and 1967.

9. Francine Rabinowitz, "Minorities in Suburbs: The Los Angeles Experience" (Cambridge, Mass.: Joint Center for Urban Studies, Working Paper #31, 1975), p. 42.

10. Ibid., p. 31.

11. Interview with Lionel Cade, April 24, 1979.

12. Ibid.

13. Edwin S. Mills and Wallace E. Oates, "Theory of Local Public Services and Finance: Its Relevance to Urban Fiscal and Zoning Behavior," in *Fiscal Zoning and Land Use Controls*, Mills and Oates, eds. (Lexington, Mass.: D.C. Heath and Co., 1975), pp. 5, 9.

14. Bruce Hamilton, "Property Taxes and the Tiebout Hypothesis: Some Empirical Evidence," in *Fiscal Zoning and Land Use Controls*, pp. 13–31.

15. Ibid., p. 13.

16. Michelle White, "Fiscal Zoning in Fragmented Metropolitan Areas," in *Fiscal Zoning and Land Use Controls*, pp. 31–100.

17. Wallace Oates, *Fiscal Federalism*, p. 58.

18. Michael N. Danielson, *The Politics of Exclusion* (New York: Columbia University Press, 1976), p. 1.

Chapter 9

1. *Los Angeles Times*, October 11, 1978.

2. Ibid., April 9, 1978.

3. Ibid., July 14, 1977.

4. Ibid., May 4, 1978.

5. Ibid., May 15, 1978.

6. Ibid.

7. Bernard Frieden, *The Environmental Protection Hustle* (Cambridge, Mass.: MIT Press, 1979).

8. Robert O. Warren, *Government in Metropolitan Regions: A Reappraisal of Fractionated Political Organization* (Davis: University of California Institute of Government Affairs, 1966), p. 247.

9. Bruce Hamilton, "Property Taxes and the Tiebout Hypothesis," in *Fiscal Zoning and Land Use Controls*, ed. Edwin S. Mills and Wallace E. Oates (Lexington, Mass.: D. C. Heath and Co., 1975), pp. 13–30.

10. James M. Buchanan, "Principles of Urban Fiscal Strategy," *Public Choice* 11 (1971): 1–14.

11. Robert L. Bish, *The Public Economy of Metropolitan Areas* (Chicago: Rand McNally College Publishing, 1971), p. 141.

12. Ibid., p. 147.

13. Ibid., p. 141.

14. Ibid., p. 147.

15. Ibid., p. 141.

16. Ibid., p. 141.

17. See, for instance, Kenneth Arrow, *Social Choice and Individual Values,* 2d ed. (New Haven: Yale University Press, 1963).

18. Benjamin Ward, "Majority Rule and Allocation," *Journal of Conflict Resolution* 5 (1961): 379–389.

Appendix

1. Vincent Ostrom, Charles M. Tiebout, and Robert O. Warren, "The Organization of Government in Metropolitan Areas," in *The American Political Science Review* 55 (1961): 831–842.

2. James M. Buchanan, "Principles of Urban Fiscal Strategy," *Public Choice* 11 (1971): 1–14. See the discussion in chapter 7.

3. *Los Angeles Times,* January 23, 1977.

4. Kenneth Arrow, *Social Choice and Individual Values,* 2d ed. (New Haven: Yale University Press, 1963).

5. Benjamin Ward, "Majority Rule and Allocation," *Journal of Conflict Resolution,* 5 (1961): 379–389.

6. Morris Fiorina, "Legislative Facilitation of Government Growth: Universalism and Reciprocity Practices in Majority Rule Institutions" (California Institute of Technology Social Science Working Paper #226, 1978); and Barry Weingast, "A Rational Choice Perspective on Congressional Norms," *American Journal of Political Science* 23 (1979): 245–262.

7. See for instance Richard E. Fenno, "The House Appropriations Committee as a Political System: The Problem of Integration," *American Political Science Review* 56 (June 1962): 301–324; John Ferejohn, *Pork Barrel Politics* (Stanford: Stanford University Press, 1974); and David Mayhew, *Congress: The Electoral Connection* (New Haven: Yale University Press, 1974).

8. *Los Angeles Times,* January 8, 1979.

9. *Serrano* v. *Priest,* 5 Cal.3d 584, 487 P.2d 1241 (1971).

10. Buchanan, "Principles of Urban Fiscal Strategy."

Index